MW00596785

The Archaeology of American Cemeteries and Gravemarkers

The American Experience in Archaeological Perspective

UNIVERSITY PRESS OF FLORIDA

Florida A&M University, Tallahassee
Florida Atlantic University, Boca Raton
Florida Gulf Coast University, Ft. Myers
Florida International University, Miami
Florida State University, Tallahassee
New College of Florida, Sarasota
University of Central Florida, Orlando
University of Florida, Gainesville
University of North Florida, Jacksonville
University of South Florida, Tampa
University of West Florida, Pensacola

The Archaeology of American Cemeteries and Gravemarkers

SHERENE BAUGHER

AND RICHARD F. VEIT

Foreword by Michael S. Nassaney

University Press of Florida

Gainesville · Tallahassee · Tampa · Boca Raton

Pensacola · Orlando · Miami · Jacksonville · Ft. Myers · Sarasota

Library of Congress Control Number: 2014934252
ISBN 978-0-8130-4971-7

The University Press of Florida is the scholarly publishing agency for the
State University System of Florida, comprising Florida A&M University,
Florida Atlantic University, Florida Gulf Coast University, Florida
International University, Florida State University, New College of Florida,
University of Central Florida, University of Florida, University of North
Florida, University of South Florida, and University of West Florida.

University Press of Florida
15 Northwest 15th Street
Gainesville, FL 32611-2079
http://www.upf.com

We thank our families for their encouragement and support

My husband, Robert W. Venables, and my son, Brant Venables
—SB

My wife, Teresa Veit, and my children, Douglas and Rebecca
—RFV

Contents

List of Figures   ix

Foreword   xiii

Acknowledgments   xix

1. Introduction: American Cemetery Studies as Above-
   and Belowground Archaeology   1

2. Belowground Archaeology: Ethics and Science   18

3. The Science in Belowground Archaeology   35

4. Beyond Death's Heads and Cherubs: Early American
   Gravemarkers   78

5. Transformations in the Design of Nineteenth- and Twentieth-
   Century Cemeteries   125

6. Ethnicity, Race, and Class within Nineteenth- and Twentieth-Century
   Cemeteries   160

7. "He Being Dead Yet Speaketh" (Hebrews 14:4): Conclusions   200

References Cited   211

Index   247

Figures

1.1. The Granary Burial Ground, Boston, Massachusetts 3

1.2. Typical colonial markers showing a death's head, cherub, and urns and willows 9

2.1. The African Burial Ground National Monument, in New York City 32

3.1. Select pressed-metal nineteenth-century coffin fittings 39

3.2. *Left*, the three lead coffins unearthed beneath the chapel in St. Mary's City, Maryland. *Right*, A reconstruction of Ann Wolsey Calvert, based on her skeletal remains 43

3.3. A modern commemorative marker at the Secaucus Potter's Field site, New Jersey 70

3.4. A Victorian cast iron mummiform coffin from Newark, New Jersey 72

3.5. Coffin plate of Senator Nicholas Ware, Spring Street Presbyterian Church Cemetery, New York 74

4.1. Mortality image for Sarah Woodruff (d. 1722), Elizabeth, New Jersey 82

4.2. Cherub marker for Samuel Vickers (d. 1785), Savannah, Georgia 83

4.3. Willow marker for Joseph Bibler (d. 1841), Granville, Ohio 83

4.4. David Gillespie carving a slate gravemarker in the eighteenth-century style 84

4.5. Cornelius Bramhall (d. 1761), Portland, Maine 85

4.6. *Left*, rubbing of the gravestone of Isaac Moses (d. 1763), Newport, Rhode Island. *Right*, rubbing of the gravestone of Cuffe Gibbs (d. 1768), Newport, Rhode Island 91

4.7. Tulip-decorated marker for Catherine Clowes (d. 1771), Elizabeth, New Jersey 97

4.8. *Top*, Hendrickson family marker showing baroque putti in Middletown, New Jersey. *Bottom*, gravemarker of Altje Brinckerhoff (d. 1749), Fishkill, New York 100

4.9. *Left*, gravemarker of George Junt (d. 1770), Ephrata, Pennsylvania. *Right*, uninscribed marker at the Bergstrasse Lutheran Churchyard, Lancaster County, Pennsylvania 104

4.10. The Moravian Burial Ground, Bethlehem, Pennsylvania 109

4.11. Edward Nott's box tomb, Bruton Parish Churchyard, Williamsburg, Virginia 111

4.12. Tombstone for Sir George Yeardley, Jamestown, Virginia 119

4.13. Headstone for Mrs. Anna D'Harriette (d. 1754), St. Philip's West Burial Ground, Charlestown, South Carolina 122

5.1. St. Louis Cemetery Number 1, New Orleans 128

5.2. Bartlett print of Mount Auburn Cemetery, Cambridge, Massachusetts 130

5.3. Lina Reiss marker, Der Stadt Freidhoff, Fredericksburg, Texas 132

5.4. *Top*, Egyptian Revival gates to the Grove Street Cemetery, New Haven, Connecticut. *Bottom*, Gothic entrance gate to Green-Wood Cemetery in Brooklyn, New York 135

5.5. "Millionaire's row," Philadelphia's Laurel Hill Cemetery 136

5.6. Albert Parsons (d. 1933) monument, Green-Wood Cemetery, Brooklyn, New York 137

5.7. *Left*, Griffith memorial, Green-Wood Cemetery, Brooklyn, New York. *Right*, Precious Georgie memorial, Green-Wood Cemetery, Brooklyn, New York 139

5.8. Congressional cenotaphs, Congressional Cemetery, Washington, D.C. 142

5.9. *Top*, Old Mortality, Laurel Hill Cemetery, Philadelphia. *Bottom*, close-up view of Old Mortality, Laurel Hill Cemetery, Philadelphia 143

5.10. *Top*, gravemarkers for Union soldiers in Gettysburg National Military Park, Pennsylvania. *Bottom*, Confederate prisoner of war gravemarkers, Elmira, New York 148

5.11. *Left*, iron marker for Anton Bernhard, St. Vincent DePaul Parish Cemetery, Crown Butte, North Dakota. *Right*, iron marker for Joseph Miller, St. Vincent DePaul Parish Cemetery, Crown Butte, North Dakota 152

5.12. *Our Drummer Boy*, a Monumental Bronze statue in Green-Wood Cemetery, Brooklyn 154

5.13. The Bruno Grandelis (d. 1905) marker, Hillside Cemetery, Metuchen, New Jersey 155

6.1. Magnolia Colored Cemetery, Aiken, South Carolina, c. 1900 170

6.2. *Left*, gravemarker of Caesar (d. 1806), Scotch Plains, New Jersey. *Right*, gravemarker of Ambo (d. 1847), Woodbridge, New Jersey 172

6.3. Modern Chinese American markers, Mansfield Cemetery, Washington Township, New Jersey 180

6.4. Jewish section of Albany Rural Cemetery, New York 183

6.5. Romany monument for Big G (George) and Loveable Rose Nicholas, Evergreen Cemetery, Hillside, New Jersey 191

6.6. The gravemarker of Mrs. Cutroneo, Oceanport, New Jersey 193

Foreword

On an overgrown wooded hillside along a gravel road in Niles, Michigan, lie two monuments that commemorate the seventeenth-century French colonization of the St. Joseph River valley. One is a large glacial erratic, said to weigh over sixty-five tons, moved from a farmer's field and dedicated to Fort St. Joseph in 1913. The other is an impressive granite cross erected at the burial site of Fr. Jean Claude Allouez, the founder of the mission established prior to the fort. Documentary sources indicate that a succession of wooden crosses were replaced by this stone in 1918 when the Women's Progressive League of Niles decided to provide the good priest with a more permanent tribute.

Monuments that commemorate death serve as physical reminders of those who came before us and the transitory nature of earthly life. Yet the messages they convey are varied depending on the observer and changing social circumstances. Nevertheless, the materiality of death is laden with cultural information of great interest to historians, anthropologists, and historical archaeologists who can use their interpretive tools to decode mortuary meanings.

All societies, from time immemorial, have employed mortuary ritual to mend the torn social fabric caused by death. Acts of commemoration invariably leave physical traces after the rituals are over, such as funeral pyres, coffin hardware, burial furniture, and shells strewn about the grave site. While Americans are not unique in this regard, the ways in which people recognize the dead and aim to soothe the grief of the living are learned behaviors that reflect in microcosm a society's values and beliefs. Thus, it is noteworthy that Americans established burial grounds and cemeteries with an eye toward permanency, unlike their European forebears who removed human remains from their places of rest to make room for new ones.

In America, European settlers often implanted their dead in earlier American Indian burial grounds, physically asserting ownership of places long held sacred. For example, along the Arkansas River about fifty miles southeast of Little Rock lies an earthen burial mound constructed and used by Native Americans about five hundred years ago. It drew the attention of C. B. Moore, that infamous American archaeologist of the late nineteenth century who arguably dug more burials in his lifetime than all currently living archaeologists combined. At the Greer site (named after the landowner), Moore remarked on the use of the mound summit to inter early Euro-American pioneers and settlers, which he was careful to avoid disturbing. As the white dominant society buried their dead in the mounds of the ancients, they often disturbed or exhumed burials associated with indigenous peoples in a powerfully symbolic act. This double standard in the treatment and care of the dead has a long history in America and is a sad legacy of our racist and colonialist past. To this day, marked white graves are seldom exhumed even for study, whereas robbing and desecration of indigenous graves was rampant in southern New England, necessitating the passage of a law in Rhode Island Colony in the 1650s that prohibited these ghoulish practices. The dead have long been used in tactics aimed to advance political agendas. Only in the late twentieth century, with the enactment of the Native American Graves Protection and Repatriation Act (1990) and the excavation of the African Burial Ground (1991), did archaeologists begin to address the legitimate concerns of descendant communities.

In *The Archaeology of American Cemeteries and Gravemarkers*, Sherene Baugher and Richard F. Veit present a comprehensive overview of the ways in which Americans have designed and used cemeteries and gravemarkers over the past four hundred years. They argue that gravemarkers are among the most evocative and informative artifacts available to historical archaeologists, who have used them to make inferences about trade networks, socioeconomic status, and religious beliefs, among other cultural practices. The authors are well acquainted with a broad body of literature drawn from various fields, which they bring to bear on the study of both belowground and aboveground archaeological remains.

They are rightly sensitive to the ethical issues involved in belowground investigations. Many Americans are understandably distraught at the thought of exhuming the dead, particularly their own ancestors; they take seriously the idea of a "final resting place." Yet cemeteries have often become lost and forgotten, particularly among the poor and disenfranchised. Their accidental discovery during urban development has necessitated the recovery of human remains. The legal frameworks under which archaeologists must operate vary by state. Suffice it to say that once legal and ethical concerns are addressed and descendants agree to investigation, careful archaeological study can yield a wealth of information pertaining to burial placement, preparation, and accouterments, as well as aspects of the individual such as stature, age, and health. Unfortunately, a comparable sample of white middle-class remains is conspicuously absent from the data sets archaeologists have at their disposal, though the few cases available exhibit interesting divergences from the high rates of traumatic injury and violent death observed among the burials of enslaved Africans in both the North and the South.

Baugher and Veit devote the majority of their synthesis to the study of gravemarkers—those publicly visible, aboveground symbols rife with meaning begging to be interpreted. Created in a near-infinite variety of forms from materials as diverse as wood, limestone, marble, granite, ceramic, metal, and concrete, gravemarkers were erected by the living to commemorate the dead and to create a means of remembrance for the living. As simple as this may seem, a multitude of decisions come into play when deciding the appropriate manner to memorialize the dead. Religious beliefs about the nature of the afterlife, human relations with a creator, and the ontology of being all come into play in the iconography and scripted messages created for what many hope will be an eternity.

Yet other, more-worldly matters intervene, such as availability of raw material, access to resources, relations with the homeland, gender, racial hierarchy, marital status, time and place of death, and a host of other factors that influence the material culture of death. The result is a tremendous amount of variability in mortuary treatment and commemoration that the authors detail as a means of monitoring cultural change and continuity. Of particular interest for the immigrant experience are the ways in which archaeologists have analyzed how the countervailing tendencies between the pressure to assimilate and the desire to maintain ethnic separateness are expressed in death. Some have argued that assimilation into the American melting pot and the potential for upward mobility among those who could claim whiteness required one to relinquish symbols of ethnic identity. At the same time, racialized groups who were excluded from full participation in American citizenship were segregated in death as they had been in life. They, in turn, ignored dominant trends in mortuary treatment and maintained their own practices. For example, Chinese Americans in the western United States often employed principles of geomancy, or feng shui, in the placement of their graves, which follow the contours of the landscape as a protection against evil spirits. They also exhumed their own dead and returned them to China, where their descendants honored them during important religious rituals.

The cemetery has also been a battleground between the powerful and the powerless. Baugher and Veit discuss studies from central New York that suggest elites were alternately distancing or aligning themselves with the working class depending on the availability of labor in urban and rural contexts. In the former case, elites erected large monuments to commemorate the dead that naturalized their positions of power in order to create and maintain a social order that served their political-economic needs. Rural elites were less likely to flaunt their status when they were dependent on local labor; hence, they downplayed ostentatious displays of death. It behooves archaeologists to remember that mortuary ritual and its material expressions are always mediated by ideology, which must be understood contextually to make sense of markers and the meanings of their epitaphs. Social identity also influences how stones are read, prompting questions about the intended audience in cemeteries. In the nineteenth century, cemeteries were designed as parklike settings that attracted public visitation, including tourists. While this practice has fallen out of favor, I recall visiting Forest Lawn Cemetery in Glendale, California, on a family vacation in 1974 to behold its statuary, ornate landscape, and memorials of the rich and famous. While the uniform appearance of markers evoked relations of equality, this place was undoubtedly segregated and socially exclusive. What becomes clear from Baugher and Veit's treatment of the subject is that mortuary remains do not always mirror social relations in everyday life. Thus, they are but one dimension of the American experience, albeit an important one.

The insights that Baugher and Veit provide on cemeteries and grave-markers demonstrate how historical archaeology can contribute to understanding an emotionally charged aspect of daily life, namely, the need to interrupt the quotidian on the occasion of the death of a compatriot. Grief is a universal human feeling; the form it takes and its fossilized traces are subject to rigorous analysis. Sentiments of sorrow and acts of commemoration embody both private and public expressions of the values of individuals, families, communities, and the nation. Our plural society is marked by a mosaic of cultures that have created an extremely diverse burial landscape in keeping with the religious freedoms Americans are accorded, in contrast with places where government edicts have limited commemoration to forms that are consistent with state values. Impromptu roadside shrines that spring up at locations where lives were tragically cut short always fascinate me, as do outpourings of affection for celebrity deaths and mass disasters that take the form of balloons, candles, flowers, and other memorabilia in public settings. Though often of a temporary nature, these commemorations point to a human need for remembrance. They also suggest the desire to mourn in community. The material manifestations of death, grief, and hope are fruitful albeit sensitive grounds for gaining a better understanding of the American experience. Archaeology can play a central role in unraveling our multifaceted and ever-changing history as written in cemeteries and gravemarkers.

Michael S. Nassaney
Series Editor

Acknowledgments

During the process of writing this book, we received useful feedback and helpful assistance from numerous individuals. Cemetery and gravemarker experts Adam Heinrich, Harold Mytum, Mark Nonestied, and Lynn Rainville all provided useful comments and suggestions. We received help with images from Tonia Deetz Rock, Eric Deetz, David and Renee Gillespie of Pumpkintown Primitives, Rabbi Joshua Segal, Mark Nonestied, Ed Morin at URS Corporation, Jacklyn Penny at the American Antiquarian Society, Meg Winslow at Mount Auburn Cemetery, Gwen Kaminski at Laurel Hill Cemetery, Silas Hurry at Historic St. Mary's City, Michael Trinkley of the Chicora Foundation, Vicki Simon, Karen Bruwelheide, and Douglas Owsley at the Smithsonian Museum of Natural History, and archaeologists Scott Warnasch and Michael Audin. Dawn Turner-Castelli is also thanked for drawing figure 1.2. We also deeply appreciate the patience and assistance of Michael Nassaney, series editor for the American Experience in Archaeological Perspective series and Meredith Babb and all of the fine folks at the University Press of Florida. Of course, any errors remain our own. We hope you enjoy the book and find it useful.

1

Introduction

American Cemetery Studies as Above- and Belowground Archaeology

In popular culture, archaeologists are often thought of as people who dig up tombs, find mummies, and unearth treasures. They are also dashing and exciting characters. This book is about what historical archaeologists—archaeologists who study the modern world—have learned from the archaeology of American cemeteries and burial places. As archaeologists, we are interested in what the aboveground artifacts found in burial grounds can tell us about the past, and especially how gravestones, tombstones, and cemetery design have evolved through time. We are also interested in the information that can be gleaned from the buried remains of our predecessors, in particular their skeletons, coffins, and grave goods. So, yes, like the archaeologists in the movies we do study tombs and graves. North American archaeologists rarely find mummies; however, they do sometimes find Victorians buried in mummiform metallic coffins. The treasures we find are not gold and silver but information and insights into how people lived and what they believed, information that often can be recovered only through archaeological research. Most of the individuals we study were not famous. They were ordinary people, but they are important for the insights that their memorials and their remains provide into our shared past. Unlike archaeologists in the movies, and sadly some archaeologists in real life, we advocate working respectfully and collaboratively with descendant populations.

This book is a guide of sorts to the world of cemetery studies in American historical archaeology. We examine American burial places and what makes them distinctive. We hope it provides you with a good foundation for your own research.

Cemeteries and burial places in general are important repositories of cultural information (figure 1.1). They reflect and embody changing ideas regarding commemoration and remembrance. Similar to other cultural landscapes, they have evolved through time; moreover, the human remains they hold can provide valuable information about the religious beliefs, socioeconomic status, and ethnic heritage of the deceased, as well as information about an individual's physiological characteristics: stature, sex, injuries suffered during life, and health.

Gravemarkers, the aboveground component of American cemeteries and burial places, are the ultimate historical artifact: they are part material culture and part document. They are generally dated and associated with known individuals. Unlike most other artifacts, which were discarded and forgotten once their useful life was over, gravestones were purposefully made to convey information to future generations. They cry out for study. Moreover, they usually remain in their original locations, and the material they were made from may provide information about craft traditions, trade networks, and local resources. At the same time, gravestone design and decoration may reflect religious or cultural traditions and other social norms. Their form, size, decoration, inscriptions and epitaphs, and location have proven to be useful indicators of gender, status, ethnicity, consumerism, and social change. American gravestones are essentially documents in stone, and their inscriptions may provide information on life spans, infant mortality, gender, occupations, military service, and religious traditions. When other sources have not survived, gravestones can often fill in the gaps left in the written records. In early America, they were one of the few forms of publicly accessible art. Gravestones and cemeteries reflect America's changing attitude toward death from a preindustrial, agricultural society to an industrial, capitalistic, and ultimately postindustrial society. For more than fifty years, diverse theoretical perspectives and research questions in historical archaeology have been reflected in the numerous archaeological studies of cemeteries and gravestones.

With so much literature available on the archaeology of American cemeteries and burial sites, why write a book? Because gravestone studies is in some ways a self-contained but interdisciplinary field, and many of the cemetery and gravestone articles written by archaeologists do not appear in the major historical archaeology publications (*Historical Archaeology, International Journal of Historical Archaeology,* and *Northeast Historical Archaeology*). Therefore, many archaeologists may not be aware of the

Figure 1.1. The Granary Burial Ground, Boston, Massachusetts. Photograph by Richard Veit.

wealth of information that exists. The Association for Gravestone Studies annually publishes a list of the new books and articles on mortuary studies. With such a growing and vast literature, a global encyclopedia of mortuary studies would be useful, but that is not the focus of our book. For a useful survey of cemetery research in the United Kingdom, the interested reader should refer to Harold Mytum's excellent *Mortuary Monuments and Burial Grounds of the Historic Period* (2004). A useful overview of Western European–style cemeteries in a worldwide context is provided by James Stevens Curl's *A Celebration of Death* (1993). Our book is focused on American cemeteries and the American experience.

Although there are some fine synthetic studies of the archaeology of death and burial (Bellantoni and Poirier 1997; Parker Pearson 1999), bibliographies on burial and related topics (Bell 1994; Sprague 2005), guides to studying and documenting gravestones (Mytum 2000, 2004; Sprague 2005), and volumes on the restoration of gravemarkers and burial grounds (Strangstad 1995), our volume is the first overarching look at the archaeology, both aboveground and below, of American burial grounds. Our book provides an overview of the important themes in the field and also provides an archaeological perspective on the American experience through the study of cemeteries.

Cemetery and burial ground publications by archaeologists often appear in diverse sources such as publications for cultural geographers, folklorists, and art historians; regional and state archaeological journals; and especially *Markers: The Journal of the Association for Gravestone Studies.* They appear in books or as book chapters (for example, Poirier and Bellantoni 1997a; Chung and Wegars 2005; Veit and Nonestied 2008). They also appear in the gray literature of masters' theses, doctoral dissertations, and cultural resource management reports (for example, Crowell 1983; Stone 1987; Veit 1991; Perry et al. 2009a). There is a wealth of important data on American cemeteries in the gray literature, especially in cultural resource management (CRM) reports that were produced for agencies and clients. Unfortunately, most CRM reports have a very limited distribution, so even other archaeologists may be unaware of the information they contain. Wherever possible we have highlighted some of the important research from gray literature.

Changing Theoretical Perspectives on Commemoration and Deathways

Anthropologists have had long-standing global interests in commemoration and human deathways. Indeed, as Richard Huntington and Peter Metcalf note in *Celebrations of Death: The Anthropology of Mortuary Ritual* (1979: 1), "What could be more universal than death? Yet what an incredible variety of responses it evokes. Corpses are burned or buried, with or without animal or human sacrifice, they are preserved by smoking, embalming, or pickling; they are eaten—raw, cooked, or rotten; they are ritually exposed as carrion or simply abandoned or they are dismembered and treated in a variety of these ways." Furthermore, burial practices, human skeletal remains, and associated artifacts have been central to the inquiries of archaeologists and biological anthropologists as they have worked to unravel the path of human evolution and document past societies.

Many of the major historical figures of sociocultural anthropology, including Alfred Kroeber (1927), Max Gluckman (1937), Arnold Van Gennep (1960), and Robert Hertz (1960), focused considerable attention on the ritual behaviors associated with death. They examined issues of liminality, transition, commemoration, and how funerary practices help structure society (Parker Pearson 1999: 22). Other anthropologists, such as Mary Douglas, have focused on issues of pollution and purity and how these practices relate to death and burial (Douglas 1966; Parker Pearson 1999: 24).

Globally archaeologists are also interested in issues related to death, burial, and commemoration and have a long tradition of studying the same (Childe 1945; Binford 1971; Chapman, Kinnes, and Randsborg 1981; Parker Pearson 1999). Human remains have much to reveal about the lives of past individuals, with the potential to provide information about stature, sex, diet, nutrition, habitual activities, injuries, disease, and many other topics (Larsen 1997: 2). Indeed, Ivor Noël Hume, the doyen of American historical archaeology, has written, "The archaeologist's concern for the preservation of human life is probably matched only by his enthusiasm for its mortal remains!" (Noël Hume 1975: 158, 160).

The rise of the New Archaeology in the 1970s saw archaeologists searching for scientific laws that would enable them to better understand human behavior. Lewis Binford, building on the work of Arthur Saxe (1970), argued that one could infer the social status of the deceased and their place within the society from the grave goods found with them (Binford 1971). Working with data from forty different societies, garnered from the Human Relations Area files, Binford tested his hypotheses and found that individuals' identities are reflected in diverse ways in burial practices (Binford 1971; Parker Pearson 1999). Other scholars have come to similar conclusions and built upon and refined the work of Saxe and Binford (Winters 1968; Ucko 1969; Brown 1971; Tainter 1978; Carr 1995). In essence, these scholars believe that differences in burial treatment accord with asymmetries once present in the living society (Peebles and Kus 1977: 421–48; Brenner 1988: 148). With the rise of postprocessual archaeology, new interpretations of mortuary remains and commemorative processes have emerged, which rather than seeing direct correlations between status and commemorative elaboration have focused on the variability of social roles across time and space. Some scholars see ideological systems as determining the expressions that are evidenced in mortuary rites (Shanks and Tilley 1982: 129; Brenner 1988: 148). One of these scholars, Ian Hodder, sees several different scenarios that may play out in mortuary rituals:

1. A naturalizing strategy where political inequalities are symbolically expressed as an integral and inherently necessary part of the hierarchical order attributed to the natural world.

2. A masking strategy wherein political inequalities are denied or hidden behind a façade of equality and egalitarianism.
3. A marking strategy wherein political relations of inequality are clearly and overtly expressed (Hodder 1982a, 1982b, cited in Brenner 1988: 148).

Other researchers have focused on ethnoarchaeology, one aspect of the New Archaeology that strove to "understand the contextual workings of material culture symbolism within particular societies" (Parker Pearson 1999: 34). In sum, the study of burial practices is a critical means of understanding past societies, including their belief systems, economies, and social structure (Binford 1971; Brown 1971; Cannon 1989; Carr 1995; Chapman, Kinnes, and Randsborg 1981; Hodder 1982a, 1982b; O'Shea 1981; Tainter 1978).

At the same time, the study of cemeteries, gravemarkers, and burials is not simply an abstract exercise in quantifying data and interpreting the past. Human remains and burial places are important here and now. Gravemarkers may be used to illustrate ideological conflict between the powerful and the powerless (McGuire 1988). Forensic anthropologists and bioarchaeologists use human remains to document crimes. Human remains, particularly Native American remains, are quite literally bones of contention. Prior to the passage of the Native American Graves Protection and Repatriation Act (NAGPRA) in 1990, scholars paid little attention to the concerns of descendant communities when excavating Native American burials. Although NAGPRA signaled a major shift in policy toward the treatment of remains (Watkins 2004), it left both sides dissatisfied: Native Americans were concerned that there were too many loopholes, while some scholars continued to protest the provisions of the law. These debates continue today.

Burial places, human remains, and monuments are major topics in anthropological archaeology. At times contentious, these studies are informed by a rich body of theory. North American historical archaeologists have built upon the foundation laid by anthropologists and anthropological archaeologists in their studies of skeletal remains, coffins and coffin hardware, grave goods, and funerary trappings. They have examined cemetery organization and the placement of individuals within the burial ground. They have also done yeoman's work in documenting gravemarkers, from the most simple fieldstone memorials to grand mausoleums. In this book, we examine the work of archaeologists and point the way toward further research.

The Study of American Gravemarkers and Commemoration

Gravestone research does not draw from the scholarly traditions of anthropological archaeology alone but is interdisciplinary in nature and is also undertaken by scholars in archaeology, art, folklore, English literature, and cultural geography. Much of the early and mid-twentieth-century research on gravestones focused on the stones either as folk art or for their literary style and epitaphs. In 1927, art historian Harriette Merrifield Forbes undertook the first major academic work on American gravestones. Her seminal work, *Gravestones of Early New England,* laid out research themes that scholars, including archaeologists, continue to address. She discussed regional styles, symbolism of the motifs, and the role of carvers and their individual styles. Her work inspired other researchers, primarily in art history and folklore studies. Their work was similar to the culture history studies being undertaken by archaeologists in the first half of the twentieth century (Mytum 2004: 5).

Social scientists began writing about cemeteries as cultural landscapes in the 1950s and 1960s (Warner 1959; Young 1960; Kniffen 1967). Cultural geographers, in particular, emphasized the relationship between burial places and "larger American settlement patterns" (Francaviglia 1971: 501; see also Ames 1981). Moreover, with the advent of the New Archaeology, American archaeologists tried to apply a more scientific approach toward their fieldwork, lab work, and analyses (Binford and Binford 1968). It was not long before functionalist and processual approaches were being applied to historic burial grounds (Saxe 1970; Binford 1971).

James Deetz, who had previously worked on precontact American Indian sites, correlating ceramic design to residence patterns in his research on Arikara Indian sites in the Midwest (Deetz 1965), brought these new perspectives to historical archaeology. In the early 1960s, Deetz became interested in historic sites including historic cemeteries. Deetz with his colleague Edwin Dethlefsen applied seriation studies to colonial cemeteries in Massachusetts and recognized the patterning in the designs on the stones (Dethlefsen and Deetz 1966) (figure 1.2). In the early eighteenth century in New England, death's heads were the common image on tombstones, by midcentury they were replaced in popularity by designs of cherubs, and in the late eighteenth century images of urns and willows became the predominant symbol. Deetz and Dethlefsen demonstrated the applicability of seriation studies to historic cemeteries. They demonstrated that gravestones were aboveground artifacts that could be analyzed for their iconographic, demographic, and textual information (Deetz and Dethlefsen 1965, 1967).

Deetz provided a structuralist perspective when he linked changes in gravestone images to changes in religion (Mytum 2004: 7). Deetz (1977: 69–71) believed that the death's head image was linked to the harsh realities of Puritanism, whereas the cherub correlated with the Great Awakening, a liberalization of Puritan theology. Deetz also surmised that by the end of the eighteenth century the new mortuary designs, particularly the urn and willow tree, reflected more secular ideas.

In his eloquently written analysis of colonial gravestones, Deetz inspired a new generation of archaeologists to focus on cemetery studies. His work challenged archaeologists to expand or refute his ideas. Archaeologists tested Deetz's theories on the link between material culture and religious change to see whether the iconography on gravestones really was tied to changes in a particular religion (Puritan) or a region (New England). The same patterns appeared in New York and New Jersey Anglican and Dutch Reformed cemeteries, suggesting broader cultural trends (Baugher and Winter 1983; Stone 1987, 2009; Veit 1991). Archaeologists working in South Carolina (Gorman and DiBlasi 1976) and in Florida (Dethlefsen and Jensen 1977) found regional variations in gravestone iconography patterns in the South. Archaeologists also found that on Long Island and in New Jersey the choice in materials (types of stone) and carving styles could be linked closely with the economics of trade networks (Stone 1987; Veit 1996).

Archaeologists, inspired by the various theoretical perspectives in postprocessual archaeology, posed a broad range of research questions relating to ethnicity, race, gender, and class. For example, in the mid-Atlantic colonies, regional differences were tied to a variety of variables: ethnicity with German Protestants in New Jersey (Veit 2000); class structure with upper- and middle-class Anglicans in Virginia (Crowell and Mackey 1990); and status in New Jersey (Veit 1996). The plain gravestones of the Quakers in Pennsylvania and New Jersey reflected a different theological perspective than that of the Puritans (Crowell 1981, 1983). In addition, not all colonists were Protestants. The gravestones of Spanish Catholics in Florida and

Figure 1.2. Typical colonial markers showing a death's head, cherub, and urns and willows. Drawn by Dawn Turner Castelli.

Sephardic (Portuguese and/or Spanish) Jews in Rhode Island are distinct and different from the northern European Protestant stones (Kerr 2009; Gradwohl 2007). However, there are some similarities between some of the Spanish Catholic and Spanish Jewish stones, which raises questions regarding the importance of images and symbols that are cultural versus those that are religious. In addition, David Gradwohl (2007) found some cherubs (similar to ones Deetz found on Massachusetts Puritan tombstones), but these particular cherubs were on the colonial tombstones of Portuguese and Spanish (Sephardic) Jewish colonists in Newport, Rhode Island. These diverse archaeological discoveries have challenged Deetz's eloquent yet simplistic correlation between religious change and gravestone iconography. Chapter 4 discusses this research in more detail.

The study of gravestones is not restricted to archaeological work on colonial cemeteries or to studies of religious change. Archaeologists use diverse theoretical perspectives from chaos theory to Marxism to analyze gravestones. For example, Suzanne Spencer-Wood (1996) applied chaos theory, also called nonlinear systems theory, to a study of 191 gravestones (dating to 1740–99) from a cemetery in Lexington, Massachusetts. In plotting the stones at five-year intervals, Spencer-Wood found two other motifs competing in popularity with death's heads and cherubs, and she found that there was not a smooth transition from death's head to cherub motifs. Spencer-Wood suggests that when one examines all the styles that appear on gravestones (not just the most prevalent styles), competition among carvers rather than religious ideology may account for the diversity in colonial gravestones. Randall McGuire (1988) used a Marxist perspective in his study of class differences and power relations reflected in the nineteenth-century and early twentieth-century working-class and elite cemeteries in Binghamton, New York. LouAnn Wurst (1991) also applied Marxist theory to the study of mid-nineteenth-century gravemarkers from Broome County, New York. She examined the stones of rural and urban elites. Wurst also noted the different ideologies of the rural elite, which grew out of the Second Great Awakening, and of the urban elite, which were more secular and scientific (Wurst 1991: 145). Furthermore, she saw rural elites working to minimize or ignore class differences, in contradistinction to their urban contemporaries, who accentuated class differences (Wurst 1991: 146).

More recently, one of us (Veit 2009) analyzed how gravestones reflect the emergence of a consumer culture. Veit examined the consumer revolution of the late eighteenth century as reflected in the growing popularity of permanent gravemarkers. At the same time, the artisans who produced the markers signed more and more of their work as they competed for markets. Joy Giguere has examined issues of gender in colonial commemoration (2007), while Adam Heinrich (2012) has seen clear linkages between styles of markers and broader artistic trends. Race and ethnicity have also been major vectors of gravemarker research (Rainville 2009; Gradwohl 1993, 1998). In essence, many of the major perspectives in social science research have been applied to gravemarkers. Moreover, cemeteries are intriguing and pleasant places to study. As James Deetz and Edwin Dethlefsen noted, "Compared to the usual field work experienced by the archaeologist, with all of its dust and heavy shoveling under a hot sun, this type of archaeology certainly is most attractive. All of the artifacts are on top of the ground, the sites are close to civilization, and almost all cemeteries have lovely, shady trees" (Deetz and Dethlefsen 1967: 37).

American Burial Places

In cemetery studies the evolving cemetery landscape is also examined. Burial places in early America included burial grounds associated with churches, synagogues, meetinghouses, family burial grounds, public burial grounds, and potter's fields (Sloane 1991: 4–5). In New England, graveyards were often located near the center of town, often adjacent to the meetinghouse (Stilgoe 1982: 266). In Virginia, having a family burial ground was seen as a mark of status (Fithian 1990: 223). The cemeteries also reflect the larger American experience. In the eighteenth and nineteenth centuries, segregation was often the norm; larger farms and plantations often have separate African American burial grounds, which often lack formal markers. In the western United States, the graves of overseas Chinese were also segregated. On occasion, individuals were buried alone outside formal burial grounds; this was particularly true for criminals, suicides, and individuals who died in military service. Archaeologist Ian Brown has noted a significant number of pioneer cemeteries located on top of prehistoric American Indian burial mounds (Brown 2007). This fascinating stratigraphy of the deceased may have been a conscious effort by settlers to claim ancient places of power as their own.

Although today the phrases *burial ground, burying ground, churchyard,* and *cemetery* are often used interchangeably, the term *cemetery* was not employed during the eighteenth century and reflects a transformation of burial practices that first became common in the nineteenth century. In the colonial period, people were buried in family burial grounds, religious-affiliated burying grounds, potter's fields, or communal cemeteries (Veit and Nonestied 2008). These types of burial grounds continued in the nineteenth century, with the addition of the carefully landscaped so-called rural cemeteries, including nonsectarian cemeteries, such as Green-Wood Cemetery in Brooklyn, New York. Chapter 5 discusses the transformation from colonial burial grounds to nineteenth- and twentieth-century cemeteries. Private, nonsectarian cemeteries developed in the nineteenth century that reflected changes in national ideology.

The nineteenth century with the Industrial Revolution, the growth of capitalism, the emergence of the middle class, and a consumer culture brought about a change in American burial grounds. In Europe individuals could purchase burial plots for a specific period of time, but in America the burial plot was regarded like any other type of American individually owned land—it had no time restriction. Elaborate corporation-owned cemeteries were established, such as Mount Auburn in Boston and Green-Wood Cemetery in Brooklyn, New York (Sloane 1991). Landscape architects were employed to design cemeteries to create peaceful and idyllic vistas with rolling hills, streams, ponds, and exotic plantings. Because this was an era of conspicuous consumption, these cemeteries displayed the wealth of the occupants with elaborate monuments, freestanding sculpture, cast iron fencing and benches, and architecturally ornate mausoleums. In the nineteenth century, the rural cemeteries had become a place for both the living and the dead—the grand nonsectarian cemeteries such as Mount Auburn in Boston and Green-Wood in Brooklyn had become outdoor museums. With the height of consumerism and the display of new wealth, these cemeteries displayed outdoor sculpture by well-known artists and elaborate mausoleums designed by famous architects. The cemeteries contained a pastoral landscape for urban dwellers to take afternoon strolls. These rural cemeteries were the forerunners of public parks. Indeed, lawn-park cemeteries, which retained much of the aesthetic of the rural cemetery movement but were smaller in scale and less picturesque, were common during much of the nineteenth and twentieth centuries. The transformation of American cemeteries reflected both changing religious and cultural views on death and the relationship between the living and the dead (as discussed in chapter 5).

Ethnicity, Race, and Class

Chapter 6 focuses on the patterns of ethnicity, race, class, and power relations, reflected in the gravestones in diverse nineteenth- and twentieth-century cemeteries throughout the United States, including cemeteries in Alaska and Hawaii. Archaeologists have analyzed how the immigrant experience and the pressures to assimilate versus the desire to maintain ethnic separateness are reflected in gravestones, cemetery mortuary art, and the design and layout of cemeteries. For example, David Gradwohl (1993, 1998, 2007) has looked for ethnic and religious differences reflected in the gravestones in nineteenth-century Jewish immigrant cemeteries. The resistance against the pressure to assimilate is perhaps more apparent when the two cultures are dramatically different, such as Chinese versus European. Chinese cemeteries in Hawaii, California, Nevada, and Oregon reflect the immigrants' adaptations and challenges to the dominant Western culture (Chung and Wegars 2005). The immigrant experience can also be studied in the American cemeteries of eastern Europeans and Italians. Sometimes the plight of immigrants can also be seen in pauper burial grounds.

Belowground Archaeology

The archaeology of cemeteries is not just about the analysis of gravestones; it also involves the excavation of burials and grave goods. Archaeologists have always been fascinated with burial sites, whether Egyptian tombs such as King Tut's or American Indian burials such as the Hopewell period burial mounds in Ohio with their elaborate grave goods. The same interest in mortuary archaeology has carried over into historical archaeology's cemetery studies. One of the earliest formal excavations of a historic American cemetery took place in 1897 when Mary Jeffrey Galt unearthed an early settlers' burial ground in Jamestown, Virginia (Noël Hume 1996: 111). The study of burials was not limited to important East Coast historic sites. During the early and mid-twentieth century, there were also numerous excavations at Spanish missions in the American Southwest and in Alta California (Cordell 1992; Costello and Hornbeck 1992; Hester 1992). Most of the people buried in the mission cemeteries were Native Americans, who were often being forced or coerced into changing their religion and their culture. Mortuary archaeologists examined burials at East Coast

Spanish missions in Florida and Georgia (Larsen 1993; Thomas 1990). By the last quarter of the twentieth century, mortuary archaeology studies had expanded from mission sites to include other ethnic and racial communities, especially in some well-publicized and published studies, such as the African Burial Ground in New York City and the seventeenth-century English Catholic burials in St. Mary's City, Maryland (Blakey et al. 2009; Miller et al. 2004). Excavation of grave sites reveals religious, ethnic, and racial diversity in burial practices. Mortuary archaeology reveals detailed information about health and disease in colonial and nineteenth-century America (Poirier and Bellantoni 1997a). Grave goods may also provide valuable insights into past cultural behaviors. Items associated with historic Native American burials may reflect cultural survival, through resistance or accommodation to the economically and politically powerful European American society (Bragdon 1999). Similarly, the items included in historic African American burials highlight cultural persistence in the face of extreme pressure to assimilate (Perry et al. 2009b).

In rare instances items of clothing survive in graves, and rarer still are even more ephemeral items such as flowers and books interred with the deceased. When they survive they provide a rare glimpse into cultural practices associated with the burial process. Shrouds, coffins, crypts, mausoleums, columbaria, and even mass graves speak to changing attitudes toward death and the human body. At the same time, the excavation of burial grounds reveals society's changing attitudes toward the treatment of the human body. Excavations of late nineteenth-century burials of Chinese Americans show a mixture of Chinese and European American artifacts that questions the nature of the Chinese immigrant resistance to assimilation and acculturation (Chung and Wegars 2005). Were these Chinese Americans able to strike a balance between two cultures? Is this evidence of transnationalism—evidence of involvement in both the home country and the new country? The excavation of these burial sites allows archaeologists to explore these diverse research questions, which are discussed in chapter 3.

Ethical Questions Regarding Belowground Archaeology

Mary Jeffrey Galt undertook early historical archaeology excavations of burials in 1897 inside the Jamestown Church. In the 1950s, John Cotter

(1958) excavated additional bodies at the Jamestown burial ground near the Jamestown Statehouse. In 2001, William Kelso (2006: 164–68) and his team from Jamestown Rediscovery uncovered the remains of seventy-two individuals from the burial ground. The Jamestown excavations provided important information on general health, disease, and cause of death and shed light on burial customs in this famous seventeenth-century English settlement. However, the law in many states prevents the excavation of European American burials unless the descendants or courts grant permission (Price 1991). Because of twentieth-century legal protections, European American cemeteries were usually not excavated unless a cemetery had to be moved. However, many historic burial grounds contained wooden markers that have decomposed, and what was once a marked burial place now appears to be vacant land. If there is no active descendant community, then these cemeteries are forgotten. These lost burial places are often encountered during construction projects and are at a high risk of destruction regardless of the ethnicity of those interred there. Moreover, construction workers, driven by tight deadlines and afraid of the consequences of discovering a forgotten cemetery, sometimes ignore the very real evidence of the burials that they encounter.

Few legal protections for burial places existed prior to the twentieth century, and many cemeteries were moved or abandoned when families and congregations relocated. Many early cemeteries were destroyed as cities expanded. Some of the early burial grounds have been uncovered during new construction projects, and contract archaeologists have been called in to excavate and remove the bodies. Urban burial grounds, regardless of the ethnicity of the deceased, are often targets for relocation or are simply paved over or built upon as land values skyrocket and changing demographics lead to the decline or relocation of associated houses of worship. Until the passage of the Native American Graves Protection and Repatriation Act of 1990, in many states Native American burial grounds were not afforded the same protection as European American cemeteries, and North American archaeologists often excavated Native American burial grounds. However, with any excavation of a grave there are religious and ethical issues that archaeologist should address. While many research questions can be answered by studying the bodies and grave goods, ethically should we be undertaking this work? What about the wishes of the descendants? When archaeological and bioarchaeological studies are completed, are the bodies reinterred? What about the grave goods? Should they be reburied too? These ethical questions and challenges are discussed in chapter 2.

About This Book

This book provides the reader with a broad overview of the diversity in American archaeological cemetery studies. We focus on how the perspectives of archaeologists shed new light on the American experience in terms of changing American attitudes toward death. But cemeteries are not just about the dead, they are also for the living. The decisions that surviving relatives made in the choice of grave site and tombstone for their dead relatives reflect the ethnicity, class, and status of both the living and the dead. Trade networks and economics could limit the availability of memorials to choose from. The study of gravestones and burials can reveal the inter-relationships between religion and culture in past societies. They can tell us how people wanted to be remembered, what they valued, and how they felt. They reveal the varied and changing attitudes toward mourning and commemoration of different populations through time. These gravestones and cemeteries also reveal the cultural diversity in America.

Chapter 2 focuses on belowground archaeology and the ethical dilemmas involved in this research. In chapter 3 we discuss the excavation of bodies and grave goods in cemeteries from the seventeenth, eighteenth, and nineteenth centuries. The rest of the chapters in this volume are devoted to aboveground archaeology and are chronologically arranged to explore changing views of death and the symbolism and iconography used in cemeteries from preindustrial to industrial to postindustrial America. Chapter 4 covers the gravestones and cemeteries of the seventeenth and eighteenth centuries. Chapter 5 covers the transformation of simple colonial burial grounds of an agricultural America into the grand, landscaped cemeteries of nineteenth- and twentieth-century industrial America. The Civil War was a turning point in America, and it also had a profound impact on burial practices and on cemetery landscapes. In chapter 6 we discuss gravestone research on ethnicity, race, and class in nineteenth- and twentieth-century cemeteries. The final chapter (chapter 7) brings the study up to cemeteries in the twenty-first century and provides some concluding thoughts on archaeological perspectives on American cemeteries.

Our book integrates case studies within each chapter to provide specific examples of what archaeological research has revealed about the changing American landscape of death and remembrance. Because most of the archaeological research for the past half century has focused on cemeteries on the East Coast of the United States from Maine to Florida, our book reflects that reality. However, whenever possible we have chosen examples from all over the United States, including Alaska and Hawaii.

With these diverse case studies we hope to illustrate how changes in mortuary practices reflect the broader changes within American society.

2

Belowground Archaeology

Ethics and Science

The archaeology of cemeteries is not just about the analysis of gravestones; it also involves the excavation of burials and all their accompanying materials, from shroud pins to coffin nails, coffins, caskets, and all manner of grave goods. These materials are valuable sources of information about individuals who lived in the past, the cultures they participated in, and the beliefs that shaped their lives. However, burials present ethical challenges to the archaeologist because we are excavating the remains of our fellow human beings. Societies and individuals past and present have held widely varying beliefs about the proper treatment of human remains. Archaeologists interested in past societies have often approached the past from a secular, scientific perspective with very little regard for the beliefs or feelings of descendant communities. Only recently have these failings begun to be addressed legislatively and ethically. This chapter examines some of the ethical quandaries involved in the study of burials. We provide a summary of the history of the excavation of graves that were dug without the permission of or input from the descendant community. We start with colonists excavating Native American graves in the seventeenth century and end with controversial late twentieth-century excavations including the African Burial Ground in New York City. We also discuss examples of cooperation and collaboration between archaeologists and descendant communities.

Excavations by European Colonists

In most cultures, cemeteries are sacred sites; they are places where the deceased can remain undisturbed. The earliest documented excavation of Native American graves was by a group of inquisitive Pilgrims who were scouting for a place to settle in what is today the community of Truro on Cape Cod in Massachusetts. In November 1620, they found a mound, dug into it assuming it was a grave, and found a pot, a bow, and some arrows, which they left (Deetz and Deetz 2000: 43). Two weeks later while exploring Indian paths and searching for a place to settle, they came upon another mound (Deetz and Deetz 2000: 46–47). The record of the discovery was published in a book known as *A Relation or Journal of the Beginning and Proceedings of the English Plantation Settled at Plimoth in New England* or, more commonly, as *Mourt's Relation,* printed in London in 1622:

> We found a place like a grave, but it was much bigger and longer than any we had yet seen. It was also covered with boards, so as we mused what it should be, and resolved to digge it up, where we found, first a Matt, and under that a fair bow, and there another Matt, and under that a board about three quarters long, finely carved and paynted, with three tynes, or broaches on the top, like a crown; also between the Matts we found Boules, Trayes, Dishes, and such like Trinkets. At length we came to a fair new Matt, and under that two Bundles, the one bigger, the other lesse, we opened the greater and found in it a great quantitie of fine and perfect red Powder, and in it the bones and skull of a man. The skull had fine yellow haire still on it, and some of the flesh unconsumed; there was bound up with it a knife, a pack needle, and two or three old iron things. It was bound up in a Saylers canvas Casacke, and a payre of cloth breeches; the red Powder was a kind of Embaulment, and yielded a strong, but no offensive smell; It was as fine as any flower. We opened the lesse bundle likewise, and found of the same Powder in it, and the bones and head of a little child, about the legs, and other parts of it was bound strings, and bracelets of fine white Beads; there was also by it a little Bow, about three quarters long and some other odd knackes; we brought sundry of the prettiest things away with us, and covered the Corps up again. After this we digged in sundry like places, but found no more Corne, nor anything else but graves. (Bradford and Winslow 1966 [1622]: 11)

This time the grave contained artifacts "deemed valuable," and the Pilgrims did not hesitate in removing (or stealing) the grave goods (Venables 2004: 75). Native Americans have viewed these actions by the Pilgrims as early examples of looting American Indian graves (Riding In 2002: 296). Sadly, the Pilgrims were the first but certainly not the last group of individuals to unearth Native American burials and wantonly remove their contents. Historian C. A. Weslager (1945) documented several colonial accounts of Native American graves being robbed for their contents, most notably wampum.

Most American archaeologists credit Thomas Jefferson with being the first American archaeologist to excavate scientifically. In 1784, he excavated a Native American burial mound on his property near the Rivanna River in Virginia (Fagan 2005: 50–51). His excavations there were motivated by a desire to better understand the Indian burial customs in Virginia (Jefferson 1999 [1787]: 104). Jefferson found multiple layers of burials of men, women, and children; the bodies were in various positions, some vertical and some horizontal, indicating that the mound had been used as a burial site for many years (Jefferson 1999 [1787]: 104–6). Jefferson did not know the age of the burials, but he did note that contemporary, eighteenth-century, American Indians knew about this mound and Indians traveled to visit it (Jefferson 1999 [1787]: 106). However, Jefferson's records indicate that he never inquired what the connection was between the contemporary Indians and this mound. Nor did it concern Jefferson that in excavating the mound he was desecrating a known Native American burial place simply for the sake of scientific inquiry (Atalay 2006: 287–88). The archaeological practice of excavating Indian burial sites without any concern for the descendant community continued until resistance from Native Americans in the late twentieth century led to legal protections for burial places (McGuire 1992).

Digging Continues in the Nineteenth and Twentieth Centuries

Since these early forays into archaeology, archaeologists have opened thousands of graves in North America; many of them were precontact American Indian graves. Archaeologists were interested in what the grave goods could reveal about past social organization. However, archaeologists studying historic period Native Americans also excavated hundreds of burial sites throughout North America. Burial grounds associated with Spanish missions in the Southeast and Southwest have been unearthed. Although many archaeologists focused on the graves of Native Americans, they also excavated the graves of early European settlers. In 1897, Mary Jeffery Galt excavated European American burials at the Jamestown Church in Virginia (Noël Hume 1996: 111). The graves of colonial elites such as the Calvert family in Maryland and forgotten slaves alike have been dug (Miller et al. 2004; Perry et al. 2009a). In the late twentieth century, archaeologists excavated the graves of Asian Americans (Rouse 2005a). Community burial grounds, churchyards, family plots, massive urban cemeteries, almshouse burial plots, battlefield mass graves, and institutional cemeteries have all felt the probe of the archaeologists' trowels. Until the late twentieth century, archaeologists in the United States were able to excavate unmarked graves and abandoned burial grounds of any religious, racial, or ethnic group as long as the archaeologist had the permission of the property owner and the police were notified to determine that the body was not a contemporary murder victim. Concern was not given to contacting religious or ethnic groups to determine whether there were any religious and/or ideological concerns; the focus was solely on the scientific value of the historic burials.

Native American graves were of tremendous interest to nineteenth- and early twentieth-century archaeologists. In part this was because of the two great archaeological research questions that inspired nineteenth-century North American archaeology: when did the first people arrive in the New World, and who built the great earthen mounds that dotted the midcontinental and southeastern United States? Moreover, as archaeologists began to develop better field methods and concerns with chronology came to the fore, the Direct Historical Approach became widely applied, in which archaeologists began excavating fairly recent deposits and working their way back or deeper to earlier deposits representing older societies (Quimby 1966). Trade goods were also seen by late nineteenth- and early twentieth-century archaeologists as sensitive markers of culture change, an idea that modern archaeologists are increasingly challenging (Gallivan 2004; Silliman 2005; Loren 2008).

It is useful to contrast some of these early excavations with more recent studies in the same general region. One particularly noteworthy case study is the Minisink Burial Ground (Heye and Pepper 1915; Hrdklička 1916; Kraft 1993; Lenik 1996). This is a historic Munsee cemetery located on Minisink Island in the Delaware Water Gap National Recreation Area, between Sussex County, New Jersey, and Pike County, Pennsylvania. The site dates from the Late Woodland and early Contact period and is in an area that served as a place of refuge for displaced Native American people increasingly forced from their traditional lands in eastern New Jersey and New York's Hudson Valley. In the mid-nineteenth century, historians recounted the discovery of Native American burials with trade goods at the site (Barber and Howe 1845: 506). Later, in 1914, a field crew led by George G. Heye, whose collection of Indian artifacts forms the nucleus of the modern Museum of the American Indian in Washington, D.C., and George H. Pepper unearthed 68 burials from a historic Munsee burial ground at the site (Heye and Pepper 1915). More recent excavators, including Charles Philhower, Herbert Kraft, W. Fred Kinsey III, Lorraine Williams, and others, carried out extensive work at the site and concluded that Minisink Island and its associated burial ground was not simply a sepulcher but an extensive habitation site (Grumet 1995: 217). In an important synthetic piece, Edward J. Lenik (1996) has written about the site as a sacred space based in large part on the large number of artistic and elaborate artifacts found there that may be linked to Native American spiritual beliefs.

Heye and Pepper were primarily interested in recovering artifacts for museum display, but they also wanted to examine processes of cultural change associated with contact with the European settlers (Heye and Pepper 1915: 76–77). The skeletal remains they recovered were studied by the pioneering physical anthropologist Aleš Hrdlička, an individual with a dubious reputation among Native Americans. He was interested in identifying what he called the "physical identity" of the Lenape Indians (Hrdklička 1916: 11). Hrdklička concluded that sixty-seven of the sixty-eight human bodies that Heye and Pepper had unearthed were Native American, and he described their burial patterns and skeletal morphology. Perhaps the most interesting aspect of Heye and Pepper's work is that it was hot with controversy. The site they were excavating was recognized by local residents, who were not Indians, as a historic burial ground, and they found Heye and Pepper's work disturbing. Unhappy with the burial ground's desecration, they took legal action. In July 1914, Heye's fieldworkers were arrested on the complaint of a local resident, John Van Sickle, who charged that Heye "did remove the remains of deceased persons to deponent unknown from their graves and places of sepulture in the Old Minisink Graveyard . . . from mere wantonness" (Heye and Pepper 1915: 3). After being convicted and fined by the Sussex County Court of Special Sessions, Heye appealed to the New Jersey Supreme Court, which reversed the decision. The court noted,

The facts show that the plaintiff in error was an anthropologist, who while looking for Indian relics in Sandyston township, Sussex

County, came across a burial place used by the Indians who inhabited that part of the state two or more centuries ago; that he removed two or three of the skeletons which he found there for the collection of the New York Anthropological Society; about the same number for the Museum of the University of Pennsylvania; and several more for the United States Government at Washington. He did this with the consent of the owner of the land upon which these remains were found. It may be that in what plaintiff in error did he violated the laws of decency and morality, but it does not seem to us that he brought himself within the purview of the 148th section of the Crimes Act.

He certainly did not remove these skeletons for the purpose of dissection; nor was it shown that he did it for the purpose of making sale of them. His conviction was rested upon the theory that his act was one of mere wantonness. We do not think this conclusion sound. He took them for a specific purpose; and a thing done for a specific purpose, whether that purpose be one which the public generally will approve or disapprove cannot be said to have been done in mere wantonness. (New Jersey Supreme Court, cited in Heye and Pepper 1915: 3–4)

This case is an interesting foreshadowing of NAGPRA, discussed later in the chapter, and it shows that some nonarchaeologists even a century ago were aware of the ethical issues involved with excavating human and particularly Native American graves.

Heye and Pepper's work was in no way unique. Donald Cadzow and others carried out extensive excavations of historic period Native American burial grounds in Pennsylvania (Cadzow 1936). Similar excavations took place in Maryland (see Curry 1999) and indeed across North America. Arthur Parker, a Seneca and New York state archaeologist in the early twentieth century, carried out some excavations on Native American burial grounds in western New York State and reported on excavations of burial grounds by other archaeologists, including several dating from the seventeenth and eighteenth centuries. Parker (1922: 166), however, noted the American Indian opposition to the excavation of burials. Parker, a trained anthropologist writing for a European American audience, emphasized what the burials and grave goods revealed about American Indian spirituality and reverence for the dead (Parker 1922: 520–21). In contrast, European American archaeologists excavating postcontact Native American burial sites in the northeastern United States focused on issues of status, subsistence, warfare, and trade, not spirituality (for example, Ritchie 1965).

By the late twentieth century, the law in many states prevented the excavation of burials in actively used cemeteries unless the descendants grant permission (Price 1991). Because of legal protections, formal cemeteries are usually not excavated unless the cemetery has to be moved. Unfortunately, these legal protections did not exist prior to the twentieth century, and many cemeteries were moved or abandoned when families and congregations relocated. Many early cemeteries were later destroyed as cities expanded. In some pauper cemeteries, wooden markers decayed and the bodies of the interred were forgotten. Sometimes these burial grounds became public spaces, as was the case in New York City's Washington Square Park in Greenwich Village. Often abandoned burial grounds are uncovered during new construction projects, and CRM archaeologists are called in to excavate the burial grounds and remove the bodies, such as in the African American Eighth Street and Tenth Street Cemeteries in Philadelphia (Crist et al. 1997). The burial grounds of the poor, marginalized, and minority groups are particularly at risk, as they may lack formal markers and clear titles (see Crist and Roberts 1996; Mooney and Crist 2007; Davidson 2004; Diamond 2006). However, property values, particularly in urban areas or along major transportation corridors, can put any burial place at risk (see McVarish et al. 2005; Yamin et al. 2007). Over the past twenty years, several massive nineteenth-century European American cemeteries have been moved in the Boston-Washington megalopolis. These include the late eighteenth- and early nineteenth-century Presbyterian cemetery of Newark, New Jersey, which was relocated for the construction of the New Jersey Devils' new stadium (Audin et al. 2005; Audin and Warnasch 2011). A few years earlier, Newark's Episcopal Cemetery was relocated for the construction of a new performing arts center and an enormous pauper's field was relocated for a new railroad station in Secaucus, New Jersey (Scharfenberger 2004; Romey 2005). Other cemeteries were moved in New York; Wilmington, Delaware (MAAR Associates 2000); and Philadelphia. Indeed, forgotten cemeteries are regularly rediscovered during urban archaeology projects (McVarish et al. 2005; Heilen 2012).

Impact of Native American Graves Protection and Repatriation Act

Until the 1990 passage of the Native American Graves Protection and Re-patriation Act (NAGPRA) regarding the protection (or lack of protection) of Native American burial grounds, archaeologists often regarded the excavation of any burial ground purely from the scientific perspective. For example, many archaeologists believe that ancient skeletal remains have a unique potential to provide scientific information about the peopling of this continent. NAGPRA has radically restructured not only the way archaeologists interact with Native American communities regarding the discovery and treatment of burials but also how archaeologists work with other descendant communities and their cemeteries (Poirier and Bellantoni 1997b: 231–32). Twenty-first-century archaeologists realize that with any excavation of a grave there are legal, religious, and ethical issues that must be addressed. Many research questions can be answered by studying bodies and grave goods, but we believe that before excavating a grave, archaeologists should seriously address a series of questions: Are there ethical issues with doing this work? What about the wishes of the descendants? Have we seriously tried to contact the descendants to obtain permission to excavate their relatives? What happens after the excavation is completed? Is there a time limit to the scientific study of the bodies? Will the bodies be reburied after the study is completed? What about the grave goods? Should they be reburied too? We believe that excavation should proceed only after these questions have been adequately addressed. Archaeologists need to be involved in "proactive planning," in which all sides discuss the issues and arrive at a jointly agreed-upon plan of action before archaeological excavations begin; this can done in both university and CRM settings (Baugher 2009: 48). Because NAGPRA has had (from our perspective) a very positive and profound change on the way archaeologists interact with all descendant communities regarding the excavation of human burials, it is important to understand the background on NAGPRA.

After analyzing all federal and state laws prior to the 1990, lawyer H. Marcus Price III (1991) concluded that most state laws offered little or no protection for Native American burial grounds. This is also true of abandoned cemeteries of the poor, such as almshouse burials and slave burials. This lack of protection for unmarked graves perhaps reflected an elitist and racist attitude by our lawmakers. Prior to NAGPRA, the accepted approach for archaeologists working on burial sites was to excavate the site without consulting Native Americans and then send any human remains and burial goods to a university or a museum to become part of permanent collections (Klesert and Powell 2000: 200–201; Quick 1985). This procedure was also used for the excavation of any burial found in an unmarked grave outside of an actively used cemetery. Descendant communities were not notified, and the human remains and grave goods became part of permanent collections—they were not repatriated to the descendant community, nor were the bodies reburied. Some archaeologists and physical anthropologists strongly defended this procedure (Buikstra 1981; Meighan 1984; Turner 1986).

While there is no single pan-Indian response in terms of the treatment of the dead, many Native Americans who follow a traditional religion support the preservation of burial grounds and sacred sites (Deloria 1969, 1994; Baugher 2005: 253). Native Americans have advocated and continue to advocate for the repatriation of human remains and burial goods (currently in museum and university collections) to American Indian tribal governments (Echo-Hawk and Echo-Hawk 1991; Jemison 1997; Mihesuah 2000; Bray 2001; Daehnke and Lonetree 2011). There are some exceptions: for example, the Navajos and the Eskimos do not want human bodies returned, because of their cultures' specific beliefs about the negative powers of the dead (Thomas 2000: 218–19). In addition, some Native Americans have viewed museums as a viable alternative for the preservation of human remains and burial goods (Baugher 2005: 253). In response to increasing Native American activism regarding burial protection and repatriation, some archaeologists tried to look for a middle ground that allowed some input from descendant communities but ensured that archaeologists would "retain for themselves the 'final court of appeal' on the disposition of human remains" (Klesert and Powell 2000: 201). A small minority in archaeology advocated an equal partnership with Native Americans in the decision-making process, with Native Americans having the final say (Zimmerman 1985, 1989).

After the passage of NAGPRA in 1990, archaeologists had to face the legal reality that they had to develop a different approach to the excavation of Native American burials. However, NAGPRA applies only to burials on U.S. government property or on tribal lands, as well as to projects involving federal funds. If burials are found on private land, the federal laws do not apply. By 2005, there were thirty-four states that had laws protecting burials on state property (Watkins 2006: 79). But if the burial is on private property, then the decisions are made between the property owner and the archaeologists. On sites not impacted by NAGPRA, some archaeologists and biological anthropologists still favor the removal of skeletal remains and grave goods to museums or universities to become part of permanent collections, because of their great value for research (Meighan 1996, 2000). However, others advocate a dialogue with the local Native American community to decide jointly what to do with any body or burial site (Zimmerman 1997, 2000; Watkins 2006, 2008).

NAGPRA has inspired a growing spirit of cooperation and trust between Native Americans and archaeologists, especially in the American Southwest and Northeast (Swidler et al. 1997; Dongoske et al. 2000; Colwell-Chanthaphonh and Ferguson 2008). In addition, books have been written about archaeologists' professional responsibilities to Native Americans and NAGPRA's impact on the profession (such as Lynott and Wylie 2000; Watkins 2000, 2003; Preucel et al. 2006; Killion 2008).

Despite progress in collaboration, there has been a continuing problem with the repatriation of human remains in museums and universities. According to the Department of Interior's regulations for implementing NAGPRA, repatriation is made with federally recognized tribes that demonstrate a clear cultural affiliation with archaeologically excavated human remains. However, archaeologists have often defined the cultural identity of archaeological collections with a particular ceramic or lithic style without making connections to any contemporary Native American tribes (Ferguson 2004: 34); these human remains are labeled as "culturally unidentifiable," which means that they do not have to be repatriated. Unfortunately, culturally unidentifiable human remains make up "80% of the collections" that are in museums or federal agencies and subject to NAGPRA (Daehnke and Lonetree 2011: 93). Some Native Americans see these narrow definitions of cultural affiliation as a way for archaeologists to prevent repatriation (Riding In 2005).

In March 2010, the Department of the Interior issued revisions to the regulations for implementing NAGPRA. The new regulations move away from the archaeologically narrowly defined cultural affiliation to a broader definition based on aboriginal territory (U.S. Department of the Interior 2010). Some Native Americans see this removal of the final barrier to repatriation as truly decolonizing archaeology (Daehnke and Lonetree 2011: 96). However, the revised regulations may increase the tensions between archaeologists and Native Americans. Some archaeologists have argued over the years that repatriating truly ancient skeletal remains, such as Kennewick Man, and grave goods to modern Native Americans based simply on proximity of the modern groups to the burial site denies the scientific value of the remains to both the Indians and all other Americans (Thomas 2000). In 2010, archaeologists and biological anthropologists, including Bruce Smith at the Smithsonian Institution, Jane Buikstra, and thirty-nine other anthropologists, sent a joint protest letter to the secretary of the interior claiming that culturally unidentifiable human remains have an "untapped research potential," especially since newer technologies, such as DNA testing, are rapidly expanding (Smith et al. 2010: 2). They stated that "if these regulations are imposed, it will result in North America's indigenous societies becoming one of the world's least known and least understood populations—in terms of ancient diet, disease, and health" (Smith et al. 2010: 2). Similar claims were made about the passage of NAGPRA in 1990 (Rose et al. 1996). Other museum archaeologists such as Chip Colwell-Chanthaphonh, curator at the Denver Museum of Science, have written in support of the new regulations (Colwell-Chanthaphonh 2010). Native American archaeologist Joe Watkins (2006: 31) believes that the conflicts over repatriation are between "American Indian philosophy and the unilateral application of American science."

The lengthy legal battles over human remains and repatriation, such as in the Kennewick Man controversy, do not have to take place. A few weeks before Kennewick Man was unearthed in the 1990s, human bones dating to 9,200 years ago were discovered in a cave on Prince of Wales Island off Alaska (Thomas 2000: 272–73). The archaeologists immediately informed all of the concerned Indian nations (the tribal government and elders) of the discovery and sought their opinions on how to handle the site and the human remains. Within a week the tribal governments of both Klawock and Craig approved analysis of the bones and the grave goods and approved further excavations (Thomas 2000: 271–72). This project worked because from the very beginning all sides were willing to discuss options, hear each other's opinions, and work cooperatively with each other. The project also may have worked because these specific Native Americans wanted to know about the age and ancestry of the individual and whether the deceased person was an ancestor of the Tlingits or Haidas or from some other group no longer living on Prince of Wales Island (Thomas 2000: 271).

Chip Colwell-Chanthaphonh and T. J. Ferguson (2008) have written about the advantages of working collaboratively with descendant communities. However, collaboration does not mean that Native Americans will agree to having the bones of their ancestors be exhumed. But collaboration could result in both sides working together, without excavating burials, to obtain a better understanding of the past. Will we move forward with cooperation and collaboration, or are archaeologists still concerned with having the ultimate power to control "who owns the past"?

African Burial Ground: Controversy and Cooperation

The ethical concerns for the protection of cemeteries and repatriation of human remains are not limited to the excavation of Native American burials. Other racial and ethnic groups have been concerned about the protection and preservation of their ancestors' graves. There have been high-profile excavations, such as the African Burial Ground in New York City, that pitted a descendant community against government officials and/or CRM companies (Harrington 1993). In 1991, coming on the heels of NAGPRA, was the discovery by CRM archaeologists of the eighteenth-century African Burial Ground in New York City. The property was being excavated because it was the site for a new federal office building and federal funds were being used. However, the story of the African Burial Ground is not simply about what the bones may tell us (discussed in the next chapter); equally important, it is also a story of politics, ethics, and community activism to protect a burial ground. Unlike the Native American burials protected by NAGPRA, unmarked African American burials can be excavated without a legal requirement to inform the descendants or stakeholders (Blakey 2009: 9). In the summer of 1991, archaeologists with the CRM firm Historical Conservation and Interpretation (HCI) discovered human remains on the former burial ground, but the U.S. General Services Administration (GSA) kept the discovery a secret until October 1991 (Harrington 1993: 28). Religious leaders and laypeople from New York's African American community were angered that they were not informed about the excavation, and the anger increased when several burials were destroyed by a backhoe (Harrington 1993: 33). The continued reluctance of the GSA to adequately excavate the site and study the human remains created a strong and powerful reaction from the African American community in

New York. A two-year battle ensued between the GSA and the African American community over the fate of the burial ground (Statistical Research 2009: 278). Because the African American community was a strong voting block (unlike Native American communities) and had the backing of politicians, including New York City's first black mayor, David Dinkins, and New York state senator David Paterson (later the first African American governor of New York), they were successful in having their voices heard (Baugher 2005: 253). The GSA eventually replaced HCI with John Milner and Associates (JMA), a firm that had experience in excavating an African American cemetery in Philadelphia (Harrington 1993: 35). Biological anthropologist Michael Blakey, then at Howard University, submitted a proposal for laboratory research on the human remains and the grave goods (Blakey 1992). In 1993, Howard University was hired by GSA to undertake the postexcavation research on the burial ground (Howson, Bianchi, and Perry 2009: 5). The archaeologists and biological anthropologists involved in the postexcavation research characterized themselves as activist scholars; they were committed to working closely with the descendant community and ensuring the repatriation and reburial of the human remains and artifacts (La Roche and Blakey 1997; Perry et al. 2009b). The research team felt that the descendant community should decide if invasive techniques could be used and if any scientific analysis should be performed, and the community approved both (Statistical Research 2009: 280). The descendant community also provided the Howard University research team with input on research questions and public interpretation (LaRoche and Blakey 1997; Perry et al. 2009b).

The role of an engaged and politically active public and descendant community also shaped how the African Burial Ground was protected and was/is interpreted to the public. As a result of the congressional hearings, GSA was ordered to cease construction on the site, and Congress appropriated funds for the establishment of a museum (Harrington 1993: 33). In 1993, the site was designated the African Burial Ground and the Commons Historic District by the New York City Landmarks Preservation Commission (Harris et al. 1993). The entire area that historically contained the burial ground was declared a National Historic Landmark in 1993, and in 2006 the site was proclaimed the African Burial Ground National Monument and became part of the National Park System (Statistical Research 2009: 20, 34). In 2003, all 419 bodies that were excavated and scientifically studied were placed in beautiful mahogany coffins made in Ghana and were reinterred at the site; seven earthen mounds mark the reburial site (National Park Service 2011). The National Park Service manages the national monument, including the museum/visitor center that opened in 2010, the reburial site, and the outdoor memorial designed by Rodney Léon (Rothstein 2010). The national monument also contains four original works of art that were commissioned by the GSA, and since 2001 the art has been on permanent exhibition in the Ted Weiss office building that borders the outdoor memorial (Taylor 2001). The African Burial Ground project provides a model for other scholars working with descendant communities and indeed highlights the importance of communities in shaping the interpretation of such sites (figure 2.1).

Archaeologists and Descendant Communities Working Together

There have been other examples of cooperation between communities and archaeologists. Other examples of archaeologists collaborating with descendant communities on burial issues include the work of one of the authors (Baugher) in New York and Patricia Rubertone in Rhode Island. In 1986, during reconstruction work on the New York City–landmarked John Street Methodist Church, human bones were uncovered; work was halted because the site could have contained burials from either a Native American or a European American burial ground (Baugher 2009: 50–51). The project did not trigger any environmental reviews or legal requirements to undertake an excavation, but Reverend Warren Danskin, the minister of the church, met with Michael Bush, the director of the American Indian Community House (representing 14,000 Indians in New York City) and Sherene Baugher as the city archaeologist to discuss how to proceed (Baugher 2009: 48–49). As a result of the discussions, a voluntary team of archaeologists and Native Americans jointly excavated the site (Baugher et al. 1991). As agreed before the excavation started, biological anthropologists analyzed the bones (no invasive techniques were used) and then the bones were reburied underneath the basement of the church in a joint Native American and Methodist religious ceremony (Baugher 2009: 54–55). For both the John Street site and the African Burial Ground, the archaeologists involved went way beyond the practice allowing a descendant community to express their opinions while reserving the right of the archaeologists to make the final decisions. We entered into an equal

Figure 2.1. The African Burial Ground National Monument, in New York City. Photograph by Sherene Baugher.

collaboration in which either partner could veto plans and compromises were reached.

Patricia Rubertone's *Grave Undertakings: An Archaeology of Roger Williams and the Narragansett Indians* (2001) examines the history of the Narragansetts and their archaeology but focuses particular attention on a cemetery known as RI-1000, which was excavated by CRM archaeologists "shortly before the Narragansett received federal recognition as an Indian tribe in April 1983" (Rubertone 2001: xvi). The cemetery had been accidentally discovered during construction activities. Although the Narragansett Tribe, the landowner, and the Rhode Island Historical Preservation Commission agreed that preservation in place would be appropriate, it was clear that given the artifacts already discovered and the development planned for the site, excavation was preferable (Robinson et al. 1985: 113). Brown University and the Rhode Island Historical Preservation Commission carried out the excavation in 1982 and 1983. Rubertone explained why the Narragansetts supported this excavation and how the burial ground was used to help solidify their modern identity. Indeed, this project is a fine example of collaborative research, which provided an opportunity to present a Native-centered history, while also helping others understand Narragansett Indian life in the late seventeenth century (discussed in more detail in the next chapter).

Conclusions

While attitudes and the legal ramifications of excavating Native American and other minority-group skeletal remains are evolving, there is also a growing public interest in forensic anthropology and osteoarchaeology. People are curious about what bones can tell us about both a person's life and the circumstances surrounding the person's death. In a dramatic reversal of what once was the case, European American skeletal remains and casts of those remains with associated objects are now being displayed in museum settings, for example, the *Written in Bone* exhibit at the National Museum of Natural History in Washington, D.C. (Owsley and Bruwelheide 2009). The *Written in Bone* exhibit even has a book written for young adults to bring the discoveries from burial sites to the next generation (Walker 2009). The message is that bones, grave goods, and even coffins can reveal information about the deceased.

But we believe that before any future belowground studies are undertaken, the ethical questions need to be addressed. Archaeologists need to communicate with descendant communities. We need to find out whether the descendants are opposed to excavation. Archaeologists should determine whether some of our research questions can be answered through oral histories, the excavation of habitation sites, and the aboveground study of cemeteries rather than undertaking the excavation of burial grounds. In some cases, the use of remote sensing can provide us with the orientation of the grave shafts without the need to excavate. If a community does grant permission for excavation of a cemetery, then all issues relating to the time limits for the analysis and the conditions regarding reburial and repatriation of grave goods must be agreed upon before excavation begins. Cooperation and collaboration between archaeologists and descendant communities should be the hallmark of any future belowground archaeological research in cemeteries.

3

The Science in Belowground Archaeology

Books, movies, and television shows have increased Americans' interest in forensic science. Skeletal remains can provide information about the stature, gender, age, and health of deceased individuals, as well as injuries they suffered during their lives and damage their bones suffered after death. From skeletal remains, forensic anthropologists can identify certain diseases (such as tuberculosis, anemia, and syphilis), identify congenital illnesses, and record evidence of trauma, habitual activities, and even childbirth. Chemical analysis of bones is being used to provide information about diet and determine where individuals lived. DNA evidence is being used to identify historic personages with some success. Grave goods are similarly revealing. At a minimum, grave goods may provide insights into religious belief systems, socioeconomic status, gender-linked behaviors, achieved and ascribed statuses, trade networks, culture change, attitudes toward age, and beliefs about death and commemoration. In burials there is evidence of ethnicity, class, religion, and racial differences.

While chapter 6 is devoted to a discussion of ethnicity and class as seen in aboveground markers, this chapter discusses ethnicity and class and how they are revealed in coffins, artifacts, and the skeletal remains of the buried individuals. Often there are significant differences between aboveground memorials and what is found belowground. Gravemarkers are in the public sphere and can be seen by anyone, whereas the material culture buried in the ground is private and is often placed there by family members, close friends, and/or morticians. The material included in the coffins or simply with the bodies reflects what grave goods families wanted to be placed with their loved ones. Native Americans, African Americans, and other groups may have been able to more freely express their ethnicity and religious beliefs with the grave goods they placed in the burials of their relatives and how these goods were buried. In contrast, the aboveground material reveals information to a wider audience. Some of the symbols on tombstones may have been purposefully chosen because they meant one thing to the dominant culture and another to the ethnic or racial minority.

In this chapter we discuss the findings from an excavation of burials of Native Americans, African Americans, Chinese Americans, and European Americans. Many of these excavations were undertaken as CRM projects when burials were accidentally discovered. But before discussing ethnic burials, we cover the general topic of grave configuration, coffins, and coffin hardware that apply to diverse groups.

Belowground Archaeology: Grave Shafts, Coffins, and Coffin Hardware

Before excavating human remains, archaeologists look for the below-ground remains of grave shafts and/or for coffins. Some people are buried without coffins, and the trenches dug for their grave shafts will leave a mottled soil outline that is distinctive. Archaeologists may find coffins, either fragmentary or whole, depending on soil conditions. In some cases all that remains is a dark outline, a stain in the soil where the coffin once was. Often, the placement of nails used to construct the coffin reflects its form. During the colonial period, both shrouded and coffined burials were employed. Shrouds were very simple. After the body was washed and prepared, it was wrapped in a shroud. This was "a long white linen or cotton garment with open back and long sleeves" (Larkin 1988: 98). Embalming was uncommon, and most shrouds were hastily prepared; in fact, some were simply a long sheet, or "winding sheet," of fabric wrapped around the remains. Copper-alloy pins held the shrouds in place, and the green verdigris left behind by copper salts is often noted on bones. For example, in the New York African Burial Ground, shrouding of the dead may have been typical, with small copper-alloy straight pins recovered from half of the 424 burials and shrouding occurred in both coffin and noncoffin burials (Perry et al. 2009b: 369).

In the colonial period, coffins were used for burials of people of different ethnic, racial, and economic classes—they were not just used by the elite. For example, in the New York African Burial Ground, 424 grave shafts were uncovered (but only 419 still contained skeletal remains) and 91 percent of the graves contained coffins (Perry et al. 2009b: 367, 369). In addition, there was diversity in coffin form, especially in the coffins for children, which may have been made by the deceased child's family rather than purchased (Perry et al. 2009b: 370). The three main types of coffins were hexagonal, rectangular, and trapezoidal (Statistical Research 2009: 218). The coffin of Burial 101 was unusual in that the coffin lid contained a heart-shaped symbol formed by "tinned or silvered iron tacks" (Perry et al. 2009b: 372). Within the heart-shaped outline, there was additional decoration and what appeared to be the date 1769 (Howson and Bianchi 2009: 239). The heart design with the interior scrolls may be the Sankofa symbol for remembering one's ancestors, a powerful design that was originally used by the Akan people of Ghana and the Ivory Coast (Perry et al. 2009b: 372). One translation of the Sankofa symbol is "learn from the past to prepare for the future" (National Park Service 2011). The use of this symbol may suggest African cultural continuity and resistance to European American acculturation (Mack and Blakey 2004: 15). However, historian Eric Seeman (2010b: 116) notes that in the eighteenth century, "hearts made out of tacks were not uncommon adornments on Anglo-American coffin lids." For white New Yorkers, the heart design symbolized the soul's ascension into a Christian heaven (Seeman 2010b: 118). It is possible that the common European American heart symbol, while used by African Americans, had a separate symbolic meaning for them or perhaps carried multiple meanings.

Coffin hardware is a particularly sensitive indicator of cultural behavior, especially for nineteenth-century populations. By the 1790s, the use of coffins among ordinary Americans was widespread (Larkin 1988: 99). Coffins were made by cabinetmakers, as well as by friends of the family or relatives of the deceased. Wealthy individuals purchased carefully finished hardwood coffins, but most were made from softwoods such as pine, which were easy to work and could be painted for a better appearance. Coffin furniture during this period was rather minimal. In urban areas, decorations such as nameplates on copper, tin, or silver and angels, flowers, and other ornaments were available (Habenstein and Lamers 1981: 160). The nineteenth century saw an explosion in coffin designs. A coffin, besides serving the utilitarian function of containing the remains of the deceased, also served to "indicate the status of the deceased through its quality of materials, workmanship, and adornment and was believed to help preserve the body" (Habenstein and Lamers 1981: 162). In the nineteenth century, coffins of cement, wood, clay, zinc, iron, rubber, and even papier-mâché were being patented (Habenstein and Lamers 1981: 163).

Inexpensive stamped and cast metal coffin hardware became the norm (Hacker-Norton and Trinkley 1984).

Arguably the most spectacular of these new coffin innovations were the metallic coffins, some of which were shaped like ancient Egyptian sarcophagi. Indeed, they have been described as containing "innovations in design that recalled at once the ancient Egyptian sarcophagus, the iron torpedo, and the strong box" topped off by a faceplate that looked like a diver's mask (Habenstein and Lamers 1981: 180). There were even patents for bizarre cemetery accoutrements such as life signals, so that the prematurely buried could alert passersby topside (Habenstein and Lamers 1981: 41)!

The Uxbridge Almshouse is a fine example of the documentation and excavation of a nineteenth-century institutional cemetery where the artifacts, particularly coffin furniture, reveal much about nineteenth-century American attitudes toward death (Bell 1990, 1991). The town of Uxbridge, Massachusetts, used the Uxbridge Poor Farm from 1831 to 1872. The cemetery was rediscovered during a road-widening project for Route 146 and was initially misidentified as either a small Quaker family burial ground or possibly an Indian burial ground (Elia and Wesolowsky 1991: 5). Concern over the possible desecration of Native American graves led to a more comprehensive archaeological study by Boston University's Office of Public Archaeology beginning in 1985. Discussing the significance of the site, Edward Bell noted, "Deathways encompasses the whole cultural system of mortuary behavior, involving emotion, ideology, symbolism, technology, and economy" (Bell 1990: 54). In particular, Bell focused on coffin hardware, especially mass-produced coffin hardware, and what it reveals about changing attitudes toward death in nineteenth-century America. Previous studies have presented coffin hardware as an indication of socioeconomic rank. As Bell notes, this is an unsatisfactory explanation for the materials recovered from a pauper's burial ground. Bell provides an alternative yet convincing explanation. Rather than seeing these mass-produced objects as reflecting true wealth, Bell views them as material evidence of the pervasive cultural notion of the beautification of death, and also as objects designed to impart a sense of socioeconomic stature otherwise not attainable for these individuals (Bell 1990: 55) (figure 3.1). This cultural shift, tectonic in scale, was linked with new romantic views of death and mourning, which came together with the rise of the funeral industry and mass production of coffin hardware in sentimental styles. There was a trend

Figure 3.1. Select pressed-metal nineteenth-century coffin fittings, similar to those re-covered at the Uxbridge Almshouse Burial Ground and other late nineteenth-century cemeteries. Photograph courtesy of the Chicora Foundation, Inc., Columbia, S.C.

toward more-decorative coffins and indeed caskets that might be seen as ostentatious status displays. The use of mass-produced coffin hardware is not unique to America but was particularly widespread here. Indeed, it, like many other aspects of nineteenth-century commemoration, was part of a trend found not only in the United States but also in much of western Europe.

Bell's case study, the burial ground associated with the Uxbridge Alms-house, apparently provided for economical but respectable burial of the dead. The archaeological evidence provides some evidence of this minimal investment in burials: gravemarkers were simple granite slabs, while cof-fins were minimalist and often poorly made (although several did display embellishments associated with the beautification of death). Bell's work cautions us that mass-produced coffin hardware should not be used as an unequivocal indication of socioeconomic rank. Rather, the coffin hard-ware may have been used to mask the nature of socioeconomic distance between classes (Bell 1990: 72). In essence, inexpensive, mass-produced coffin furnishings, often stamped from metal, allowed poorer families to decorate their relatives' coffins in ways that were similar to those of wealthier individuals. This served as part of a masking strategy whereby the social distinctions so real in day-to-day life could be hidden in death.

The movements from graveyards to cemeteries, from gravestones to monuments, and from shrouds and coffins to caskets were part of a pervasive transformation of the nineteenth century, which has been described as the beautification of death. Although death rates remained shockingly high, attitudes toward death were changing. As Edmund Gillon notes, "Victorian epitaphs, reflecting the change from gray-slate markers to softer-seeming white marble, were more cheerful, more restrained: the deceased was 'asleep,' 'at rest,' 'gone away'" (Gillon 1972: 7). With changing religious attitudes, especially the growth of Arminianism, which argued that individuals could be saved through good works, more people felt certain of eternal life (Sloane 1991: 72). The graves of young people received special treatment during this period, as romantic notions of death as worthy of prolonged and intense mourning. Coffins, simple boxes to hold the remains of the deceased, were replaced by beautifully made and lavishly ornamented caskets, not unlike jewelry boxes.

The excavations at seventeenth-century St. Mary's City in Maryland, one of North America's most intensively studied seventeenth-century sites, provide information on coffins, colonial burial practices, and the health of a much earlier group of Americans. Unlike other colonial cities, St. Mary's City was a bastion of Catholicism in the predominantly Protestant English North American colonies. The chapel, which stood at the center of a large colonial burying ground, has seen considerable study (Riordan 1997, 2009).

St. Mary's City's first chapel was constructed circa 1638 and was initially an earthfast structure, which may have burned down during the Protestant rebellion of 1645 (Riordan 1997: 29). A substantial brick chapel replaced it in the 1660s (Riordan 2000: 1-5). In 1704 the brick chapel was closed, and it was torn down shortly thereafter (Riordan 1997: 29). Aside from the extensive subterranean archaeological traces of the chapel, no aboveground remains were associated with the structure, though a splendid modern reconstruction now stands on the site.

Initially excavated in the 1930s (Forman 1938: 249–51), the chapel was completely exposed by archaeologists from Historic St. Mary's City in 1989–90 (Riordan 1997: 29). The property was excavated using a 5 percent random sample followed by block excavations around known or suspected buildings. The graves were recorded, their fill content was sampled, and evidence of markers was noted (Riordan 1997: 30). Although grave shafts may seem decidedly less interesting than the skeletal remains that are recovered from them, their location, orientation, fill, and associated features can provide important insights into a society's beliefs. Generally speaking, in traditional English Christian burial, graves were oriented with their long axes on an east-west line, with the deceased's head to the west. Riordan found that while many of the graves were oriented east-west, there was some variation, which he attributes in part to these graves being oriented parallel to some of the structures and other landscape features present in the cemetery. Indeed, Riordan was able to demonstrate that some graves predate, while others postdate, the chapel based on their orientation.

Finally, unlike New England's iconographically rich burial grounds, Maryland's early burial places have very few stone gravemarkers. Indeed, carved stone tombstones were not common at all before the mid-eighteenth century. Riordan (1997) examined grave shaft orientation and found post molds indicating the locations of once-ubiquitous wooden gravemarkers. Roughly 16 percent of the burials found in the cemetery show evidence of what were likely wooden markers (Riordan 1997: 36). These may have been crosses, grave rails, or dead boards, wooden gravemarkers consisting of two posts set in the ground and a panel above. Some were oriented parallel to and above the graves, while others were perpendicular to the heads of the graves. So even in sites where there appears to be very little to say about the burials, considerable information can be gleaned from the stains in the soil, as seen at the Chapel Burying Ground.

In St. Mary's City, of the fifty-eight burial shafts, forty-seven shafts contained skeletons and 68 percent contained coffins (Riordan 2000: 5-1). Riordan (2000: 2-3) examined seven seventeenth-century burial sites in Maryland and Virginia and noted that there was a trend from infrequent use of coffins and just shaft burials in the 1600s to nearly universal use of coffins by the late 1600s. In examining the coffins at St. Mary's City, Riordan found a movement from diverse coffin shapes in the early seventeenth century toward more regular coffin construction with an emphasis on hexagonal coffins by the late seventeenth century (Riordan 2000: 6-3). Riordan (2000: 6-2) also discovered that Catholic English practices at St. Mary's City reflected the same changes occurring in Protestant burial practices in England and noted that "while the Marylanders may have been Catholic, they were also English."

The archaeologists at St. Mary's City found that burials occurred both in the cemetery and under the floor of the church: in addition to the fifty-eight unmarked graves outside the church, thirty-five graves were found inside the church (Riordan 2000: 1-10, 3-2). In the chapel, three extraordinary graves containing tightly sealed lead coffins were identified. This presented a unique archaeological opportunity, not just to identify who these noteworthy individuals were but also the possibility that seventeenth-century air or pollen was preserved within the coffins. A team of experts in atmospheric science, geology, palynology, conservation, history, forensics, and other fields was assembled to study the coffins and the human remains inside the coffins (Miller et al. 2004).

Henry Miller and Silas Hurry from Historic St. Mary's City enlisted the help of numerous experts, including NASA for air sampling and non-destructive analysis, the Smithsonian Institution and the army's Walter Reed Hospital for forensics, the Armed Forces Radio-Biology Institute for gammagrams (a form of imaging) and logistics, the U.S. Army Reserve and U.S. Navy for logistics and security, and the Maryland Historical Trust for archaeological assistance (Silas Hurry, pers. comm., July 2013). One challenge was imaging through the lead, so that the investigators could tell the condition of the remains. The army provided a nuclear physicist who was able to create images using gamma radiation. The army also provided a mobile laboratory to process the images. A specialist from the navy working with NASA atmospheric scientists designed a machine to extract air from the coffins without introducing outside air (Project Lead Coffins n.d.). Craftsmen from the Patuxent Naval Air Station also developed a cradle that could cut under the coffins; using a gantry and a bomb cart, they were able to transport the heavy lead coffins to a study tent (Project Lead Coffins n.d.).

The three coffins contained the burials of a man, a woman, and a female child (figure 3.2, *left*). Identifying the deceased in the three coffins took detective work worthy of Sherlock Holmes. Certain characteristics such as high status, wealth, and adherence to Roman Catholicism were assumed, since burial in a Roman Catholic church in a lead coffin indicated that the individuals had to fit these profiles. They must have passed away after the 1660s, when the brick chapel was completed, and before 1704, when the chapel's doors were locked by order of the royal governor. The three individuals also had to live close enough to St. Mary's City for them to have been buried there. This greatly narrowed the list of wealthy, high-status

Figure 3.2. *Left*, the three lead coffins unearthed beneath the chapel in St. Mary's City, Md. *Right*, a reconstruction of Anne Wolsey Calvert, based on her skeletal remains. Photographs courtesy of Historic St. Mary's City.

Catholics. The archaeologists finally identified the man as Philip Calvert, governor of Maryland, the youngest son of the first Lord Baltimore; Philip Calvert died in 1682 when he was about fifty-six years old (Riordan 2004: 329, 345). The woman buried next to him was probably his first wife, Anne Wolsey Calvert (Riordan 2004: 329, 345) (figure 3.2, *right*). The rarity of lead coffins indicated that the child was the offspring of high-status parents, but the identity of the child was still a bit of a puzzle. Philip, after his first wife's death, married Jane Sewell, but he died shortly thereafter; the child is likely to have been the product of this second marriage, given the child's burial location (Miller et al. 2004: 366).

But what did the archaeologists learn by analyzing the three bodies? Scientists at the Smithsonian Institution and the Armed Forces Institute of Pathology performed a detailed skeletal analysis of the remains. The Calvert child was about six months of age when she died. She had some serious health problems. Her bones indicate a deficiency of vitamins C and D, and she had rickets and perhaps scurvy (Miller et al. 2004: 362). She also had a cranial infection that caused lesions on her skull that may have led to her death. The middle coffin contained the exceptionally well preserved remains of an older woman, Anne Wolsey Calvert. Not only were her remains in good shape, but silk ribbons were intact and there was even a bit of plant material that turned out to be the herb rosemary, a symbol of remembrance (Miller et al. 2004: 359–60). Despite her wealth, Anne

Calvert had caught some of the slings and arrows of life's misfortunes. She had suffered a badly broken leg; when the bones healed, her right leg was several inches shorter than her left leg (Miller et al. 2004: 360). Her bones also showed that she suffered from additional health problems— there was evidence of osteoporosis; she had advanced arthritis in her back and neck; and she had lost most of her teeth, with the eight teeth that remained containing cavities and/or abscesses, making eating difficult—but she managed to survive until she was at least fifty-five years old (Miller et al. 2004: 360). Biological anthropologist Douglas Owsley, who has studied other colonial period burials, found that rich women such as Anne Calvert "suffered far more severe dental problems than common people," perhaps because of greater access to sugar in their food and drinks (Miller et al. 2004: 371). The third and largest coffin, weighing roughly 1,500 pounds, contained the remains of Philip Calvert. Quite a bit of engineering was required to unearth it. When it was opened, it was found to contain a perfectly preserved wooden coffin. However, the remains within the coffin were very poorly preserved. The man had been in his early fifties when he died. Despite the poor preservation, the biological anthropologists were able to determine that he was about five foot six inches tall, right handed, and "somewhat corpulent," and the "muscle markings on his bones indicated [that] he led a relatively sedentary life" (Miller et al. 2004: 356). Neutron activation analysis of crystals on his body indicated that he was embalmed, an indication of high status, as very few individuals were embalmed in the seventeenth century (Miller et al. 2004: 357).

Pollen analysis was also brought to bear. According to the pollen analysis by Gerald Kelso, the child had been buried in the spring, the woman was buried in the fall, and the man died in the winter (Miller et al. 2004: 357, 360, 362). The wooden coffins of the man and the woman had been either constructed or stored in a building where European grains were stored. Again this points to the wealth of the deceased. The use of diverse scientific techniques, such as neutron activation and pollen analysis, helped the archaeologists determine who was buried in the coffins and the conditions of their life and death. The rest of this chapter focuses on what archaeologists have learned in studying the human remains of postcontact Native Americans, African Americans, Asian Americans, and European Americans.

Excavation of Historic Period Native American Burial Grounds

The interaction of Native American and European American populations in colonial America has seen intensive archaeological study. Many of the best-known sites from this period in the Northeast are cemeteries (Simmons 1970; Gibson 1980; Turnbaugh 1984; Robinson et al. 1985; Brenner 1988; Crosby 1988; Bragdon 1999; Hodge 2005). An early example is the work of Foster H. Saville, who excavated a Montauk cemetery at Easthampton, Long Island, in 1917. Saville unearthed a total of fifty-eight skeletons. The report is typical of the time, in that the artifacts are simply described, including bottles of dark green glass, shell beads, clay pipes, fragments of cloth bags, beadwork, and spoons. Scratched on the shoulder of a glass bottle Saville unearthed is the name Wobetom, a seventeenth-century Montauk chief. No interpretations are provided, though the report was well illustrated (Saville 1920). However, by the late twentieth century the level of analysis and sophistication had increased measurably.

Indeed, the rich burials of the Narragansetts have seen considerable study by archaeologists. For example, the site RI-1000 (discussed in chapter 2) was discovered accidentally during construction in 1982. Excavating the site became part of a process of revealing the Narragansett peoples' lives. Tacking back and forth between the archaeology of the site and Roger Williams's (1936 [1643]) *A Key into the Languages of America* provides some clues into the lives of the Narragansetts during this period. Orderly graves, dug perhaps with shovels, were found generally reaching about three feet below the ground surface. Native textiles seem to have been included in many graves and were apparently used to line the graves, providing a secure resting place for the deceased (Rubertone 2001: 135). The graves were in arable soil, perhaps indicating that the relationship between life and death was a continuous cycle of renewal. Graves were clustered, perhaps reflecting a sort of sociability (Rubertone 2001: 131). While the Catholics at St. Mary's City placed their relatives oriented east-west, the Narragansetts placed their graves facing southwest. Forty-seven graves were identified; the buried individuals were flexed in a fetal position, likely signifying a symbolic connection between death and birth, and placed on their right side facing east, both life-associated social directions, affirming Narragansett well-being (Rubertone 2001: 133). Grave goods tended to be placed east of the corpse near the upper half of the body, though some items were placed directly upon the body. Grave goods were carefully selected, including numerous trade goods. The Native Americans had also reworked European kettles and spoons in their own designs; they cast buttons and made tokens using lead and pewter; and they created beadwork designs of incredible beauty (Rubertone 2001: 138). As Rubertone notes,

> European trade goods uncovered in the RI-1000 graves were much more than an index of how accustomed those buried in this cemetery had become to new forms of technology and material culture, or how they unwittingly acquiesced to more profound changes in their lives and surroundings. These items suppose a much more complicated scenario than one that can be captured in a "continuous narrative" with an inevitable outcome of emerging Anglicization and disappearing "Indianness." They [the Narragansetts] came to rely on many of these things for their survival, but they also imposed their imprints on them. As part of their everyday lives and sacred traditions, they became the tools of their resistance. (Rubertone 2001: 139)

In many instances, the remains contradicted what Williams had written. For example, Roger Williams noted that in life children generally went naked, but in the cemetery they were buried with clothing on (Rubertone 2001: 143). Children received different goods than adults did, including bells, and scaled-down or miniature items of adult goods.

Young women had goods appropriate to their daily lives. Several skeletons showed physical evidence for the injuries their bodies had suffered during life. There was evidence for malnutrition, and one showed what may have been evidence of venereal disease (Rubertone 2001: 152). Older women wore no beads or other body ornamentation; they were sometimes buried with hoes, pestles, awls, and kettles, reflecting their lives and perhaps the fact that "their social position within the community had become redefined in terms of their own life experiences and increasing sense of independence" (Rubertone 2001: 155).

Men's graves were quite different from those of the women. Many men's graves also contained tools, although these were for metalworking and wampum production; some bodies were decorated near their heads with wampum or bone combs (Rubertone 2001: 161). The majority of the men were buried with pipes, both imported and Native made. Indeed, Rubertone even reported a finely wrought steatite pipe, perhaps one of the "great pipes" mentioned by Williams, buried in an intrusive pit above an earlier grave (Rubertone 2001: 171). Michael Nassaney (2000) has written about the pipe that Rubertone reported and the possibility that it was buried later by someone who was returning it to its owner. Nassaney recounts a Wampanoag folktale titled "The Silver Pipe," which tells of how Massasoit gave one of his warriors a great silver pipe. When the warrior was about to die, he charged his wife to bury it with him. His wife kept it but found that when she went to use the unburied pipe, it moved away from her on its own accord. Frustrated, she then buried the pipe in the warrior's grave (Nassaney 2000: 422). The parallels between this tale and the past behaviors reflected in the archaeological remains seen at RI-1000 are intriguing.

The site is also noteworthy for the incredible preservation. Preserved by contact with copper salts, fragments of decayed clothing were recovered from several graves (Welters et al. 1996: 231). These scraps provide evidence about the role of trade cloth in the transformation of Indian culture and in textile history, and they also represent the types of materials available in early America. It is also worth noting that textiles may have been used in ways unintended by their European producers, such as shrouds, wrappers for grave goods, and medicine bags (Welters et al. 1996: 231).

Rubertone's study is important for elucidating differences between the grave goods of men and women and also those of old and young and tying these differences to cultural behaviors that confirm and in some cases refute Roger Williams's writings. Perhaps it is even more important for showing how important commemorating the dead through time was (and still is) for Algonquian-speaking peoples in the Northeast. According to Rubertone (2001: 166), this could involve creating piles of stone, digging small holes in the ground to "renew their memories of 'many great things of antiquity,'" celebrating important events, or visiting former burial sites. The RI-1000 project tells us about not only Narragansett attitudes toward burial in the colonial period but also the persistence of Native American beliefs into the modern period. Finally, Rubertone (2001: 175) notes how historical documents indicate that even in the early colonial period, Native American graves were being plundered of their trade goods by greedy colonists.

Another noteworthy study of a historic Native American burial place was Moreau Maxwell and Jim Brown's excavation of the Fletcher site in Michigan (Mainfort 1979, 1985). This was a burial ground from a mid-eighteenth-century village likely occupied by Ottawas. No formal coffins were present, but wooden slabs lined the graves. The archaeologists were interested in researching the status differences in this community and in looking at how archaeology can provide insights into the rise of social inequality (Mainfort 1985: 555). The site was excavated by Michigan State University, between 1967 and 1970, and contained some two dozen graves. Grave goods were almost entirely French, likely indicating the site's abandonment near the end of the French and Indian War in 1760 (Mainfort 1985: 557).

Historical evidence indicates that the Central Algonquian communities, such as this one, moved away from an egalitarian form of organization as trade goods were distributed through chiefs to other community members. Using a statistical analysis of the artifact assemblage, Mainfort concludes that the burial ground was associated with an incipient ranked community. Moreover, using contemporary accounts, he was able to calculate the value of trade goods in beaver pelts. European trade goods such as kettles, axes, mirrors, silver gorgets, muskets, and the like became status markers. Using this scheme, he was able to rank the burials by the wealth with which the dead were interred. Moreover, this wealth seems to have been concentrated with particular families, presumably those of community leaders. Furthermore, he noted differences between the locations of high-status burials, as well as differences by age and gender. Some of this may be due to different clans competing for wealth and status (Mainfort 1985: 572). Mainfort's work is an early and important example of how careful analysis of burial data can reveal important information about social patterns.

Post-NAGPRA, there has been minimal excavation of American Indian burial grounds, but archaeologists are reanalyzing material from earlier excavations. Christina J. Hodge (2005) analyzed artifacts from archaeologist Harry Shapiro's 1924 excavation on the Waldo Farm in southern Massachusetts. Property owner John Lincoln Waldo unearthed the remains of three individuals, and then Shapiro unearthed an additional thirty-four graves. The site is likely associated with a burial ground donated by Quaker John Slocum to the local Native American population, and this burial ground was used for the first half of the eighteenth century.

As Hodge notes, scholars focused on documenting the presence and quantity of trade goods in an effort to trace the supposed decline of Native American communities and their increasing level of acculturation. Hodge notes that Native American burial grounds differ from those of European Americans in their spatial organization, in the choice of gravemarkers, and in the presence of grave goods. Hodge's study focused on the Waldo Farm site. Christianized Wampanoags used the cemetery during the early eighteenth century (Hodge 2005: 74). Unlike many Native American burial grounds from this period, such as Minisink Island, and RI-1000, Waldo Farm Burial Ground contained very few grave goods. Rather than abandoning this project in frustration, Hodge examined why this was the case. By employing a holistic approach including folk history, historical documentation, tribal oral histories, and archaeological data, she was able to "explain the absence of grave goods in light of accommodation, ambivalence, and a persistent Wampanoag identity" (Hodge 2005: 75). This area's first European settlers were Quakers who arrived in the mid-seventeenth century. During King Philip's War (1675–76), the area saw considerable conflict, and some captured Wampanoags were sent to the West Indies as slaves while some remained in New England (Hodge 2005: 76).

With the exception of shroud pins, no grave goods were recovered with the bodies. This is noteworthy, as Quakers employed shrouds for burials while Native Americans during this period often buried individuals fully clothed. Simple fieldstone gravemarkers are present, which fits well with Quaker beliefs, which eschewed elaborate gravemarkers. The cemetery appears irregular in form and grave orientation is somewhat variable, though over 17 percent of the Waldo burials have the head to the west, thereby conforming to contemporary Christian practices (Hodge 2005: 80). Complicating matters, this would also fit with Wampanoag beliefs, which placed the dwelling of the creator to the southwest.

Hodge employs postcolonial theory in her attempt to interpret the burial ground. As she notes, "Postcolonial theory mandates the critical investigation of colonizer and colonized interaction in its multiple, dynamic, and situationally dependent forms" (Hodge 2005: 84). Untangling the relationship between the colonizer and the colonized is not straightforward. The colonized may have mimicked and imitated European norms, but how they understood these actions is open to interpretation.

During the colonial period, the Quakers established no missions and oversaw no praying towns, but they preached the gospel to both Native Americans and European Americans (Hodge 2005: 87). The lack of grave goods may reflect a lack of tension regarding social structures. Hodge concurs with Kathleen Bragdon, who has argued that in some cases "Christianity played a positive role in the maintenance of distinct native communities in the eighteenth century" (Hodge 2005: 88). Hodge believes that Native Americans may have found Quaker beliefs particularly attractive during a period of societal redefinition and change.

Archaeologists from museums, universities, and CRM projects have undertaken numerous studies of Native American burials from mission sites in Florida, Georgia, and the islands off the coast of Georgia and the Carolinas. Some archaeological testing of mission sites and their cemeteries was undertaken in the 1940s and 1950s, but intense study of Florida missions took place during the last quarter of the twentieth century (Gannon 1993). The most detailed excavation has been the multiyear excavation of the Spanish Catholic mission of Santa Catalina de Guale on St. Catherines Island off the coast of Georgia. David Hurst Thomas and a team of specialists from the American Museum of Natural History in New York City uncovered the cemetery underneath the floor of the second mission church (1604–80); the cemetery contained 431 individuals (Thomas 1993: 9, 13). Before excavating the cemetery, Thomas tried to find descendants of the Guale Indians who were buried at the mission. When Thomas was unable to find Guale descendants, he contacted the Catholic bishop of Savannah to obtain permission to excavate the cemetery; Bishop Raymond Lessard granted permission with the agreement that all the bodies would be reburied in the original cemetery once the analysis was completed (Thomas 1988: 38–39). While the bones were poorly preserved because of the acidic soil, some analysis was possible. The individuals were buried in supine, extended positions with hands folded over the torso; the large number of burials in a limited area resulted in later burials disturbing earlier burials (Larsen 1993: 325).

The burials provided some insight into the Catholic conversion of the Guale Indians. The precontact Guale Indians buried their dead with grave goods, and the Christianized Guales continued this practice, only replacing Native religious items with crosses, medallions, religious medals, and "Jesuit" rings (Thomas 1988: 35, 51–52). The burials contained numerous grave goods including tens of thousands of glass beads; the majority of the beads were sewn onto clothing, while other beads were from jewelry or rosaries (Thomas 1993: 13). A few individuals maintained some Guale traditions with the burial of some projectile points, a chunky stone, and a rattlesnake-etched shell gorget (Thomas 1993: 13). The large number of grave goods in the Guale graves contrasts with the Spanish burials in the Soledad cemetery in St. Augustine, where there were no grave goods except for one burial, perhaps of a parish priest, with a silver crucifix and a rosary (Thomas 1990: 384).

When the British destroyed the Santa Catalina Mission in 1680, Guale Indians and missionaries relocated to Amelia Island off the coast of Florida (near the border of Georgia and Florida); there they built a new mission church with burials under the clay floor of the church, which was burned by the British in 1702 (Saunders 1993: 35–37). Intensive excavation of the burials took place first by a CRM firm in 1985 and then by staff at the Florida Museum of Natural History from 1986 to 1990. One hundred and eighty burials were excavated (Saunders 1993: 38, 51). Burial positions were similar to those on St. Catherines Island except there were very few disturbed burials, reflecting the short-term use of the cemetery (Larsen 1993: 326). The burial posture, with the hands across the chest, is typical of all the mission burials of Christian Indians in Florida as well as the Spanish burials in the Soledad cemetery in St. Augustine (Thomas 1990: 383). The practice of burying individuals under the floor of the church was found not only in the Guale missions on St. Catherines and Amelia Islands but also in excavations of two Apalachee Indian missions—one at Patale (Marrinan 1993) near Tallahassee and the other the San Luis de Talimali Indian mission in Tallahassee (Larsen 1993: 333–34). This practice differed from the burials of Spaniards in the Soledad Catholic cemetery in St. Augustine, where some graves were under the church floor while others were in a cemetery adjacent to the church, with class distinctions dictating who could be buried inside the church (Thomas 1990: 383–84).

The study of Native American burial practices from the historic period has evolved considerably since the early twentieth century. Early researchers showed a rapacious interest in Native American burial grounds and rarely evinced much regard for the concern of descendant populations. The insensitive attitudes of these pioneering investigators did great harm to later relations between scientists and descendant communities. Early approaches, such as seen in Foster Saville's work, tended to be descriptive and historical and were carried out to enrich museum and personal collections. Physical anthropologists, such as Aleš Hrdlička, focused on identifying physical differences between skeletal populations. This was followed by a period in which grave goods were used as markers of acculturation, often following the rather simplistic notion that more trade goods reflected the demise of traditional cultures. More recently, archaeologists have begun to examine more carefully issues of gender, identity, resistance, and cultural resilience using materials associated with graves. Postcolonial approaches such as that employed by Hodge have allowed for more sophisticated understandings of a very complicated period in our history. And increasingly, archaeologists are partnering with Native American groups to develop better-informed understandings of the varieties and meanings of burial practices seen in North America.

African American Burial Sites

The African Burial Ground in New York City is the most well-known study of a colonial cemetery of enslaved and free people of color. The CRM project (discussed in the previous chapter) unearthed 419 burials, as well as a significant collection of artifacts and coffins. The cemetery dates from at least 1703, when Trinity Church assumed management of the town cemetery and banned the burial of "Negros," but Africans may have used the burial ground site in the 1600s, and documents show that they continued to use the burial ground until 1795 (Howson, Bianco, and Barto 2009: 35–36, 43, 53–55). The recovery of a substantial collection of African American skeletal remains from a colonial urban setting provided an unprecedented opportunity to study the population's geographic origins, investigate the physical quality of life for these people who were primarily enslaved, and learn about "the biocultural transformations of these people from African to African American identities" (Mack and Blakey 2004: 10).

The approach taken by the team investigating these burials is best termed "biocultural and biohistorical" in that "it examines the historical interactions of biology and culture such that data on each inform the other and . . . that human biology is interpreted within historically specific, sociocultural contexts" (Mack and Blakey 2004: 11). One challenge that the researchers faced is that earlier scholars tended to lump African American artifacts and human remains together rather than treating them as representative of distinct populations (Jamieson 1995). Despite the challenges, the Howard University team tried to connect the individuals from the African Burial Ground with more-specific regions and cultures in Africa. For example, the DNA samples from thirty-two individuals show similarities to populations in Benin, Nigeria, Senegal, Niger, and other parts of West Africa, while the crania measurements are more similar to people from Ghana and the Ivory Coast (Mack and Blakey 2004: 11). In addition, there were also dental indications of their African heritage, with some individuals having dental modifications similar to those seen in West African populations.

A study of the teeth and bones showed the effects of the high level of disease and poor diet among the enslaved Africans. For example, there were high levels of lead in the teeth of children born in New York, and the bioanthropologists noted that "a poor intake of calcium would have increased the absorption of lead" (Blakely et al. 2009: 270). There was a high rate of tooth loss, caries, and abscessed teeth, with females having a higher rate of dental problems (Mack et al. 2009: 165–66). Analysis of the bones indicated that nearly 82 percent of the men and 60 percent of the women showed muscle and ligament tears or persistent strain "associated with heavy lifting and moving" (Mack and Blakey 2004: 12).

The site is also important for looking at evidence both of resistance and of the violent punishment that was experienced by many African Americans. Twenty-three males and eighteen females had fractured bones, and four of those skeletons had multiple fractures that could have been the cause of their death (Statistical Research 2009: 210). The most dramatic case of violence is Burial 25, a twenty- to twenty-four-year-old woman who was beaten (she had broken bones) and shot "with a musket ball lodged in her rib cage" (Wilczak et al. 2009: 224–25).

Despite the incredible hardships suffered by the enslaved Africans, the burial ground provides evidence of the attempts to maintain their culture. For example, the woman in Burial 340 had modified teeth, suggesting that she had been born in Africa, and wore "an African-style strand of beads around her waist" (Perry et al. 2009b: 371). In Ghana and Nigeria, women wore waist beads similar to those found in Burial 340 (Bianco et al. 2009: 329). The waist beads served as an "under belt" to keep a garment in place, and the garment was tucked around the beads. The archaeologists note that the waist beads were used by African women "to apportion the public and private sides of their lives," since the beaded belt would be seen only by "people who lived in emotional and physical proximity to the weaver" (Bianco et al. 2009: 329). The woman in Burial 340 was buried with two strands of beads made up of blue, yellow, and amber glass beads, as well as cowries, and cowries held symbolic importance to West Africans (Statistical Research 2009: 233). The blue glass beads have been found at other African American sites and have been associated with West

Africans, especially with the Yoruba (Statistical Research 2009: 234). The waist beads suggest that the woman in Burial 340 was committed to maintaining her African heritage (Perry et al. 2009b: 371).

Burial 340 contained an unused clay smoking pipe, and unused pipes were also found in two male burials (Burials 158 and 165); these pipes may have been included in the burials "as a talisman or a memento" (Perry and Woodruff 2009: 357). In addition, many of the grave shafts contained fragments of clam and oyster shells, and some burials had whole shells, suggesting deliberate placement of the shells in the graves (Perry and Woodruff 2009: 354). The placement of shells in burials has been found in West and West Central Africa and symbolizes the "deceased's passage through the water to the spirit world" (Perry and Woodruff 2009: 355). The shells and blue glass beads in the African Burial Ground both suggest the continuation of some African burial practices and African spirituality.

A nineteenth-century but equally intriguing excavation of an African American burial ground is the work done at the First African Baptist Church cemeteries in Philadelphia (Crist et al. 1997). As these authors note, "Where archaeology reveals the existence of historic cemeteries representing disenfranchised groups, a broad-based multi-disciplinary approach can be brought fully to bear on questions regarding historical aspects of America that cannot adequately be addressed by other sources" (Crist et al. 1997: 19). Their research looked at two early nineteenth-century burying grounds associated with this congregation, including the examination of the skeletal remains of 225 individuals.

Early nineteenth-century Philadelphia was one of America's most important industrial centers, as well as a major port. Its population grew rapidly, from 81,000 in 1800 to 408,000 by 1850 (Crist et al. 1997: 20). It was also a major center of the abolition movement and an important center of African American life and culture. Sadly, increasing economic competition, with the growth of industrial capitalism, eroded the social and economic gains African Americans had made in the very early nineteenth century. Many individuals suffered from physical attacks by whites, and while some African Americans were quite successful, others experienced economic decline and were quite poor.

The Baptist Church with its egalitarian underpinnings and emphasis on faith proved appealing to African Americans, and they joined the First Baptist Church in some numbers. On May 13, 1809, they requested to be released from the Baptist Church to form their own independent church. The Philadelphia congregation soon established its own burying ground. By 1816 the congregation had split, though the exact reasons for this are not clear. The group that had split off established its own congregation. Both cemeteries were closed by the end of the nineteenth century and had been built over by the twentieth century. The Eighth Street Cemetery was excavated by John Milner Associates, Inc., in 1983 and 1984, while the Tenth Street Cemetery was excavated in 1990, also by Milner (Crist et al. 1997: 25). Both excavations took place because of the construction of the Vine Street Expressway (U.S. Route I-676). The human remains from both cemeteries were reburied after analysis because of the interests of the descendant community.

The Eighth Street Cemetery contained 135 individuals sufficiently intact to be analyzed, while the Tenth Street Cemetery yielded the remains of 89 individuals suitable for analysis (Crist et al. 1997). Both groups had short life expectancies, with the average age of men in the mid-forties and women in the late thirties. The infant mortality rate was high, largely because of endemic diseases such as dysentery, fevers, and cholera. As Crist and his colleagues note, "Children under 16 years of age accounted for 37% of the interments identified at the Tenth Street site and 44% of the burials at the later Eighth Street Cemetery" (Crist et al. 1997: 34). Evidence for trauma in the form of fractures was noted among both groups, and two individuals in the Tenth Street group showed evidence of gunshot wounds.

The archaeologists and biological anthropologists highlight how the differences in these two skeletal samples relate both to status differences within the African American community and to the declining socioeconomic status of African Americans in nineteenth-century Philadelphia. Curiously, the earlier Tenth Street population shows more lesions related to violent trauma than the later Eighth Street population does, perhaps contradicting ideas about the earlier period being less violent (Crist et al. 1997: 37).

Rural African American populations have also been studied. Sharon Ann Burnston (1997a) carried out a CRM study of an African American burial ground associated with Catoctin Iron Furnace in Frederick County, Maryland. There thirty-five burials were excavated, which date from 1790 to 1840. Very few artifacts, only a handful of coffin nails, and a small number of buttons and shroud pins were associated with the burials. Only four individuals showed evidence of having been buried in clothing. Average age at death for the males was 36.7 years and for the females was 33.1 years (Burnston 1997a: 95). Here the distinctive burial practices sometimes seen in African American burial grounds were missing. As Burnston noted, these individuals were "as invisible to us in some ways as they were to society in their own lifetimes" (1997a: 102).

An example of an archaeological study of a post-1890 African American burial ground is the salvage excavation of the Cedar Grove Baptist Cemetery in rural southwestern Arkansas. This study was one of the earlier comprehensive studies of an African American burial ground in the American South. The cemetery was rediscovered in 1980 when human bone was noted eroding out of a bank of the Red River. Initial assessment of the site indicated that a significant prehistoric site was present. As work proceeded, it became clear that a very large historic cemetery was present. Under ordinary circumstances, cemeteries were not considered eligible for the National Register: "The intent of this exception was to limit the inclusion of consideration of cemeteries, a ubiquitous property type that commonly carries considerable sentimental associations, but which individually may not have been subject to objective scholarly analysis to determine historic significance. However, cemeteries may embody values beyond personal or family specific emotions; therefore, the National Register criteria allow the listing of cemeteries as exceptions when a cemetery is significant because of age, distinctive design features, graves of persons of transcendent importance, or association with historic events" (Limp and Rose 1985: 3). In this case, the cemetery was deemed significant because of its potential to provide new information about the lives of formerly enslaved African Americans and their descendants living in the late nineteenth and early twentieth centuries in rural Arkansas.

This was a cotton-growing area. After the Civil War, wage labor replaced slave labor (Maish et al. 1997: 107). Cedar Grove Church was established in 1881. Because of a pair of disastrous fires, most of its historical records have been lost. The burial ground appears to date from 1890 to 1927. The remains of eighty individuals were excavated from the cemetery. Children died at a fairly high rate and there appears to have been minimal investment in their burials. Ninety percent of the individuals exhibit pathological lesions, many related to systemic infections. Pulmonary tuberculosis is suggested by some of these lesions, while congenital syphilis is suggested by others (Maish et al. 111). Dietary deficiencies are indicated by cribra orbitalia, and orbital bone expansion indicates extensive anemia. Many children appear to have died during the weaning process, likely indicating that childhood diets were not nutritionally adequate. Males also show excessive bone porosity exceeding that of the females, which may indicate very poor nutrition. This was a population highly stressed by diet and disease, living in an extraordinarily challenging situation (Maish et al. 1997: 114).

James M. Davidson's (2004) excavation of the Freedman's Cemetery in Dallas, Texas, was a landmark study, which recovered the remains of over 1,157 individuals. This was the primary burial place for Dallas's African American community between 1869 and 1907. Relocation of the cemetery was necessitated by the expansion of the North Central Expressway through Dallas. At the time there were few aboveground traces of the cemetery, which had been partially paved over and turned into a park. No gravemarkers were present. Indeed, hundreds of broken tombstone fragments had been used in the 1920s as road fill for nearby streets (Davidson 2004: 96). Davidson frames his work around the contrasting themes of consumerism as part of the larger beautification of death movement and the retention of community derived belief systems.

Dallas has a long history of unhappy race relations. The period of Reconstruction, after the Civil War, saw a variety of heinous abuses perpetrated on the local African American population. It was during this period that the Freedman's Cemetery was established. In the twentieth century as other African American burial grounds were established, the Freedman's Cemetery was supplanted, ultimately desecrated and almost forgotten.

In his detailed analysis of the burials, Davidson found extensive evidence for the use of mass-produced coffins and accoutrements, reflecting the African American community's fight for an equality in death that was denied them in life. Indeed, Davidson provides extensive documentation for the African American participation in fraternal associations that assisted with burial expenses, and he delves deep into the primary documents to examine regional African American burial practices (Davidson 2004: 117). At the same time, he documents extensive participation in vernacular folk traditions, involving the inclusion of plates, bottles, and coins in burials. Ultimately, these two different practices—the Victorian sentimentalization of death versus the practice of folk grave decoration and grave inclusions—served to mediate the experience of Dallas's early African Americans and reflect their participation in some aspects of the larger society's practices and at the same time highlights their resistance to the strictures imposed upon them.

Chinese American Cemeteries

Chinese American burials have been found during CRM projects or as a result of accidental discoveries by local communities. Compared to the number of cemeteries of other racial and ethnic groups, very few Chinese American cemeteries have been excavated. For example, in Nevada the sites of some nineteenth-century Chinese cemeteries were destroyed without archaeological investigation by twentieth-century construction (Chung et al. 2005: 111). The nineteenth-century Chinese cemeteries were primarily burials of adult males rather than the mixed ages and genders found in cemeteries of other ethnic and racial populations. Chinese laborers first arrived on the West Coast of North America in the mid-nineteenth century. The Chinese population was primarily male because the Page Law of 1875 (supposedly to stop prostitution) stopped female immigration from China, and later the Chinese Exclusion Act of 1882 prevented Chinese laborers and their wives from entering the United States (Greenwood 2010: 275). The Chinese communities, because of cultural and religious beliefs, maintained strong ties to their families and ancestors in China. In the nineteenth century, the Chinese abroad depended on the local Chinese community to handle a temporary burial and to later exhume the body and ship it back to China so that the deceased could be reburied with his ancestors (Chung and Wegars 2005: 6). In 1855, there was the earliest recorded shipment of Chinese human remains back to China from the United States; the shipment was from San Francisco to Hong Kong (Chung and Wegars 2005: 6). Because the Chinese American bodies were going to be exhumed, the burials were shallow—only "eighteen inches deep rather than the more traditional six feet, permitting easy exhumation" (Abraham and Wegars 2005: 154). Archaeologists studying Chinese cemeteries in Warren, Pierce, and Florence, Idaho, and in Baker City, Oregon, found visible exhumation pits; the graves were not backfilled once the body was exhumed (Abraham and Wegars 2005: 154).

Jerald Johnson and Melissa Farncomb and their students in archaeological field courses from California State University in Sacramento excavated two nineteenth-century Chinese cemeteries in Virginiatown, California

(Rouse 2005a: 81). They excavated thirty-seven shallow graves and found that all the bodies were exhumed, but twenty-one graves contained food vessels (Rouse 2005a: 82, 93). The vessels included rice bowls, a cup, a stoneware food jar, a stoneware soy sauce jar, and two cans plus diverse animal bones that were food offerings to "provide the deceased with the necessary sustenance in the afterlife and were also used to satisfy the appetites of any lingering evil spirits" (Rouse 2005a: 93). Chinese coins were placed in six graves and could have been symbols of "fertility or wealth for future generations" or to ward off evil spirits (Rouse 2005a: 95). The grave goods also contained personal items, including eyeglasses, paintbrushes, pens, inkwells, a whistle, pipe stems, and one opium pipe bowl (Rouse 2005a: 95–97). Even though no bodies were found, the Chinese buttons found in the graves indicated that seven of the individuals were buried in traditional clothing while European American buttons and Levi Strauss jean rivets indicate that the other individuals were buried in European American–style clothing (Rouse 2005a: 93–94). While some of the individuals were adapting to a more European American lifestyle in clothing and personal possessions, the surviving members of the local Chinese community made sure that the deceased would be returned to their ancestors' home and their bones were shipped back to China.

Differing from other Chinese cemeteries, the nineteenth-century Carlin Chinese Cemetery in Carlin, Nevada, contained some graves that had not been exhumed. This cemetery was discovered by accident when, during grading for the construction of a new home, a coffin was uncovered. The project did not lead to a formal cultural resource investigation, however, because it was on private land and involved private funds. The dig was a voluntary excavation by professional archaeologists Fred Frampton and Timothy Murphy, as well as community members (Chung et al. 2005: 107). Carlin was a railroad terminal, and its repair shops provided a source of steady employment for Chinese immigrants; the community developed its own Chinatown, with stores, boardinghouses, and religious centers. The census records indicate a small Chinese population in Carlin: in 1870 there were forty-nine Chinese residents, in 1880 there were forty-six, and in 1900 there were only thirteen Chinese individuals living in Carlin.

Thirteen male bodies, each in a wooden coffin, ranged in age from mid-twenties to mid-sixties; all the bodies showed evidence of having broken bones during their lives, and two individuals had suffered violent deaths

(Chung et al. 2005: 122–24). Burial 8's clavicle, sternum, and ribs were broken, "perhaps from a severe beating and Burial 10 also appeared to die from a beating with facial and rib fractures (Chung et al. 2005: 124). In the nineteenth-century American West, violence against the Chinese "was not uncommon" (Chung et al. 2005: 124). The archaeologists suggest that these thirteen men were probably too poor to have prepaid for their exhumation and to have their bones shipped back to China, but it is possible that they chose to remain in Nevada, perhaps because they had family and friends in Nevada (Chung et al. 2005: 110–11).

The dates for some of the burials were estimated based on hairstyles, specifically, the presence of queues (braided hair), which were mandatory for men prior to the 1911 anti-Manchu revolution in China (Chung et al. 2005: 125). The archaeologists do note that Chinese who did not plan to return to China may have adopted American hairstyles, thus short hair did not automatically mean a post-1911 burial. The clothes on some of the bodies showed a mixture of European American styles—western shirts and boots—with Chinese clothing, but seven graves contained more-traditional Chinese clothes and also more grave goods (Chung et al. 2005: 125–26). The grave goods included pipes, coins, incense sticks, and ceramics. In three graves, identification bricks were found with their names, hometowns, ages, and dates of death (Chung et al. 2005: 126, 129, 131–33). This small cemetery shows both traditional Chinese burial practices and the gradual transformation of those practices in the early twentieth century. Although the individuals in the cemetery could not be fully identified, they may represent the culture and experience of a larger group of Chinese immigrants in the American West.

Excavations of European American Cemeteries

When the Howard University team studying the African Burial Ground in lower Manhattan sought published data from excavations of eighteenth-century European American cemeteries to compare with their data, they found that

1. European American populations are rarely disinterred and/or studied; and
2. When European American populations are excavated, they are predominantly from poorhouses or almshouses.

In trying to find comparable populations of European American middle-class burials, Jodie O'Gorman (2000: xiv) notes that archaeologists "have been far more likely to move the dead poor and treat them in a scientific manner than those in upper or middle-class burial contexts." Indeed, unmarked burial grounds, small burial grounds such as family plots and farm burials, and cemeteries with ephemeral or vernacular markers such as those associated with ethnic minorities and the poor are at great risk of development and desecration. Larger, incorporated, active burial grounds with formal markers and landscaping that fit modern notions of cemetery aesthetics are less likely to be excavated and moved than small burial grounds. In part, these distinctions may be seen as reflecting prejudice in a racialized society. The descendants of middle- and upper-class whites in urban and suburban cemeteries may be easier to identify than those of poor rural folk. Moreover, their graves may be more readily recognizable to modern eyes as burial places and better protected from desecration. The issue of scale is also important here. Many of the burial grounds that academic researchers have studied are modest in size, unmarked or minimally marked aboveground, and associated with minority or marginalized populations. It is hard to imagine a researcher requesting to dig up a large urban burial ground with aboveground markers and thousands of interments simply for research purposes. However, we found that these large urban nineteenth-century burial grounds have been excavated for CRM projects.

The bottom line seems to be that there is no such thing as a safe place for an historic burial ground. Abandoned European American cemeteries (meaning cemeteries that are no longer actively being used or cared for) that have standing gravestones have been destroyed by urban development. High property values in urban areas put all but the most famous historic burial places at risk. Rural burial grounds seem to be particularly easy to forget, and many have been lost to the plow and to the encroachments of suburbia.

We searched for examples of archaeological excavations of European American cemeteries, and we found that most of the excavations of cemeteries were because of CRM construction projects rather than the comparable academic projects by colleges, museums, historical societies, and/or park services purposefully excavating nonendangered American Indian burial grounds. In part this may be due to the scale of some of these projects. Archaeologists have studied enormous nineteenth-century cemeteries, sometimes containing thousands of interments, but projects of this scale require resources and budgets rarely available for academic undertakings.

We also found that the results of these CRM reports are often not in published journal articles or book chapters. Unfortunately, these CRM reports are often produced in very limited quantities and filed only with the client and the government agency overseeing the work. The accessibility of these reports is uneven, with some states maintaining computerized files and others listing only the title of the report (such as "Phase 2 Archaeological Investigation of the Route 23 Extension in Broom County") with no summary or indication of the contents of the report. Moreover, the reports are rarely found in easily accessible archives.

One of the best examples of a non-CRM excavation of an early European American cemetery is the St. Mary's City seventeenth-century cemetery (discussed earlier in this chapter). Another example of non-CRM archaeological investigation at an early European American cemetery comes from Jamestown, Virginia. In 1954 and 1955, archaeologists with the National Park Service uncovered seventy grave shaft outlines and uncovered bones from seven graves buried below the Jamestown State House (Kelso et al. 2001: 9). In 2000, the Jamestown Rediscovery team undertook a more detailed excavation of the cemetery. They uncovered seventy-two individuals, with ten graves holding two individuals and one grave holding three (Kelso 2006: 164). Some of the graves were shallow and haphazardly aligned or contained multiple burials, and it appeared to the archaeologists as if the graves were dug quickly (Kelso et al. 2001: 11). However, this was not a paupers' cemetery. While many were buried in shrouds, three individuals were buried in their clothing, which would indicate death from infectious disease, since clothing in the early 1600s was considered part of a person's estate (Kelso 2006: 164, 166). Seven people were buried in coffins, which in the early 1600s in colonial Virginia indicated a person of wealth (Kelso 2006: 166). The bones from the cemetery are undergoing various forensic tests, but William Kelso (2006: 166) believes that these graves were dug during the "starving time" of 1609–10. In 2013, Jamestown archaeologists unearthed evidence of cannibalism during the starving time (Horn et al. 2013). Physical anthropologist Douglas Owsley from the Smithsonian Institution examined the skull, jaw bone, and leg bone (tibia) of a fourteen-year-old girl and found evidence of multiple cutting and chopping marks on the bones (Neely 2013). The bones were found in a trash pit and provide the first forensic evidence of the cannibalism that had been reported in the historical documents written by the Jamestown colonists (Horn et al. 2013).

CRM excavations in Albany, New York, revealed the burial ground of a Lutheran churchyard. However, only three burials dating from the late seventeenth through the early eighteenth century were recovered; two were males of European descent and one was a female (Phillips 2003: 59). The remains of the three bodies were subjected to stable isotope analysis. There is a clear relationship between the chemical composition of human bone and the types of food consumed by the individual while alive that allows the study of diet from human bones (Ubelaker 1989: 141). Although individual food items cannot be identified, certain food groups can be studied. For instance, on prehistoric sites, the introduction of maize agriculture can be reconstructed using human bones (Ubelaker 1989: 141). Plants with three carbon atoms (C3) plants differ from C4 plants. The former category includes "temperate grasses, all trees and shrubs, all fruits and nuts, and cultivated roots and tubers, while C4 plants are mostly tropical grasses, such as corn, sugarcane, sorghum, and some amaranths" (Keegan 1989: 227). Corroborating historic accounts make clear that corn was an important part of the Dutch diet in upstate New York. Nitrogen isotope analysis also allows the amount of terrestrial or marine foods in a diet to be examined (Ubelaker 1989: 142). In the Albany skeletons, domestic and wild animals made up a large part of the diet. Trace elements such as copper, zinc, and strontium were also examined. Copper and zinc are common in foods originating from animals, while calcium and strontium are more common in plant resources (Sandford 1992: 83). Shellfish can also increase strontium levels, and this appears to have been the case in Albany (Fisher 2003: 63). Zinc is also linked to shellfish consumption, as is copper consumption. The elemental analysis suggests that the two males consumed more root crops while the female ate more leafy vegetables. One of the males consumed more meat and shellfish, which may reflect a different, higher, social status (Fisher 2003: 67). Lead can relate to status differences: eating off pewter plates, drinking from pewter tankards, and eating off lead-glazed ceramics would all have increased lead values, as would exposure to lead paint and lead-based hair dyes. Lead was also used in medications (Fisher 2003: 66). One of the male skeletons contained significant amounts of lead, perhaps reflecting a higher social status and the greater use of pewter and lead-glazed ceramics (Fisher 2003: 67). Even with this very small sample, trace element and stable isotope analysis have the potential to provide intriguing clues to past behaviors. While we did find a few archaeological examples of excavations of seventeenth-century European American burials (as discussed in this chapter), we concur with Michael Blakey and the African Burial Ground team that there are relatively few archaeological examples of excavations of eighteenth-century European American burial grounds.

In contrast to the scarcity of eighteenth-century excavations, we found that archaeologists have excavated numerous nineteenth-century European American burial grounds. For example, an excavation of a white middle-class nineteenth-century cemetery was undertaken by the Center for American Archaeology (CAA) as a CRM project. In the cemetery in Grafton, Illinois, they uncovered 252 graves dating from 1834 to 1873 (Buikstra 2000: 142–43). Despite the poor bone preservation, the biological anthropologists were able to come to some conclusions about the health of the people buried in the cemetery. Analysis of the bones yielded only eight individuals showing evidence of traumatic injury: six had broken bones, one 25–35-year-old male was an amputee with a leg brace and a wooden foot, and a 15–20-year-old female was a murder victim with a lead ball found in her cranium and another lead ball in her thorax (Houdek et al. 2000: 98). This small number of white middle-class individuals with traumatic injury and violent death is in dramatic contrast with the burials of enslaved African Americans. While eighty-eight individuals in the Grafton cemetery had some dental problems, the main condition being caries (in 33 percent of the skeletons), four individuals had dental restorations, including gold fillings and porcelain false teeth, indicating individuals with some wealth (Houdek et al. 2000: 98). The study of carbon and nitrogen isotopes showed that the Grafton residents "consumed quantities of protein-rich foods, including freshwater fish as well as terrestrial wild game and domesticated animals" that suggests a more middle-class diet (Houdek et al. 2000: 113). The choice of coffins changed over time, with pine coffins being replaced by more expensive black walnut and red oak, and some coffins had more expensive brass hardware (Rotman et al. 2000: 90). On the whole the Grafton cemetery suggests that these were people with the means to maintain good health, in contrast to individuals buried in cemeteries for the working class, paupers, or the enslaved.

The Wier Family Cemetery in Manassas, Virginia, is a high-status, nineteenth-century, rural white plantation burial ground that was investigated by Barbara J. Little, Kim M. Lanphear, and Douglas W. Owsley (1992). Descendants had asked for the burials to be moved because of recent construction activities adjacent to the site. In 1988 the cemetery was cleared and mapped. There were fifteen marked graves. Using a backhoe, investigators stripped away topsoil to reach the grave shafts. One grave contained a burial in a cast iron coffin, which was well preserved. A second coffin had been lined with metal sheeting of a lead/tin alloy but had collapsed. Apparel fragments were recovered, including a very complete set of clothes associated with Walter Wier. A pessary, an intrauterine device used to reposition a prolapsed uterus, was recovered from another grave, providing an interesting glimpse of nineteenth-century medical techniques. With the exception of the remains from the cast iron coffin, the bones were so fragmentary that no gross paleopathological analysis could be accomplished (Little et al. 1992: 404). Walter Wier's well-preserved skeleton showed evidence for anterior facial trauma, evidenced through fractured "vertical fractures on all anterior teeth" (Little et al. 1992: 406). He had an active tooth abscess and was missing his first molar, and he may have suffered from a septic infection derived from the tooth abscess that led to his death (Little et al. 1992: 406). Generally speaking, the high economic status of the Wiers seems to have given them access to above-average nutrition and medical care. Although they had a comparable number of caries to those of other contemporary populations, many had received gold fillings, a clear sign of wealth (Lanphear 1988). The archaeologists also linked the burying ground to the beautification of death movement, in which there was "a marked increase in the expense and ritual associated with death, demonstrated in mourning clothing, adornment of the home of the deceased with funeral crepe and wreaths, erection of elaborate grave markers, and encouragement of decorative commemorating death or memento mori. The rural cemetery movement in the United States and England was connected with this trend as cemeteries became parks for the living" (Little et al. 1992: 411).

During four different periods of use, there are clear variations in the kinds of material culture associated with the burials: during the earliest period, there is very little evidence for elaborate mourning customs; then, before the Civil War, there was a move toward elaboration and the use of manufactured coffins and coffin hardware; after the Civil War, as old social norms broke down and status and wealth were not as clearly correlated, there was an elaboration of the beautification process, perhaps reflecting a need to reassert status through grave goods; and finally, this trend diminished in the late nineteenth century (Little et al. 1992: 414).

An interesting and curious example of mortuary archaeology comes from the Walton Family Cemetery in Griswold, Connecticut. This site was discovered by accident during a gravel mining operation in the fall of 1990. A family burying ground associated with the Walton family had been located there from the mid-eighteenth century into the early nineteenth century before being abandoned. There was one marked stone, which had been lost before the site was rediscovered. Because of the instability of the soils in the sand and gravel quarry, excavation of the remaining burials was necessary. Two human crania had been discovered by boys playing in the quarry (Bellantoni et al. 1997: 132–33). Archaeologists from the University of Connecticut and Public Archaeological Survey Team, Inc., a private CRM firm, working with local volunteers carried out the mapping and excavation. Twenty-seven individuals were recovered from twenty-eight grave shafts. They are generally orderly in their organization. There is a cluster of seven graves in close proximity that may represent a disease epidemic that carried away many members of a family (Bellantoni et al. 1997: 137). Coffin hardware was minimal, consisting of hand-wrought nails and pins. Two burials were placed in stone and unmortared brick crypts. While the skeletal remains generally reflect the vicissitudes of life in early New England, Burial 4 presented something extraordinary. This was the grave of a 50–55-year-old male who had been interred in a stone-lined crypt; the skull and femora were found in what might be termed a skull and crossbones orientation and the coffin, now fragmentary, was marked with the initials "JB 55." Nicholas Bellantoni, Paul Sledzik, and David Poirier (1997: 148–49) argue that the curious position of this individual's bones relate to a folk belief in vampires and an attempt to stop the activities of a vampire. Contemporary newspaper articles refer to deaths blamed on vampires in this area during the early nineteenth century, and the arrangement of the bones fits with New England folk beliefs about destroying a body to prevent the return of a vampire (Bellantoni et al. 1997: 146, 148). Moreover, lesions likely associated with pulmonary tuberculosis were also present on the rib cage, likely indicating that the deceased suffered from this disease, which was highly infectious. His contemporaries, however, may well have believed him to be a vampire. Following the close of the project, the skeletal remains were reburied in a local cemetery with extensive involvement from the local community, family descendants, and, of course, the archaeologists.

A classic study of a nineteenth-century institutional burying ground is Ricardo Elia and Al B. Wesolowsky's (1991) investigation of the Uxbridge Almshouse burying ground in Uxbridge, Massachusetts (discussed earlier in the chapter in the discussion of coffins). Historical research showed that the growth of Uxbridge and its increasing industrialization as a mill and factory town, coupled with the shift to a cash economy, increasingly put individuals at financial risk and necessitated the construction of the almshouse. Owners provided no compensation for the unemployed, so towns bore the costs of poor relief (Cook 1991: 50). As a result, the town of Uxbridge established its almshouse in 1830. The almshouse or poor farm produced some of its own food to help defray the costs incurred by the community supporting the indigent. Ultimately thirty-one graves, containing thirty-two individuals, were excavated; only seventeen of the individuals buried there had stone gravemarkers (Elia and Wesolowsky 1991: 18). With the exception of one professionally carved marble headstone—for Nancy Adams, "A respectable colored woman"—the other markers were all blocks of minimally modified fieldstone. Individuals died from diseases of the lungs, as well as typhoid, typhus, old age, and suicide (Cook 1991: 78–79). In general they reflect the varied health of the almshouse residents.

More-recent European American burial grounds have also been the focus of archaeological study. While most of the excavations discussed in this chapter have uncovered a few hundred burials, there are a couple of examples of large CRM projects unearthing thousands of European American burials. A good example of a noteworthy relocation of a modern burial ground is Louis Berger and Associates' excavation of the Secaucus Potter's Field in Hudson County, New Jersey. This project was completed in advance of the construction of a new exit on the New Jersey Turnpike, which was designed to connect with a new railroad terminal in Secaucus (Scharfenberger 2004). The cemetery was associated with a variety of Hudson County institutions, including a poor farm, insane asylum, penitentiary, smallpox hospital, children's eye infirmary, and tuberculosis hospital (Scharfenberger 2004: 2). It was in operation from about 1855 until 1962. The scale of this project was massive, with over 2,896 grave shafts identified, containing 4,571 burials and over 113,000 artifacts (Scharfenberger 2004: 1). The bodies and artifacts provide extensive information about the lives of institutionalized and indigent individuals in late nineteenth- and early twentieth-century America. One of the driving forces behind the project was a lawsuit instituted by Patrick Andriani, whose grandfather Leonardo was buried in the cemetery.

Leonardo Andriani was an Italian immigrant, who came to America in the hopes of creating a better future for himself and his family. In 1948, the disoriented Andriani was hospitalized in the Hudson County Hospital for Mental Diseases (Romey 2005). He passed away shortly thereafter. His son would later move to America but was unable to find his father's grave. Ultimately, his grandson discovered that he was buried in the Hudson County Burial Grounds, only to learn that it no longer existed. The county buildings had been razed in the 1930s, and the cemetery was buried under landfill. Unaware of the magnitude of the burial ground, the New Jersey Turnpike Authority acquired the property for a $235 million highway-interchange project. As archaeologists and historians researched the burial ground, they realized that rather than the six hundred or so interments believed to be present, the burial ground had once held over nine thousand burials (Romey 2005). Although the Turnpike Authority had planned to exhume the burials, the Authority had to notify descendants, including Andriani. Andriani wanted his grandfather to be identified, which was accomplished after much legal wrangling and considerable scientific sleuthing.

Excavations at the site took eight months. Very few of the graves had markers, and those were generally numbered ceramic tubes; however, a surprising number contained grave goods, including religious and military medals, tobacco pipes, clothing, embalming paraphernalia, prostheses, and even coins. The most common artifacts were, not surprisingly, coffin nails, followed by buttons (Romey 2005). Tobacco pipes were present with several graves, including one grave that contained fifty-seven clay pipe fragments distributed across the body and found within the coffin. Scharfenberger (2004: 3) argues that they may have been deposited there during an informal ritual carried out by friends of the deceased. Hundreds of complete bottles were recovered, including eighteen empty embalming fluid bottles (Scharfenberger 2004: 3). Some appear to have been tucked into coffins and disposed of when the deceased was buried. Jewelry, including wedding bands, and collar studs were present, and the collection of clothes was extensive, including some fairly stylish items. Prosthetics, including most notably glass eyes, were present. A surprising number of coins were recovered from the burials, including an 1879S Double Eagle, a twenty-dollar gold coin (Scharfenberger 2004: 4). Military medals indicate service during the Civil War—there were two from the Grand Army of the Republic, or GAR (a Civil War veterans group), and several from the Spanish American War. Catholic rosaries, medals, crucifixes, and Greek Orthodox crosses were all recovered (Scharfenberger 2004: 6). Children's toys, sometimes associated with adults, shaving kits, harmonicas, and toothbrushes were also found.

Coffin forms were variable and included hexagonal, rectangular, and tapering coffins, as well as Ziegler Boxes—a wooden coffin lined with sheet metal, used to transport bodies long distances. There were also quite a few surprises, including what appeared to be a child's coffin, which actually held the amputated leg of an adult male!

Coffin plates are often found on nineteenth-century coffins; however, in this case, coroner's identification numbers were found, indicating the individual responsible for the burial rather than the interred. Most of the coffins were simple and utilitarian, but two were quite elaborate, which may indicate that these individuals were interred in the burial ground for medical reasons, such as to prevent the spread of contagion, rather than because of financial hardships. The skeletal remains were analyzed on site and showed (unsurprisingly, given the size of the population) a wide range of pathologies, including "lesions, vertebral fusion, untreated fractures, and developmental defects; and blunt force traumas" (Romey 2005).

All of these items speak to the lives of individuals living in late nineteenth-century America, from anonymous and unclaimed immigrants brought to the cemetery from the bustling urban centers of Hudson County for burial to the institutionalized and indigent members of society who lived out their lives in the county hospitals and the almshouse. They present a very different picture of society than we see in Edward Bell's landmark study of the Uxbridge Poor Farm burials. At the Uxbridge Poor Farm, most burials were minimally marked and were bereft of personal possessions. At the Hudson County Poor Farm, we see many individuals buried with personal possessions, including military medals and jewelry, and even in some cases with money still in their pockets. Toys and even purses were recovered. Although it appears that the deceased had only the most modest of ceramic markers aboveground, for the markers had been removed long before the project began, the artifacts speak to the individuality and the varied circumstances of these individuals.

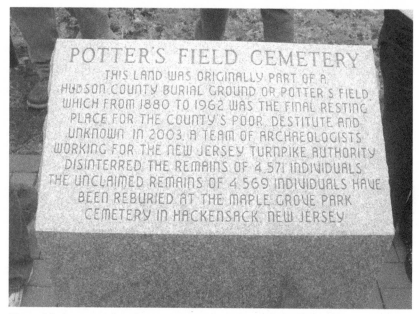

Figure 3.3. A memorial marker commemorating the Secaucus Potter's Field in New Jersey and the archaeological excavations that took place there. Photograph by Richard Veit.

Urbanization, industrialization, and international migration, combined with new scientific understandings of the human condition, transformed nineteenth-century life. Although with only a handful of exceptions (including Mr. Andriani's grandfather Leonardo) these individuals were anonymous, their remains and the artifacts found with them speak to individual lives and experiences, in a "population that was a reflection of society from all levels brought together by circumstances that knew no racial, economic, religious or class boundaries" (Scharfenberger 2004: 6).

Ultimately 900 of the disinterred remains were identified, out of 4,571 that were excavated (Romey 2005). The remains of all the deceased and their personal effects were reburied in modern concrete vaults in Maple Grove Cemetery in Hackensack, New Jersey, and monuments were erected in the cemetery and on the site of the original burial ground commemorating the deceased (figure 3.3). Leonardo Andriani's remains were returned to his kin for private reburial (Romey 2005).

Another noteworthy large-scale CRM project that was carried out in New Jersey was the excavation of Newark's Old First Presbyterian Burial Ground, which was, rather ironically, impacted by the construction of the new New Jersey Devils' arena (Audin et al. 2005). This cemetery, located on Broad Street in Newark, was in use from the late eighteenth century until the 1950s. An earlier cemetery located across the street, which dated from the seventeenth and early eighteenth centuries, had been relocated to a vault known as the Old Settlers' Vault in Newark's Fairmount Cemetery in the late nineteenth century. Despite the fact that these burial grounds held the remains of many of the leading families in Newark, both fell prey to rising real estate values. Indeed, the Presbyterian Church had petitioned the New Jersey Superior Court to exhume the burials from the burial ground in 1957 and reinter them in a common grave behind the church. Their petition was successful, and in 1959 they reported that the project had been completed (Audin et al. 2005: i). However, an environmental assessment of the property performed in 2004 revealed that very few of the burials had in fact been relocated to the common grave. Ultimately, some 2,320 individuals from 2,592 grave shafts were excavated (Audin et al. 2005: i). Neither the remains nor the numerous fragmentary headstones found at the site were subject to a detailed analysis. Ultimately the remains were cremated and interred under a memorial behind the church.

In the early nineteenth century, this cemetery was associated with Newark's most prominent church and was the final resting place of many of its most illustrious citizens. The presence of two collapsed family vaults (popular with the wealthy in the early nineteenth century), finely carved gravemarkers, and coffins with silver nameplates all point to the congregation's wealth. One hundred and seventeen of the graves had nameplates. These date from 1811 to 1854 and are generally associated with higher-status burials (Audin et al. 2005: 43–44). Also recovered were two mummiform cast iron coffins (Audin and Warnasch 2011) and several lead- and zinc-lined coffins. Cast iron coffins were an interesting Victorian response to the issue of protecting and preserving human remains. They have been found at nineteenth-century sites across much of the United States (Owsley and Mann 1995; Owsley and Compton 1997; Owsley et al. 2006; Rogers et al. 1997). The cast iron coffins from Newark are currently undergoing detailed analysis at the Smithsonian Institution (figure 3.4). Sadly, without an energized descendant community to advocate for an adequate study and preservation, this cemetery received only minimal analysis.

Another early nineteenth-century European American high-status burial ground that has been archaeologically examined is the Spring Street Presbyterian Burial Ground in Manhattan. Here archaeologists from URS

Figure 3.4. The Fisk Metallic Burial Case of Captain William A. Pollard (d. September 3, 1854). This cast iron mummiform coffin was found in Newark, New Jersey, during excavations at the First Presbyterian Church's cemetery. Photograph by Michael Audin.

Corporation investigated a series of burial vaults that were unearthed during the construction of a proposed new hotel on the site. The church was established in 1810 and thrived for much of the nineteenth century. However, by the mid-twentieth century it was badly in debt and the size of its congregation was shrinking (Mooney et al. 2007). The church was destroyed by fire in 1966 and, in what seems to be a common fate for abandoned urban burial grounds, replaced by a parking lot.

Construction equipment destroyed one of the four vaults before the archaeological investigation began. When the construction workers discovered human bones, the New York Police Department and the Office of the Chief Medical Examiner were contracted (Morin 2010). It soon became clear that the remains were historic, and an archaeological work plan was put in place to investigate the site. It consisted of background research on the site, an attempt to identify descendant communities, collecting and documenting the previously disturbed skeletal remains, exhuming any additional remains that were present, analyzing and inventorying the human remains and associated artifacts, reburial of the skeletal remains, and preparation of a report (Mooney et al. 2007). In many ways this is a model procedure for similar projects.

The church had an interesting history, and for periods in the early nineteenth century it was ministered to by Reverend Samuel Hanson Cox and

Reverend Henry G. Ludlow, ardent abolitionists. In 1834 the interior of the church was destroyed in an antiabolitionist riot (Meade 2010: 13). Soon thereafter, a new, more fashionable church was constructed; however, the middle and late nineteenth century saw the fortunes of the congregation oscillate considerably, with the dissolution of the congregation in the 1960s.

Vaults were a common feature of early nineteenth-century burial grounds and were often associated with wealthy families. The vaults at the Spring Street Burial Ground appear to have used between 1820 and 1846 (Mooney 2010: 19). As might be expected, working in what had been an active construction site was challenging for the archaeologists. The northern two vaults had stone walls and coarse sand floors, while the southern two vaults had brick walls and floors. The latter were probably constructed in 1831 (Mooney 2010: 26). The vaults displayed arched or vaulted ceilings and lacked the benches or shelves common in contemporary structures. Perhaps in an effort to support the vaulted ceilings of the structures, columns were installed in some of the vaults.

All of the vaults contained skeletal remains; however, Vaults 2, 3, and 4 contained greater quantities, with the most contained in Vault 4. Vault 3 showed the greatest degree of articulation of its skeletal remains, while Vault 4 contained the largest quantity of remains. Ninety-three burials were identified, representing individuals at all stages of life. Preservation of the coffins was quite poor, but all were likely hexagonal. Some were painted in bright colors, such as yellow and red. Although personal items were quite rare, some thirty coffin plates were recovered, which, with one exception, had become disassociated from the skeletal remains (Mooney et al. 2007: 4.24). In England, burials placed in vaults typically had an outer wooden coffin with a coffin plate, enclosing a lead shell and an inner wooden coffin (Mooney et al. 2007). Here, only a single wooden coffin was used, and the coffin plates were more modest in scale than those employed in England. Engraved with the name of the deceased and vital statistics, coffin plates were made of silver, silvered copper, and other white metal alloys such as brittania metal. The two most common forms were oval and rectangular with rounded corners, with larger plates for adults than for youths, which in turn were larger than for infants (Mooney et al. 2007: 5.3). Sadly, none of the plates were still attached to the coffins. The earlier plates were oval in shape, while those made after 1826 were more rectangular (White and Mooney 2010: 44).

Figure 3.5. Coffin plate of Georgia senator Nicholas Ware, buried in the Spring Street Presbyterian Church Cemetery, New York. Reproduced courtesy of the URS Corporation.

Meticulous cleaning revealed the identities of some of those interred in the vaults. They included Senator Nicholas Ware, who was visiting New York City from Georgia (figure 3.5); Rudolphus Bogert, a merchant; Louisa Hunter; and many others. Letters or figures that could be nailed to wooden coffins as a means of identification were also present (Mooney et al. 2007: 5.13). Small quantities of coffin hardware and linings were also noted. One coffin also showed evidence of a viewing window, whereby the deceased could be viewed through a small glass portal. Curiously, three ceramic saucers were found in association with burials in Vaults 2, 3, and 4. Placing ceramic vessels on graves has been noted in both African American (McCarthy 1998) and European cemeteries (Fremmer 1973: 58). Indeed, studying the contemporary First African Baptist Cemetery in Philadelphia, John McCarthy found plates placed inside several coffins (McCarthy 1998). Another possibility is that the plates held disinfectant concoctions used to dispel the noxious odors present in the vaults (Mooney et al. 2007: 5.34).

The Spring Street Church vaults excavation identified the remains of at least 101 discrete individuals (Crist 2010: 70). These remains were meticulously studied. The skeletal remains are particularly revealing, as they date from a period when Manhattan's population was undergoing significant changes. Unsurprisingly, many of the deceased were children, with the first eighteen months of life being particularly dangerous (Mooney et al. 2007: 6.3). However, life expectancies in general during this period were much shorter than those of today. The archaeologists note that "of the 42 adults studied in this population, only eight (19%) lived past their 45th birthday, and only three (<1%) lived beyond the age of 60" (Mooney et al. 2007: 6.3). Women faced particular health risks because of the dangers associated with childbirth. Indeed, the remains of one woman carrying a full-term fetus were unearthed during the project (Mooney et al. 2007: 6.4). As Thomas Crist noted,

> Virtually every disease and disorder described in the city's historical accounts are represented among the Spring Street Church congregants' remains. These include cases of syphilis and tuberculosis; nutritional disorders including anemia, rickets and scurvy; a small number of accidental fractures; a possible case of abdominal cancer; and one poignant burial where a mother and her baby had apparently both died during childbirth. Almost half of the 85 individuals presented evidence of skeletal infection or inflammation and about 10% of the adults had a healed fracture[;] not one of the fractures resulted from injuries of a violent nature. About one-third of the 34 infants and children appeared to have suffered from anemia and at least five of them may have had scurvy. (Crist 2010: 91–92)

The remains of the children also showed a high rate of rickets, associated with a vitamin D deficiency (Ellis 2010: 130). There was even evidence that two of the individuals had been subjected to some type of postmortem examination (Novak and Willoughby 2010: 148).

The Spring Street Church vaults excavation is a model for fieldwork on this type of site and highlights the sort of information that can be recovered from the careful excavation of nineteenth-century European American burial grounds.

Of course, not all burials occurred in cemeteries, and sometimes burials are encountered accidentally during an archaeological excavation or during a construction project. For biological anthropologists and forensic specialists, all burials hold scientific value, no matter where they are found. Remains of murder victims not buried in a cemetery are sometimes found.

For example, William Kelso's excavations at seventeenth-century Jamestown, Virginia, have unearthed casualties of the colony's first few years. These include the remains of a young woman given the moniker Jane, who died during the "starving time" of 1609–10 and was cannibalized by her compatriots (Horn et al. 2013), and an early shooting victim known by his alphanumeric designation, JR102C (JR for Jamestown Rediscovery, the name of the project). JR102C was a European male who had been buried in a hexagonal coffin, a sign of some social standing; he died young (he was in his late teens or perhaps twenty) and stood about five foot nine (Kelso 2006: 126). Most surprisingly, he had been shot in the lower leg with a musket ball and buckshot, a wound that nearly severed the leg and probably led to his death in a very short period of time (Kelso et al. 1998: 7). Chemical analysis was used to determine his place of origin. As Kelso (2006: 128) notes, "Of particular interest in the bone chemistry is the relative presence of two types of stable carbon isotopes: the C3 isotope, found in the bones of people who primarily eat wheat, and the C4 isotope, found in the bones of those who primarily eat corn. The bones of recent English immigrants in America, according to this theory, would show a wheat diet, while the bones of American Indians and seasoned English immigrants at Jamestown would show a corn diet" (Kelso 2006: 128). Curiously, this skeleton showed a strong corn signature, perhaps indicating that JR grew up outside England, because millet has the same C4 isotope signature as corn and is eaten in Italy and in the Caribbean (Kelso 2006: 128). A second isotope test for lead, strontium, and oxygen from drinking water (but embedded in teeth) indicated that JR spent his childhood in southwestern England or in Wales (Kelso 2006: 129).

Numerous other noncemetery burials have been excavated. Perhaps the best-known victims were the bodies excavated by Ivor Noël Hume and his staff at Martin's Hundred in Virginia. The bodies were of colonists murdered during an Indian revolt in 1622 (Noël Hume 1979, 1983). Also, archaeologists have found bones of babies in privies. For example, on a CRM project in Philadelphia in 1973, Sharon Burnston found bones of two eighteenth-century babies in a privy: one nine months old or full term and one seven months old, a premature newborn. Burnston concluded because of the age of the remains, the deaths were not the result of abortions (Burnston 1997b: 54). The conclusion that Burnston eventually came to is that these tiny skeletons represent cases of eighteenth-century infanticide. Additionally, during a CRM project archaeologists uncovered nine thousand human bone fragments from nineteenth-century cadavers near the Medical College of Georgia building in Augusta (Blakely and Harrington 1997). These colonial and nineteenth-century noncemetery burials are important for what they reveal about the diversity of the human experience: murder, infanticide, and medical study all result in the disposal of human remains, sometimes illicitly. As archaeologists and anthropologists, we can learn much about past cultures and their practices from these remains.

Conclusions

As science advances, especially DNA research, biological studies of burials may be able to link African American burials to specific tribes in Africa. DNA studies could also link Chinese bodies to specific regions in China. However, excavations of comparable populations in Africa and China are needed in order to make valid comparisons. While Michael Blakey noted, and we agree, that there are relatively few colonial, nonpauper, white burials for comparison with other racial groups, biological anthropologists are interested in expanding that data set. The study of the colonial poor confirmed their poor health conditions, but the three elite burials in St. Mary's City revealed the health problems that plagued even the wealthy in the seventeenth century. Were these three elite burials an anomaly? To have a wider colonial sample, more elite and middling European American burials need to be excavated. Grave goods also provide insights into changing cultural practices and provide evidence of assimilation as well as the maintenance of cultural traditions. To enable a better understanding of the pressures of immigrants and enslaved peoples to assimilate into American society and their resistance and determination to maintain their traditional culture, comparable grave goods from African, Asian, and European burials need to be studied. It is also critical that what researchers have learned about historic burial practices through CRM archaeology be shared with a wider audience through publication in books, journals, and websites.

4

Beyond Death's Heads and Cherubs

Early American Gravemarkers

> And know, reader, that though the stones in this wilderness are already
> grown so witty as to speak, they never yet that I could hear of, grew so
> wicked as to lye.
>
> Cotton Mather 1853 [1702]: 118

Early American gravemarkers, with their stark imagery and poignant inscriptions, have a strong hold on the popular imagination. The leering
skulls and smiling cherubs found in New England's early burying grounds
are, for many researchers, the ultimate in mortuary art. Even for some archaeologists, gravestone studies are synonymous with the study of religion
and death practices in colonial New England. However, the reality is that
archaeologists study colonial cemeteries throughout the eastern United
States, from Maine to Florida, not just in New England. The results of
those studies have provided significant new insights into early American
society, particularly issues of religion, art, demography, and social structure. While there were colonial settlements in the American Southwest
and California, unfortunately very few early gravestones have survived.
Therefore, this chapter examines colonial burying grounds from the eastern United States and the gravemarkers they contain, with a view toward
understanding what they reveal about early American culture. Issues of
religion, socioeconomic status, trade networks, gender, race, ethnicity, regional culture, and consumer behavior can all be examined through gravemarkers. As Cotton Mather noted over three centuries ago, the colorful
slate, sandstone, granite, and marble markers of early America have many
tales to tell. Over the past forty years, archaeologists have worked hard to
reveal these stories. This chapter examines some of their contributions.

The Origins and Growth of Colonial Gravestone Research

Early American gravemarkers have long been of interest to genealogists and local historians. In the early nineteenth century, collections of epitaphs were published for the edification of readers (Alden 1814). John Barber (1837, 1848) and William Howe (Barber and Howe 1844, 1845), authors of a series of mid-nineteenth-century state histories, frequently used gravemarkers to illustrate discussions of historical figures. Similarly, Benson Lossing (1972 [1852]: 101–2), the peripatetic historian of the American Revolution, recorded curious epitaphs and used illustrations of historic gravemarkers in his magnum opus, *Pictorial Field-Book of the Revolution*. During the late nineteenth and early twentieth centuries, as many colonial churches celebrated significant anniversaries, they published lists of gravemarker inscriptions and photographs of particularly noteworthy markers (Harris 1869; Wheeler and Halsey 1892; West 1908). However, it was during the twentieth century that interest in the material culture of commemoration grew significantly.

The first significant book to come out of this interest was Harriette Merrifield Forbes's *Gravestones of Early New England and the Men Who Made Them, 1653–1800* (1927). Unlike previous antiquarian studies, Forbes's book approached gravemarkers as an art form to be catalogued and studied in the way that art historians might study paintings, silver, or furniture. Individual carvers were identified, their styles described, and their work cataloged. Forbes's work also debunked several common myths. Most notably, she was able to show that New England's slate gravemarkers were produced by local craftsmen and were not, as many of her contemporaries believed, imported from England or Wales (Forbes 1927). Forbes's work was truly significant, and her notes, original photographs, and glass-plate negatives survive. However, with a handful of exceptions (see Lichten 1946; Barba 1954), it would take several decades for other scholars to see the scholarly value of early American gravemarkers.

Gravemarkers Rediscovered: The Work of James Deetz and Edwin Dethlefsen

In the years running up to the Bicentennial, interest in the arts and industries of colonial America blossomed. It was at this time that art historians, artists, and folklorists rediscovered gravemarkers (Ludwig 1966; Parker and Neal 1963; Tashjian and Tashjian 1974). Indeed, the basic premise underlying their interest in gravemarkers and indeed the broader study of material culture is that "material culture as a study is based upon the obvious fact that the existence of man-made objects is concrete evidence of the presence of human intelligence operating at the time of fabrication. The underlying premise is that objects made or modified by man reflect, consciously or unconsciously, directly or indirectly, the beliefs of the individuals who made, commissioned, purchased or used them and by extension, the beliefs of the larger society to which they belonged" (Prown 1982: 1). But it was James Deetz and his colleague Edwin Dethlefsen who drew the attention of archaeologists to gravemarkers through a series of significant articles published in the 1960s and 1970s (Deetz and Dethlefsen 1965, 1967, 1971; Dethlefsen and Deetz 1966, 1967).

Deetz and Dethlefsen's interest in the topic began in the summer of 1963 when, according to one of their former students, Anne Yentsch (1992: 23), "Jim and Ted Dethlefsen found the past facing them in Massachusetts cemeteries; it was the year Jim jumped for glee, seeing in the faces staring out of the gravestones the stylistic proof that historians sought." There in the Concord cemetery they "were sitting in the midst of the orderly stylistic change" (Yentsch 1992: 37). Gravemarkers provided Deetz and Dethlefsen with material support for the theory of seriation employed by archaeologists dealing with prehistoric artifacts. Briefly, the dating procedure known as seriation, developed by archaeologist James A. Ford (1962), assumes that specific artifacts, such as a particular pottery style, grow in popularity, reach a peak, and then die out. The popularity cycle of these artifacts can be graphed, and ideally the graph will be a battleship curve with the peak of popularity forming the widest (middle section) of the battleship. Deetz and Dethlefsen set out to demonstrate that when one studies a colonial cemetery one will find this clear seriation pattern in the iconography on the tombstones.

Deetz and Dethlefsen's first article was titled "The Doppler Effect and Archaeology: A Consideration of the Spatial Aspects of Seriation," published in the *Southwestern Journal of Anthropology* (1965). The authors presented the article as an attempt to refine the methodology of seriation and used the Doppler Effect, a concept from physics, which argues that there will be the appearance of a change in the frequency of a sound wave, or other frequency wave, for an observer moving relative to the wave. More simply, if a particular type of artifact was first produced at one site and distributed from there, it would appear later at the places it was distributed to than at the place where it originated. Furthermore, one would expect more examples of a type as one moved toward its place of origin (Deetz and Dethlefsen 1965: 199). Deetz and Dethlefsen employed this concept in their interpretation of seriation graphs (Deetz and Dethlefsen 1965: 199). Then they tested their theory using colonial gravemarkers from eastern Massachusetts carved by Jonathon Worcester and found the results quite effective at looking at seriation with the addition of a spatial component (Deetz and Dethlefsen 1965: 206).

The second of their articles, "Death's Heads, Cherubs and Willow Trees: Experimental Archaeology in Colonial Cemeteries," was published in 1966 in *American Antiquity* (Dethlefsen and Deetz 1966). It was based on an earlier paper presented at the 1964 Society for American Archaeology meeting. In this article, they argued that colonial gravestones provide an excellent proving ground for archaeological methods because they were "produced by a literate people whose history is known . . . [and] show design variations in time and space which can be projected against known historical data, thereby detailing the dynamics of change in material objects as a function of changes in the society which produced them" (Dethlefsen and Deetz 1966: 502). They went on to elaborate on the characteristics that made gravemarkers useful for study, noting that they were folk products and therefore similar to the handmade artifacts with which prehistorians often work, and they were produced for a local population in a decorative tradition. Because most are dated, they also provide excellent chronological control. Moreover, gravestones contain kin-based information as well as age of death, epitaphs that allow values regarding death to be examined, and decorative elements that can be investigated in relation to other areas of change. Essentially, gravemarkers provided a ready-made laboratory for archaeologists studying material culture. Dethlefsen and Deetz then outlined their study, which focused on an area approximately one hundred miles long and fifty miles wide running north to south along the Atlantic coast and centered on Boston. Their temporal focus was the period from 1680 and 1830 (Dethlefsen and Deetz 1966: 503). After concluding, as Forbes had before, that the gravemarkers were locally produced, they presented their now-famous tripartite evolutionary scheme, in which they noted that there were three major iconographic forms represented on the gravemarkers (figures 4.1, 4.2, and 4.3): death's heads or mortality images (generally winged skulls, sometimes combined with hourglasses, coffins,

Figure 4.1. Mortality image for Sarah Woodruff (d. 1722) in the churchyard of the Elizabeth First Presbyterian Church, Elizabeth, New Jersey. Photograph by Richard Veit.

and palls); cherubs or angels (winged human faces); and finally urns and willow trees. Furthermore, they outlined a fieldwork procedure, consisting of photography of all stones, accompanied by detailed recording of inscriptions, that most subsequent archaeologists have emulated.

Dethlefsen and Deetz also noted that when they plotted these gravestone designs over time, the data produced battleship-shaped curves or histograms. Dethlefsen and Deetz (1966: 508) correlated the popularity of the death's head motif with Puritanism and speculated that the shift away from this design and the equally grim epitaphs that accompanied it might have to do with religious change and the Great Awakening. Moreover, they noted that a similar change from death's heads to cherubs had occurred some seventy years earlier in England than in New England (Dethlefsen and Deetz 1966: 507). They observed that urban congregations made the shift from mortality images to cherubs before their rural counterparts did. Finally, they linked the demise of cherubs and the rise of the urn and willow motif to the rise of Methodism and Unitarianism, and they believed that the urn and willow motif served as a depersonalized memorial (Dethlefsen and Deetz 1966: 507–8).

ve: Figure 4.2. The cherub-decorated grave-
e of Samuel Vickers (d. 1785) in Colonial Park
etery in Savannah, Georgia. The marker was
ed by Ebenezer Price on sandstone. Price was a
er from Elizabeth, New Jersey. Photograph by
k Nonestied.

t: Figure 4.3. A highly stylized willow tree
rates this early nineteenth-century gravemark-
r Joseph Bibler (d. 1841) from the Old Colony
ying Ground in Granville, Ohio. Photograph by
ard Veit.

Figure 4.4. David Gillespie carving a slate gravemarker in the eighteenth-century style. Photograph by Renee Gillespie.

Dethlefsen and Deetz were aware of the role of individual carvers and how the carver's design of the death's head or cherub reflected the carver's individual style (figure 4.4). For example, they noted curious Medusa-like death's heads in the Plymouth-Scituate area (figure 4.5) and observed differences between urban and rural gravemarkers (Dethlefsen and Deetz 1966: 505). In that sense, they were aware of what archaeologists now would call "the agency of the carvers," meaning the carvers' choices or the free will to make those individual choices.

Their 1966 article was a widely influential piece and was followed up one year later by an equally important article in *Natural History* magazine titled "Death's Head, Cherub, Urn, and Willow" (Deetz and Dethlefsen 1967) in which they reiterated the ideas outlined in their previous work and cited the contemporary research by art historian Alan Ludwig, who called the use of cherubs among iconoclastic Puritans nearly heretical (Deetz and Dethlefsen 1967: 30). Their 1967 article was also important for expanding their research into two new areas. First, they examined in detail how the work of a particular carver, in this case Ebenezer Soule, can be tracked through time and how changes in his work can be seen as reflecting both larger issues of cultural change and individual issues of design. They also expanded their geographic range and looked at differences in stylistic change over space. Using an approach that focused on what later scholars would call agency, they documented the seemingly disproportionate influence of a single carver on the material record found in the burial grounds. Moreover, they noted the importance of their fieldwork in recording otherwise inaccessible demographic data, and they discussed how different studies could be developed including those of political units—counties, townships, and colonies. They described the value of their fieldwork for

Figure 4.5. Marker for Cornelius Bramhall (d. 1761), Portland, Maine. This is the type of design that Deetz and Dethlefsen characterized as a Medusa head. Farber Collection, reproduced courtesy of the American Antiquarian Society.

historic preservation, pointing out that the photographing of over 25,000 gravemarkers (Deetz and Dethlefsen 1967: 37) that had occurred as part of their fieldwork would serve to preserve these gravemarkers for the future.

In another 1967 article, "Eighteenth Century Cemeteries: A Demographic View," they presented the view that gravemarkers may often be more-useful sources of demographic and biological information about deceased individuals than the skeletons themselves (Dethlefsen and Deetz 1967: 40). Although their focus was on New England, much of what they observed there they felt would hold true in other locations. They noted the extensive biographical information contained on gravemarkers, such as the deceased's date of death and age, marital status, gender, and sometimes kinship information such as the name of the father and mother or husband (Dethlefsen and Deetz 1967: 41). Dethlefsen and Deetz further suggested some studies that might be carried out comparing the data from one cemetery with another to determine family size, assess marriage patterns, and compare community composition (Dethlefsen and Deetz 1967: 41). Finally, they noted some preliminary demographic insights from their own work. For instance, they found that mortality was highest for sub-adults during the summer and for the aged in the winter. Women in the peak childbearing years, ages twenty to thirty-nine, saw their mortality peak in the period from May to July (Dethlefsen and Deetz 1967: 42).

In their 1971 article "Some Social Aspects of New England Colonial Mortuary Art," they refined their ideas regarding iconographic change, noting that in urban areas, specifically Cambridge, the choice of the cherub motif was a function of social class, with the well-educated, socially, and economically elite choosing cherubs, and that this preference diffused outward into rural areas on the order of one mile per year (Deetz and Dethlefsen 1971: 31). This article separated out urban change and rural or folk change and argued that as the Great Awakening spread across New England in urban areas, gravestone purchasers could opt for either cherubs or mortality images. In rural areas that were still relatively close to Boston, there was a modification of the death's head pattern in which the death's head slowly evolved into a cherub. Those carvers in the most remote areas, such as Plymouth, engaged in something Deetz and Dethlefsen termed radical evolution and replacement, in which death's heads were modified into something that was neither cherub nor death's head (Deetz and Dethlefsen 1971: 33). Essentially, whereas urbanites opted for one of two styles (traditional-mortality images or the new cherubs), those in very rural areas saw radical modification, and in between there was direct modification.

This series of articles was summarized in Deetz's classic introduction to historical archaeology, *In Small Things Forgotten* (1977). In it, Deetz laid out a series of coherent eloquent arguments regarding the evolution, distribution, and research potential of early American gravemarkers and modeled a rigorous research methodology that formed the foundation for decades of subsequent scholarship. Deetz also stressed the link between gravestone images and religious change. Deetz and Dethlefsen made profound contributions to gravestone studies and inspired a whole generation of archaeologists to view gravestones as aboveground artifacts worthy of study.

Soon Deetz and Dethlefsen's students were busy documenting markers across much of New England. With this data in hand, a series of articles followed that provided a coherent, theoretically informed understanding of iconographic change. Deetz and Dethlefsen's work stands as a good example of the New Archaeology and its emphasis on science and hypothesis testing. At the same time, their research reflected part of a broader challenge that historical archaeology was mounting to the then-accepted view of archaeology: by working with relatively recent gravemarkers, they challenged the ideas that archaeologists had to dig for their data and that archaeological sites had to be old to be significant (see Rathje 1979: 2). In fact, their research and that of other early historical archaeologists may be seen as central to a redefinition of archaeology as "a focus on the interaction between material culture and human behavior and ideas, regardless of time or space" (Rathje 1979: 2). Their studies were also useful for teaching and testing archaeological principles, doing the archaeology of today, and relating our society to past societies (Rathje 1979: 3–4).

Challenges to Deetz and Dethlefsen

In spite of the inspiration that Deetz and Dethlefsen provided to archaeologists, not all of their ideas went unchallenged. The link between gravestone iconography and religious change sparked reactions from scholars. Deetz and Dethlefsen saw their tripartite evolution of death's head motifs to cherub motifs to urn and willow motifs reflecting these religious changes in the eighteenth century. They linked the death's head motifs to what they believed was the harsh and grim religion of the Puritans.

Historian David Hall stated bluntly, "These stones are not connected to Puritanism" (Hall 1976: 23). Hall argues, building from the work of the French *Annales* school historian Philippe Aries, that early American gravemarkers, particularly those with mortality images, were not related to Puritanism but to a much earlier memento mori concept: "Such stones were meant to be read by the living[:] they were not really commemorating the dead, they were telling the living, look, you, too are going to die and therefore act in a certain way. . . . Remember . . . that time is flying, 'shape up!'" (Hall 1976: 29).

Historian Peter Benes studied death's head images on gravestones in Plymouth Colony that were carved by descendants of the Pilgrims. Like Hall, Benes believed that the death's heads reminded the viewer of the brevity of life (Benes 1977: 56). In addition, Benes found that the death's head motifs continued to be carved long after cherubs became popular throughout New England, and he noted that there was not the evolution into the cherub style that Deetz and Dethlefsen associated with the Great Awakening (Benes 1977: 33–56). Benes (1977: 155) asserted that "religious attitudes, particularly those during the Great Awakening revivals, seldom followed socially quantifiable patterns." He discussed in detail the complex seventeenth- and eighteenth-century religious schisms within communities in Plymouth and also the various competing Protestant sects, including Anglicans, Quakers, and Congregationalists (Puritans). Benes believed that the death's head images that continued to be carved throughout the eighteenth century in Plymouth Colony could have reflected the communities and carvers continuing Puritan orthodoxy throughout the eighteenth century (Benes 1977: 56). Benes (1977: 150) acknowledged that the diversity in the death's head designs and the appearance in the late eighteenth century of cherubs and portrait images reflect "a multitude of factors[,] many of [which] are difficult to pin down. Not the least of them is the personality of the carvers themselves."

Art historian Alan Ludwig analyzed New England cemeteries at the same time as Deetz and Dethlefsen but came to markedly different conclusions. Rather than arguing for a three-part evolution reflecting religious change, Ludwig argued that the New England stone-carving tradition reflected a distinct repertoire of symbols, including symbols of death, sin, time, transformation, resurrection, life, and more. Ludwig believed that these designs represent the soul in transition between earthly and heavenly domains. He divided New England stone carving between 1650 and

1815 into "a coastal Provincial tradition informed by succeeding waves of borrowing from baroque to neoclassical; and a rural inland ornamental tradition," which he believed was much more inventive and abstract (Ludwig 1966: 416). Ludwig asserted that after 1815, imported neoclassical designs almost entirely replaced the local vernacular styles (Ludwig 1966: 421).

Kevin Sweeney, in examining Connecticut Valley gravestones in western Massachusetts, found no correlation between religious revivals and gravestone iconography. In his words, "The religious enthusiasm of the valley revival of 1735, a precursor of the Great Awakening, left not a mark" (Sweeney 1985: 4). Instead, the selection of particular gravestones by certain carvers seems to relate almost entirely to patronage networks between certain leading families and their preferred artisans. Sweeney notes the irony of the situation:

> Johnson cherubs [produced by the Johnson family of carvers] found favor with Col. Israel Williams, who publicly opposed the visit of the itinerant revivalist George Whitfield to the county [Old Hampshire County] in 1745; with Rev. Jonathan Ashley, one of the region's first clerical critics of the Great Awakening; and with Lt. Col. Oliver Partridge, Colonel Williams's ally, who sat on the council that voted to dismiss Rev. Jonathan Edwards in 1750. These individuals were very self-conscious consumers, and it is hard to believe that they would have knowingly purchased emblems suggesting religious enthusiasm or association with the Awakening. The purchase of such stones probably indicated nothing more nor less than a desire to keep up with funerary art down river and to affirm their kinship with leading gentry families in the lower valley who also patronized the Johnsons. (Sweeney 1985: 11)

Sweeney also found other evidence that contradicts the view put forth by Deetz and Dethlefsen, including the use of diverse folk motifs by late eighteenth-century carvers, and a focus in newspaper advertisements on the medium or stone being carved rather than iconography.

Finally, archaeologists have noted that if the death's head motif was associated with Puritan ideology, then this image should not be found in non-Calvinist cemeteries. However, researchers found that was not the case. Death's head motifs were found in abundance in Anglican cemeteries in New York City (Baugher and Winter 1983) and in nearby New

Jersey (Veit 1991). A death's head image is even found on the gravestone of Jacob Lopez, a Portuguese Jew buried in a Jewish cemetery associated with Touro Synagogue in Newport, Rhode Island (Gradwohl 2007: 36–37). The death's head may simply have been a cultural symbol of death and mortality rather than a symbol reflecting a particular religious ideology. Archaeologist Harold Mytum (2004: 171), in studying gravestones in England and Ireland, found that "both Protestants and Catholics could use the mortality symbols with their own particular emphasis on sin and the way to salvation."

Beyond the death's head motifs, Deetz and Dethlefsen associated the cherub motif with the Great Awakening. Dethlefsen and Deetz (1966: 508) believed that the Great Awakening was "characterized by a newly placed stress on the joys of life after death and resurrection of the dead rather than on the stern emphasis on judgment and mortality." Deetz especially pointed to Great Awakening revivalist preacher Jonathan Edwards as an example of this new liberal approach to religion (Deetz 1977: 71). Jonathan Edwards actually preached a return to the Calvinist teaching of the early 1600s (Hall 1976; Miller 1971). Jonathan Edwards in his most famous sermon, "Sinners in the Hands of an Angry God," was preaching a return to early seventeenth-century ideals of Puritanism; Edwards believed in predestination and original sin and believed that people needed to emotionally and spiritually return to a strict Calvinist version of Christianity (Miller 1971: 290–93).

Deetz and Dethlefsen neglected to mention that in the seventeenth century, the Enlightenment with its focus on science challenged religious thinking. Historian Carl Bridenbaugh (1966: 423) notes that one of the religious outcomes of the Enlightenment was the development of Deism with staunch supporters such as Benjamin Franklin and Thomas Jefferson. Historians have noted that the Great Awakening in the eighteenth century was a complex religious reaction to the Enlightenment and to social changes, not a reaction against Puritan ideology (Bridenbaugh 1966; Bushman 1971). The Great Awakening involved evangelical religious revivals where people experienced an emotional religious experience as they declared themselves Christians; this emotionalism did not, however, imply a liberal theology. The Great Awakening was actually a series of religious revivals that ranged from conservative to liberal ideas and lacked a uniform message (Howard 2001: 171). For example, in New York City the aftermath

Figure 4.6. Gravestone rubbings. *Left*, gravestone carved for Isaac Moses (d. 1763) from the cemetery associated with Touro Synagogue in Newport, Rhode Island. Note the date in the Jewish calendar and the cherub. Rubbing by Jessie Farber. *Right*, gravestone of Cuffe Gibbs (d. 1768), God's Little Acre, Newport, Rhode Island. Rubbing by Sue Kelly and Anne Williams. Rubbings in Farber Collection, reproduced courtesy of the American Antiquarian Society.

of the Great Awakening left the city with more-pronounced religious differences and religious rivalries (Howard 2001: 171).

Like the death's head motif, cherubs have been found as images on stones of diverse ethnic and religious groups (Baugher and Winter 1983; Stone 1987; Veit 1991). The cherub motif was even found on stones in the colonial Sephardic Jewish cemetery associated with Touro Synagogue in Newport, Rhode Island (Gradwohl 2007: 36–37) (figure 4.6, *left*). Clearly the families erecting these Jewish tombstones were not choosing a cherub design because it reflected their liberal Protestant views on the afterlife or the conversion experience they had as a result of attending the Great Awakening revival meetings. Archaeologist David Gradwohl (2007: 38) notes that the cherub designs are especially interesting, particularly given the "traditional Hebraic taboo against the use of graven images." However, Gradwohl (2007: 38) adds that "sculptural depictions of humans are not unknown in Sephardic cemeteries of the 17th and 18th centuries in the Caribbean and Europe." One for Rebecca Polock even has an inscription in Hebrew. Gradwohl (2007: 39) rightly points out that it is not clear that these anthropomorphic motifs had the same religious connotations to the Jews of Newport as they did for their Christian contemporaries.

Moreover, Deetz noted that the urn and willow motif that appeared at the end of the eighteenth century and was used well into the nineteenth century was a symbol of commemoration (Deetz 1977: 69, 72). Dethlefsen and Deetz (1966: 508) asserted that the third stage in their religious and gravestone evolution was the linking of the urn and willow with the rise of Methodism and Unitarianism and a "depersonalization of death." Deetz (1977: 72) further noted that the early nineteenth century was a period of the "secularization of religion." Historian David Hall (1976: 26) criticized Deetz's lumping together of Methodism and Unitarianism, which are distinct faiths, and linking them to the rise of secular culture.

Methodists are a Protestant group that branched off from the Anglican Church in the eighteenth century, not the early nineteenth century. During the Great Awakening, the Anglican/Methodist George Whitefield was actively preaching in the colonies from Georgia to Massachusetts (Bushman 1971: 299). Benjamin Franklin, while not at all swayed by the sermons, noted that Whitefield was a charismatic preacher with a booming voice who could be heard a few blocks away (Franklin 1987: 1409). Two of the other founders of Methodism—John Wesley and Charles Wesley—also were preaching in Georgia in the 1730s (Ahlstrom 1972: 324). Methodist congregations were established in the colonies before the nineteenth century. The first Methodist congregation in New York City was formed in 1766 (Rogers 1984: 1).

Unitarians are quite distinct from Methodists. Unitarians are a religious group, but they are not "Trinitarians," that is, they do not share the belief that there is "one God in three distinct persons, called Father, Son, and Holy Ghost"—the Unitarians believe that there is one being, God the Father (Ahlstrom 1972: 395). Unitarians view Jesus as a great teacher, not as a son of God (Ahlstrom 1972: 401).

Countercurrents: Art Historians, Folklorists, and Scholars of Religion

Working at roughly the same time as Deetz and Dethlefsen, other scholars, particularly art historians, began cataloging, photographing, rubbing, and casting historic gravemarkers (Ludwig 1966; Farber 1975; Wasserman

1972). Like Deetz and Dethlefsen's studies, art historian Alan Ludwig's work in 1966 was seen, at the time, as iconoclastic. It represented a direct break with the focus on elite culture then popular in art history (Ludwig 1999: xxvi). In the preface to the third (1999) edition of his classic book, Ludwig attributes his interest in gravemarkers to "getting lost on his way to an outdoor pig roast [where he found himself] . . . looking at the Thomas Cushman stone of 1727 in Lebanon, Connecticut," and ultimately concluded that it looked a lot like modern art (1999: xxv). He became fascinated with understanding why Puritans "cut graven images for their tombs but would not allow the same imagery into their meetinghouses." While Deetz and Dethlefsen's work might be seen as structuralist because of its focus on the binary oppositions between death's heads and cherubs and, later, cherubs and urn and willow symbols, Ludwig divided New England stone carving between 1650 and 1815 into two traditions: a rural, inland folk tradition and a more urban coastal tradition (Ludwig 1999: 416) (figure 4.6, *right*). After 1815 or so, the imported neoclassical ideas almost entirely replaced the local vernacular styles (Ludwig 1999: 421).

By the 1970s and 1980s, the number of individuals researching and publishing on colonial gravemarkers in the eastern United States, particularly the Northeast, had grown tremendously. They included artists and art historians (Neal and Parker 1970; Tashjian and Tashjian 1974; Wasserman 1972; Farber 1975; Rauschenberger 1977; Duval and Rigby 1978; Trask 1978), cultural geographers (Zelinsky 1976; Jordan 1982), folklorists (Glassie 1968), religious scholars (Hall 1976), and, of course, anthropologists and archaeologists. Indeed, in 1977, the Association for Gravestone Studies was founded as a result of this burgeoning interest in early American gravemarkers.

The meanings and interpretation of early New England markers, mortality images, cherubs, and urns and willow trees remained central during this period. Ann and Dickran Tashjian's masterful book, *Memorials for Children of Change: The Art of Early New England Stonecarving* (1974), took a holistic view of funerary art and highlighted the imagery and meaning of New England gravemarkers in their cultural and historical context.

Peter Benes (as noted earlier in this chapter) also wrote a significant book on gravemarkers from Plymouth County, Massachusetts, which looked at stylistic change through time. He noted that there were marked changes on what he calls "masks" (skulls and faces) that coincided with the Great Awakening and the Revolutionary War. Benes (1977: 151) states that the masks/faces appeared to be "animated during the Great Awakening religious revival, frenzied in the years just preceding the Revolution, martial during the Revolution itself, and phlegmatic in the waning years of the century." Benes is perhaps most important for noting that "nowhere . . . in the voluminous letters, literature, and documents of the period is there any reference to the purpose of the symbols, to their meanings, or to their propriety" (Benes 1977: 12).

Ultimately, folklorists (Glassie 1968), geographers (Francaviglia 1971; Jordan 1982; Zelinsky 1976), historians (Welch 1983, 1987), and other scholars (Prioli 1979; Little 1998; Luti 2002; Patterson 2012) have explored various aspects of gravestones, such as the history of individual carvers and the evolution of their style, the epitaphs on the stones, the genealogical data, and data on community history.

So while Deetz and Dethlefsen had opened the door to a new understanding of early American gravemarkers, other researchers went in very different and sometimes contradictory directions. However, for many anthropologists and archaeologists, Deetz and Dethlefsen's work provided a model to be tested and replicated in other locations within the Atlantic English colonial world, as well as assumptions to be challenged. Although archaeologists were deeply involved in this research, many published their findings in nonarchaeological journals and proceedings volumes, such as *Puritan Gravestone Art I* and *II* and its successor publication, the journal *Markers*.

Death's Head to Urn and Willow Redux

Deetz and Dethlefsen's students caught the gravestone bug, and papers on the topic proliferated (Yentsch 1963, 1978; Earle 1963). As Yentsch has noted (1992: 37), some focused on design motifs (Dethlefsen and Jensen 1977; Dethlefsen 1992), others on kinship (Allen 1968), and still others carried out detailed studies of carvers and stylistic analysis (Brown 1992), while others examined rites of passage (Yentsch 1978).

Deetz and Dethlefsen's early work was also important for establishing a model for rigorous recording of gravemarkers. All told, they recorded about twenty-five thousand gravemarkers (Deetz and Dethlefsen 1967: 37). Typically scholars document the style/motif of the gravemarker, age at death, month and year of death, stone material, epitaph, preface, kinship, cause of death, and titles (Tibensky 1983: 257). Other researchers also recorded the form or shape of the marker, as well as its dimensions, which proved useful for addressing issues of status, gender, and age; the presence of secondary motifs; the gravemarker orientation; the name of the carver, either by signature or by stylistic attribution; and the condition of the stone (Stone 1987; Veit 1991; Oakley 2003). Generally all the markers are photographed and keyed to the database. Lynn Rainville's (1999) comprehensive study of Hanover, New Hampshire, gravemarkers is a model of proper gravemarker recording, in documenting not only the physical characteristics of the markers but also extensive archival information about the deceased.

Like ripples from a stone thrown into a pond, the scholarship continued to expand. We, along with other researchers, were applying and testing Deetz and Dethlefsen's ideas in other parts of the country (Goodwin 1981; Crowell 1981; Baugher and Winter 1983; Fitts 1990; Levine 1978a, 1978b; Mackie 1986; Veit 1991). We soon discovered that rather than a single unified cultural pattern in New England, there was considerable regional variation, reflecting the places of origin of early settlers (Allen 1968; Benes 1977).

One of the first published studies was the work of Frederick Gorman and Michael DiBlasi (1976, 1981) of Boston University, who examined eighteenth- and nineteenth-century gravemarkers in South Carolina and Georgia. Building from the assumption that gravemarkers are material correlates of mortuary ideas, they examined three hundred gravestones in six southeastern colonial cemeteries and drew comparisons between the beliefs of eighteenth-century South Carolinians and Georgians with those of colonial New Englanders. They characterized their work as ethnohistory. They examined cemeteries in Midway, Sunbury, and Savannah, Georgia, and three cemeteries in Charleston, Carolina. Gorman and DiBlasi explicitly focused on coastal cemeteries, because of the coast's earlier settlement and perceived cosmopolitan nature. They also examined cemeteries of different religious denominations (Gorman and DiBlasi 1981: 82). Midway and Sunbury in Georgia were rural Congregational congregations; St. Phillips and St. Michaels in Charleston were Episcopal/Anglican, as was Savannah's Colonial Park Cemetery; while the Huguenot Cemetery in Charleston was French Protestant, and Savannah was interdenominational. Gorman and DiBlasi (1976: 80–83; 1981: 83) recorded the motif, denomination, age at death, date of death, sex, occupation, birthplace, material composition of stone, and identity of the carver. Their study is one of the most statistically informed of any examined. Many of their results contradicted those noted by Deetz and Dethlefsen in New England. Although Gorman and DiBlasi (1976: 86) argued that colonial gravestone motifs were part of a single iconographic tradition, the heterogeneous nature of early settlement in the Southeast was different from that seen in New England, and the predictable patterns of diffusion noted in New England were not common in the Southeast. Furthermore, they found that the spatial pattern of the religious iconography was not linked to mortuary concepts, nor did they find that the spatial patterning of gravestone iconography was significant. Social factors such as immigration and status preferences also failed to be useful indicators of iconographic patterning (Gorman and DiBlasi 1981: 92). However, the importation of New England carved gravestones was significant, and the use of imported gravestone motifs might signify either status or social preference. Interestingly, the evolution of gravemarkers noted in New England also occurred in the Southeast, reflecting the interregional scope of this phenomenon and, perhaps more important, trade networks. Moreover, the Doppler Effect noted by Deetz and Dethlefsen in New England was not present in the South (Gorman and DiBlasi 1981: 95).

In 1983, Frederick A. Winter and I (Sherene Baugher) published an article in *Archaeology Magazine* titled "Early American Gravestones: Archaeological Perspectives on Three Cemeteries of Old New York." We presented the results of our examination of colonial New York's three largest surviving cemeteries: Trinity in Manhattan, St. Andrew's on Staten Island, and Gravesend in Brooklyn. New York City had a much more ethnically diverse population than colonial New England. Trinity Church on lower Broadway in Manhattan, the earliest and largest surviving colonial Anglican English burying ground in New York, was associated with the city's elite and is located in the urban core. St. Andrew's is an Anglican Cemetery in Richmondtown, Staten Island, an area with close ties to neighboring Perth Amboy and Elizabeth, New Jersey, that served as an outlying trade center, and the cemetery served the English, Dutch, and French settlers in the village. Gravesend in Brooklyn was a rural, farming, predominantly English community within the Dutch colony of New Netherland; the cemetery was nonsectarian and contained stones of both English and Dutch families (Baugher and Winter 1983: 48, 53).

Of the three burial grounds examined, Trinity was by far the largest, with over 350 pre-1815 gravemarkers (Baugher and Winter 1983: 51). The urn and willow–decorated markers that Deetz and Dethlefsen noted in New England at the end of the eighteenth century were conspicuously absent from Trinity Churchyard. Indeed, undecorated markers were much more common. A careful analysis did show the expected evolution from mortality images to cherubs, but we found no clear-cut correlations between the decoration of the gravemarkers and the age and sex of the deceased (Baugher and Winter 1983: 52). A similar pattern was noted at St. Andrew's Cemetery. However, in St. Andrew's cemetery, floral designs were found only on the gravestones of individuals with French and Dutch surnames (figure 4.7). Additional documentary research revealed that

Figure 4.7. A tulip-decorated marker representative of the style used for young women and girls in colonial New York and New Jersey. This marker commemorates Catherine Clowes (d. 1771) and is located in the burial ground of the First Presbyterian Church of Elizabeth, New Jersey. Photograph by Richard Veit.

some of the graves and gravestones were reinterments from family plots and homestead graves of non-Anglican individuals and families, and we noted that "religious affiliation obviously cannot be assigned simply on the basis of an individual's presence within the cemetery" (Baugher and Winter 1983: 52). Our discovery reinforced the need to undertake documentary research beyond simply recording gravestones in a cemetery.

At Gravesend, a mix of English- and Dutch-language inscriptions were found. There was little difference between the English inscriptions found on stones with English and Dutch surnames and/or the inscriptions in English and in Dutch. Interestingly, the same carver created cherub stones for Dutch families in Gravesend cemetery and for English families in Trinity cemetery (Baugher and Winter 1983: 51, 53). Unlike Trinity and St. Andrew's cemeteries, there were no death's head images in Gravesend.

The markers in Trinity Churchyard, when graphed, come the closest to replicating the battleship curves for death's heads and cherubs noted by Deetz and Dethlefsen in New England; however, even there the patterns are not as uniform as expected and no urn and willow markers were found (Baugher and Winter 1983: 50–51). Interestingly, the similarities between markers for individuals of English and Dutch descent and of Anglican and Dutch Reformed faiths led us to suggest that the iconography on gravestones may reflect a shared Western cultural tradition rather than a specific religious ideology (Baugher and Winter 1983: 53).

Adam Heinrich, building on the work of earlier scholars, undertook extensive research on the same question of whether death's heads and cherubs reflect religious changes or whether they are part of a secular cultural tradition. Instead of seeing the cherubs on colonial-period gravemarkers as being inspired by the Great Awakening, Heinrich attributes them to wider contemporary artistic trends, especially the rococo, which influenced the ornamentation of a wide variety of material culture including gravemarkers, furniture, and architecture. For Heinrich (2012: 1), the markers "reflect the fashions observed on contemporary material culture and therefore reflect the consumer and not the religious ideology of those who purchased the stones." As Heinrich notes, there seem to be no clear religious boundaries to the colonial-period gravestone symbols. Though infrequent, mortality images and cherubs both appear in Jewish, Catholic, and even, on rare occasions, Quaker burial grounds. In his view, the winged skulls that Deetz and Dethlefsen attributed to the Puritan mindset are more closely linked to the medieval European tradition of memento mori, which saw the body as corruptible and stressed life's brevity. This view was also voiced by historian David Hall (mentioned earlier in this chapter). Similarly, Heinrich, like Alan Ludwig (mentioned earlier in the chapter), notes that the urns and willows of the very early nineteenth century reflect the growing popularity of neoclassical fashions and adds that they were in part inspired by "then current archaeological discoveries in Italy and Greece" (Heinrich 2012: 7). In between came a new style, later labeled the rococo, based on its use of natural and stylized rocks and shells (*rocaille* and *coquilles*). These designs, which emphasized natural forms as well as allegorical figures (such as satyrs and putti), were seen as emphasizing notions of love and freedom (Heinrich 2012: 8). This style quickly spread to England and the American colonies and can be seen in furniture such as Chippendale-style chairs, silver, and mass-produced English ceramics such as the ubiquitous shell-edged pearlware (Heinrich 2012: 10). Cherubs, or *putti* (genderless, winged infants), were part of the rococo stylistic vocabulary (figure 4.8, *top*). There is, however, some question as to whether putti were religious or secular designs, and it seems likely that they were understood differently in different contexts. Heinrich's work is important for tying cherubs to broader cultural and artistic trends rather than simply seeing the iconography as reflecting religious movements.

Working just to the east of New York City, Gaynell (Levine) Stone has spent decades documenting and interpreting Long Island's colonial gravemarkers (Levine 1978a, 1978b; Stone 1987, 2009). Much of her research focused on what gravemarkers can reveal about trade networks. Long Island, an enormous glacial moraine, lacks carvable stone, though fieldstones were used for informal markers (Stone 1987: 13). Gravestones are also particularly useful for examining trade networks on Long Island, as the island has few documentary shipping records from the colonial period. Initially she began by examining the surviving premarble gravestones of Long Island's earliest English settlements: Southold, East Hampton, Southampton, Setauket, Smithtown, and Huntington (Levine 1978b: 47). Long Island is interesting, as an area situated between the cultural hearths of New England and the Middle Atlantic (Glassie 1968: 37–40; Levine 1978a: 49). Stone found that 99 percent of the extant gravestones on Long Island came from a handful of production centers: New York City; Newark and Elizabeth, New Jersey; Boston and Plymouth, Massachusetts; Providence and Newport, Rhode Island; and Coastal Connecticut and the Connecticut River valley (Levine 1978a: 51, 56). She noted that neither

Figure 4.8. *Top*, a pair of baroque putti under a cloudy sky. This marker was broken when the Hendrickson Family Burial Ground in Middletown, New Jersey, was demolished by a misguided condominium association. The association erroneously believed that they owned the cemetery and had the markers broken and removed, when in fact a descendants' group held title to the cemetery. Photograph by Richard Veit. *Bottom*, the gravemarker of Altje Brinckerhoff (d. 1749), wife of Abraham Adrianse, Fishkill, New York, is inscribed with her maiden name, as was the Dutch custom. It was carved by Johannes Zuricher. Photograph by Richard Veit.

ease of transport nor political ties determined trade networks. Moreover, there was no response to known historical events such as epidemics or to religious shifts and little change due to the Great Awakening (Levine 1978a: 53). The American Revolution did lead to a drop in the number of extant stones, likely because British naval forces effectively shut down the coastal trade. On Long Island, social and family connections and, perhaps most important, economic ties seem to have influenced gravestone choice (Levine 1978a: 57).

Stone followed up on her M.A. thesis, which was limited to six communities, with an even larger study of all of Long Island's pre-1820 gravestones that included two boroughs of New York City, Brooklyn and Queens Counties, which are on Long Island. For her 1987 dissertation, "Spatial and Material Aspects of Culture: Ethnicity and Ideology in Long Island Gravestones, 1670–1810," Stone photographed and inventoried more than 4,300 gravemarkers from 164 cemeteries and coded them for forty-four variables. Because Long Island lacked its own carvers until the 1790s, imported markers from New England, New York City, and New Jersey filled the island's burial grounds. Long Island is also interesting in terms of its early settlement and the presence of both English and Dutch settlers. Stone examined these markers in light of issues of ideology, ethnicity, settlement hierarchy, social organization, and geographic setting. Perhaps most important is that she used gravemarkers to define and examine the distinctions between regional ethnic cultures in eighteenth-century New York. Stone also attempted to seriate the markers as Deetz and Dethlefsen had in New England. However, she found that the New England patterns were not replicated here, and she postulated that this was because Long Island was part of two different culture spheres located between New England and the "'Dutch' culture sphere of New Amsterdam/New York" (Stone 2009: 142). Although many of Long Island's early houses, particularly in heavily urbanized western Long Island (Brooklyn and Queens Counties), have been lost, gravemarkers have survived and reflect the intersection of the New England and New Netherland cultural hearths on Long Island.

Both New York and New Jersey were multiethnic colonies. For example, historian Patricia Bonomi (1971: 24–25) notes that in addition to the Dutch and English there were also waves of immigrants from France, the German Palatine area, Scotland, Ireland, Sweden, and Portugal (primarily Spanish Jews who fled first to Portugal), as well as enslaved people from Africa. The spread of English language and English culture threatened the vitality and integrity of these diverse ethnic groups (Howard 2001: 168). Ethnic intermarriage promoted acculturation. In the eighteenth century, there was a push for locally trained ministers and services in English (Howard 2001: 171). In addition, there were economic incentives for men to become "more English" to more easily participate in business and trade with the English citizens and government officials (Cantwell and Wall 2001: 184). However, some historians, such as Joyce Goodfriend (1992), note that the acculturation was slow. The Anglicization of colonial New York and New Jersey clearly was a lengthy process occurring over numerous decades. This persistence of ethnic separation and ethnic identity can be seen in the gravestones.

Gaynell Stone found on the Long Island gravestones that the language of choice reflected the ethnicity of the deceased. Stone (2009: 152) noted that the Dutch language was used on stones until 1817, even though Long Island had been part of the English colony of New York since 1664. Long Island gravestones also revealed ethnic and gender differences in the inscriptions for Dutch and English women. Gravestones for Dutch women noted the woman's family of birth by using her natal name and then her husband's name (figure 4.8, *bottom*), whereas only a small portion of gravestones of high-status English wives contained the information "wife of" and "daughter of" on their stones (Stone 2009: 152–53).

The persistence of the Dutch culture can be also seen in studies of individual carvers. For example, we found that the New York City carver John Zuricher carved stones inscribed in both English and Dutch (figure 4.8, *bottom*). Markers cut by Zuricher in cemeteries in Brooklyn are almost exclusively inscribed in Dutch, while those found in Trinity Churchyard in Manhattan are inscribed in English (Baugher and Veit 2013). Moreover, those Dutch stones in Brooklyn generally have brief inscriptions. Deetz (1977: 88) states that "religious institutions and their artifacts are known to be the most conservative aspects of a culture, resisting change." Therefore, in gravestones, including Zuricher's stones, we see evidence of maintenance of cultural boundaries and cultural separation in some of the Dutch stones with the use of the Dutch language (Baugher and Winter 1983; Stone 1987, 2009; Baugher and Veit 2013).

New Jersey's early gravemarkers, which represent multiethnic and multireligious communities, have seen considerable study (McLeod 1979; Welch 1983, 1987; Crowell 1981, 1983; Veit 1991, 2000; Heinrich 2003; Veit and Nonestied 2008; Zielenski 2004). Northeastern New Jersey was part of the Dutch cultural sphere and, like New York City and Long Island, had stones inscribed in both Dutch and English. Northwestern New Jersey contained a large German community, and their gravemarkers are inscribed in German. One of us (Veit) studied these German-language markers of northwestern New Jersey. The stones were generally more iconographically restrained than those found in New England and New York but were beautifully lettered and often contained funeral *leichen*, or texts read at the funeral of the deceased (Veit 2000). A few were decorated with floral motifs and other designs. These designs and the colorful fieldstones they were carved upon continued to be produced throughout the late eighteenth century. One example is the work of John Solomon Teetzel, a bilingual carver, who was able to tailor very different markers to the German and English populations of northwestern New Jersey (Veit 2000). Teetzel had a disproportionate effect on the gravestones of a particular region for a little more than a decade (1789–1800). For his German clients, he produced markers with beautiful German calligraphy, complete with funeral texts and tympanums ornamented with flowers, while for his English clients he used English lettering and ornamented the markers with the deceased's monogram. Other German carvers in Lancaster County produced strong bas-relief mortality images and cherubs (figure 4.9). They also carved a wide range of other images—including the man in the moon, floral motifs, and stars—on their markers.

The Dutch-language markers of the Hudson River valley and adjacent parts of New Jersey have been studied by Brandon Richards (2007). Richards sees parallels between the simple fieldstone gravemarkers employed by the Dutch and much earlier wood and stone folk monuments dating back to the Viking rune stones. He notes that these markers, though made from stone, were rough-hewn and appeared much like wooden planks. Richards characterizes these early markers as plank, post, and trapezoidal or pointed markers. Many are quite simple and may have been made by individuals who were not professional gravestone carvers (Richard 2007: 34–35). Rarely decorated, these folk markers persisted well into the eighteenth century.

Northern New Jersey's burial grounds reflect New Jersey's exceptional cultural diversity during the colonial period. Veit examined the colonial burial grounds of Middlesex County, New Jersey, in another attempt to replicate Deetz and Dethlefsen's work outside of New England. Middlesex and adjacent Union County's markers are replete with iconography:

Figure 4.9. *Left*, a German-language gravemarker for George Junt (d. 1770), at the Bergstrasse Lutheran Churchyard, Ephrata, Lancaster County, Pennsylvania. Note the skull, long bone, hourglass, and sickle displayed near the base of the marker. Photograph by Richard Veit. *Right*, an uninscribed marker at the Bergstrasse Lutheran Churchyard in Lancaster County, Pennsylvania. Markers like this probably had painted inscriptions. Photograph by Richard Veit.

leering skulls, crossbones, hourglasses, winged cherubs, and even, on occasion, more startling images, such as God's arm, emerging axe in hand, to cut down a fully leafed tree! The first two stages of Deetz and Dethlefsen's evolutionary scheme held true in much of northern New Jersey, where death's heads were followed by cherubs (Veit 1991). However, markers decorated with the monogrammed initials of the deceased or in some cases plain markers became the norm at the end of the eighteenth century. Urns and willows did appear in the early nineteenth century but in fairly small numbers.

We, along with other scholars, found that Presbyterians, Baptists, Anglicans, and Dutch Reformed settlers purchased markers from the same carvers. John or Johannis Zuricher, a New York City carver able to produce markers in either English or Dutch, seems to have been the favorite carver of some Dutch settlers (Baugher and Veit 2013).

Elizabeth Crowell examined eighteenth-century gravemarkers in Cape May County, New Jersey, for her doctoral dissertation at the University of Pennsylvania. Though located at the southernmost tip of New Jersey, colonial Cape May County was an area settled by New Englanders, many of whom were whalers and had migrated south in search of better whaling grounds. Indeed, culturally, Cape May, New Jersey, though located in the Middle Atlantic region, might be considered an extension of New England. Although Cape May was initially settled at the end of the seventeenth century, the population was relatively small. Presbyterians, Baptists, and Quakers were the primary religious denominations. Religious revivals associated with both Baptists and Presbyterians occurred in the early 1740s (Crowell 1983: 31). By the 1780s, Methodism had also been introduced to the region, and it grew to be a very popular denomination. However, Crowell (1983: 9) found that the gravestones were not similar to those in colonial New England and there were very few decorated markers: "The initial observation of Cape May County gravestones shattered all previous illusions. The overwhelming majority of Cape May County gravestones were undecorated . . . [and] the burial patterns were also different from New England patterns. New Englanders buried their dead in churchyards in nucleated villages. In Cape May County, most early burials took place on plantations[,] and later in the eighteenth and early nineteenth centuries burials took place in churchyards." Crowell carried out a comprehensive study of Cape May County's cemeteries dating from 1740 to 1810 and recorded 233 gravestones in twenty-six burial grounds, as well as some displaced markers. Crowell noted some problems with patterning, among other things, as family plantations and farms were sold and in some cases gravemarkers and burials were moved—though, making matters more confusing, only some individuals were moved, and often only stones, not bodies, were moved (Crowell 1983: 56). This same pattern of moving bodies and stones from farm burials to church burial grounds was also found at Staten Island at St. Andrew's Cemetery (Baugher and Winter 1983). Crowell attributed the popularity of home burial as relating to problems transporting bodies of the deceased to distant churchyards. She also noted some interesting burial patterns. She noted that women were buried with their husband's family, typically to the right of their husband (Crowell 1983: 74).

Confounded by the lack of iconography, Crowell strove to understand why the markers were so plain. Rather than focusing on decoration, she focused on the form of the markers. These did show an evolution over time. Although devoid of decoration, the forms of the markers reflected a change from a cherub shape to an urn-shaped or neoclassical form (Crowell 1983: 20). In essence, the tympanums or tops of the earliest markers consisted of a central lobe with smaller subsidiary lobes on the sides, reflecting a shape similar to a winged cherub. Later markers had tympanums that were shaped to accommodate the form of a funeral urn.

One of the factors influencing Cape May County's colonial gravemarkers was that the county is essentially devoid of local stone (just like Long Island), so there was no local stone carving industry; individuals who wanted formal gravemarkers had to import them. Unlike Long Island communities, which imported their gravestones from New England, New York, and northern New Jersey, the Cape May County residents primarily imported their stones from Philadelphia. Indeed, several of the markers bear signatures of Philadelphia carvers, while receipts and other family papers corroborate the importation of markers from Philadelphia (Crowell 1983: 85). A few of these documents are so detailed that they note exactly how much it cost to cut the stones, breaking it down on a letter-by-letter basis.

Philadelphia's stonecutters primarily employed marble or limestone quarried in Montgomery and Chester Counties in Pennsylvania (Crowell 1983: 86). Even more important, Crowell argues that those same Philadelphia carvers were influenced by the strong Quaker presence in Philadelphia, which emphasized that undecorated stones or no gravemarkers at all be employed (Crowell 1983: 86). Although many of Cape May County's settlers were the descendants of Puritans from New England, they imported their gravemarkers from the Quaker stronghold of Philadelphia and lived in a part of New Jersey where their neighbors were often Quakers. Crowell further notes that many individuals received no gravemarkers at all or would have used wooden markers or wooden grave rails, which unfortunately no longer survive. Grave rails were wooden gravemarkers that resembled small sections of fence and consisted of two upright posts and a cross bar, inscribed with the name of the deceased. Rather than being placed at the head of a grave, they ran parallel to and above the grave itself.

Crowell also discovered that marker inscriptions were a fruitful source of information. For instance, husbands' names were listed on wives' markers, but not vice versa. This is the same pattern Gaynell Stone found on

English markers on Long Island. Crowell found that sentiments conveyed by epitaphs could be divided into those mentioning or reminding the reader of death; those mentioning death but promising eternal life; and those promising life after death (Crowell 1983: 219). Furthermore, Crowell pointed out significant differences between New England burial grounds, where markers are numerous and ornamented and the bodies are in churchyards, and the Cape May burials, where there is largely an absence of carved iconography and the earliest burials were on plantations and only later in the eighteenth century were citizens buried in churchyards (Crowell 1983: 221).

Crowell also did important early work on Philadelphia gravemarkers, again modeled on the studies of James Deetz and Edwin Dethlefsen in New England. Although there are a handful of soapstone or steatite gravemarkers in and around Philadelphia, the vast majority of markers were made from a rather low-grade marble with a high limestone content that is very sandy in consistency and is mercilessly attacked by acid rain (Crowell 1981: 23). Moreover, those markers that survived were generally lacking in religious motifs. What was particularly interesting here is that Philadelphia was a city with a strong Quaker presence. Quakers sometimes left graves unmarked or used ephemeral wooden or very modest stone markers. In Philadelphia it appears that settlers belonging to other religious denominations such as Anglican, Presbyterian, Lutheran, and others may have deferred to the Quaker style (Crowell 1981: 24).

Quakers, more properly members of the Society of Friends, were an influential and distinctive religious group in early America. Their burial grounds, found in Pennsylvania, New Jersey, Delaware, Rhode Island, and elsewhere, are often devoid of formal gravemarkers. Quakers valued simplicity and equality; therefore, they saw no need for elaborate gravemarkers. However, in the mid-eighteenth century when the professionally carved gravemarkers became more common, some Friends seem to have succumbed to the temptation to erect more-permanent memorials (Bromberg and Shephard 2006). To quote Pearson Thistlethwaite, gravemarkers were a "stone of stumbling" for Quakers (Fischer 1989: 521). In the 1760s the London meetings recommended that all gravemarkers be removed from burial grounds. Even earlier some local coreligionists had taken this task on themselves. The February 18, 1751, minutes from the Woodbridge, New Jersey, Friends meeting notes, "Some Friends having been concerned in setting up grave Stones in our Burying ground, John Vail and Joseph

Shotwell are desired to treat with them and to desire them to have them removed" (Dally 1873: 209). Similarly, in Shrewsbury, New Jersey, when Friends erected gravemarkers a member of that meeting "applied sledge-hammers to the most prominent stones and only ceased when the debris of many was thrown into the highway as a warning to others" (Stillwell 1903: 375). Later, in the nineteenth century, these rules were relaxed.

Much like the Quakers the religious group known as Moravians believed in the equality of all humans. Moravians lived in communal societies primarily in North Carolina and Pennsylvania. In 1741, they set up their first town (in Bethlehem, Pennsylvania, followed by Nazareth in 1742); between 1753 and 1766 the Moravians established three towns in North Carolina (Reps 1980: 269–71). The Moravian settlements in North Carolina have seen extensive archaeological study (South 1999; Ferguson 2011). Similarly, Bethlehem, Pennsylvania, was the site of early archaeological investigations (Foley 1965: 61–64). However, the results of the Bethlehem excavations were not widely disseminated, and other Moravian communities in Pennsylvania and New Jersey have not been extensively examined.

Archaeologists have only begun to examine Moravian commemoration. Moravian gravemarkers were simple, often just plain slabs of stone, roughly the size of a legal pad. They were inscribed with the deceased's name, age, year of death, and sometimes birthplace and place of death (figure 4.10). Brian Thomas's article "Inclusion and Exclusion in the Moravian Settlement in North Carolina, 1770–1790" (1994) explores the question of how Moravian leaders balanced maintaining the integrity of their community with participation in the larger Anglo-American society. Thomas argues that the Moravian leadership employed "the built environment, mortuary practices, language, and the regulation of marriage to maintain social cohesion" but could when necessary deemphasize these practices to "give the appearance of Moravian inclusion in the larger Anglo-American society" (Thomas 1994: 15).

Thomas argues that one way the Moravians reinforced their ideas of community was through the built environment. This is particularly true in the half-timbered buildings they constructed that clearly reflected their Germanic heritage. Later buildings were more similar to those of their Anglo-American neighbors. God's Acre (as they called their cemeteries) was balanced by a strangers' burial ground used to inter non-Moravians. God's Acre is laid out in large squares by choir, containing flush numbered gravemarkers, professionally lettered and measuring fifteen inches square

Figure 4.10. The Moravian Burial Ground, Bethlehem, Pennsylvania. Note the small uniform gravemarkers arranged by choir, or social group, rather than as families. From a stereoview titled *No 4, Old Moravian Burying Ground—Winter* and inscribed "Photographed and Published by M. A. Kleckner, Bethlehem, PA." From the collection of Richard Veit.

(Little 1998: 87). The Moravians struggled to retain conformity with their guidelines, while those buried in the strangers' burial ground contained both Moravian-style markers and more-typical headstones (Little 1998: 89).

More recently, Leland Ferguson (2011) has studied the Moravian community of Old Salem, today part of Winston-Salem, North Carolina, and more specifically, St. Philip's African American Moravian Church and its associated Strangers' God's Acre. Ferguson (2011: 195) identified some eighty-five burials, thirty-one gravestones, and the site of a log church dating from 1823. However, what Ferguson discovered goes well past these

plain numbers. The chance discovery of several carved gravestones under the hallway floor of St. Philip's Church and more-modest Moravian
memorials under the granite front steps of the church led Ferguson and
his students on an archaeological odyssey, which allowed them to document and confront the Moravian community's changing perspectives toward slavery. As Ferguson notes, the first Moravian settlers, who arrived
in the area in the late eighteenth century, eschewed slavery, as they strove
to create a "worldwide Christian nation . . . and establish themselves as an
example of the earthly as well as heavenly rewards of pious Christianity"
(Ferguson 2011: 195). However, in the first decades of the nineteenth century, racial and status differences increasingly manifested themselves and
became engrained in Moravian practice. In part, this included the segregation of burial space, with non-Moravian and African American Moravians relegated to the Strangers' God's Acre rather than the congregational
God's Acre. The latter, employed by the white congregants, crowned a high
hill, while the former was at the bottom of Salem Hill. Ferguson's work is
important not only for documenting the past but also for exposing "racist scars on the landscape" (Ferguson 2011: 199) and helping the modern
Moravian community move toward reconciliation.

In the Tidewater area of Virginia there was no locally available stone,
and like the people on Long Island, the Virginia residents had to import
their gravestones. After examining public records, Elizabeth Crowell and
Norman Mackie (1990: 111) found that the majority of the stones were imported from England at a price between two and nineteen pounds sterling,
and only 2 out of the 184 stones were from a quarry in northern Virginia.
Because gravestones were expensive and imported, the stones represented
primarily the elites of Virginia. Crowell and Mackie (1990) documented
colonial gravestones in eleven Tidewater Virginia counties and found only
184 stones. Unlike the stones found in the other colonies, which were primarily headstones, only 21 Virginian stones were headstones. The other
stones were as follows: 53 box/chest tombs (a stone box with a ledger top),
1 table top (a ledger on four legs), 2 obelisks, 80 ledgers for outdoor sites,
and 27 ledgers for burials within churches (Crowell and Mackie 1990:
118–21) (figure 4.11). While ledgers and box tombs were found in the other
colonies, the predominant style, regardless of class, was the headstone,
but this was not the case in Virginia (Crowell and Mackie 1990: 133). The
Virginian headstones were primarily for nonelite individuals, whereas the
box tombs and ledgers (because of the cost) were primarily for the elites.

Figure 4.11. Edward Nott's monumental box tomb, likely carved in Great Britain, in Bruton Parish Churchyard, Williamsburg, Virginia. Notice the putti, or cherubs, at the top of the curtain, or pall, and the skull, or mortality image, below. Photograph by Richard Veit.

In the box/chest tombs, the dead were interred belowground, but these large and sometimes lavishly cut tombs served to advertise their status. Indeed, following the old adage in real estate that location is everything, many Virginia elites were buried inside churches, beneath ledgers noting their accomplishments.

The majority of the Virginian stones were undecorated. However, one-third of the stones bore a coat of arms, and in "nearly all of these the individual was designated as a 'gentleman'" (Crowell and Mackie 1990: 123). Rank was also seen in inscriptions with titles such as *honorable* or *esquire*; the term *mister* was reserved for individuals who were not entitled to a coat of arms but were of a status above a yeoman (Crowell and Mackie 1990: 126–28). The use of Latin in the inscriptions, along with the coat of arms or the use of a title in the inscriptions, indicated elite status. Women with inherited wealth were listed as "the daughter of," but women who married a man of a higher status were simply listed as "wife of," and a woman of wealth who married into wealth was listed as both a daughter and a wife (Crowell and Mackie 1990: 128). The Virginian gravestones also reflected their owners' concerns with status and with maintaining their ties to the elites in England through the use of family coat of arms.

The cemeteries in New England and in the Middle Colonies reflected various Protestant denominations. In Maryland, Georgia, and Florida there were Catholic cemeteries. Many of the markers in these colonial Catholic cemeteries were made of wood and have not survived. One of the cemeteries with many wooden markers was the Tolomato Cemetery in St. Augustine, Florida. The Spanish Catholic Tolomato Cemetery was established in 1777 on the grounds of the former Tolomato Indian Mission, 1720–63 (Kerr 2009: 6–8). In two 1880 photographs, numerous large wooden crosses are still standing throughout the cemetery, but none of these wooden markers have survived (Kerr 2009: 23). In 2009, there were only two extant colonial and early nineteenth-century markers, and they were box tombs. Similar to elite English Protestants in Virginia, the elite Spanish Catholics in St. Augustine buried their dead in the ground and placed the box tomb over the grave site. These two Tolomato box tombs consist of marble slabs sitting on a box made of coquina (Kerr 2009: 51). Coquina is a local shellstone, a conglomerate of marine shells, found in Florida (Manucy 1992: 156). Floridians used coquina (carved into brick-shaped forms) for the construction of colonial residential, commercial, religious, and military structures (Manucy 1992). Beyond its use for architecture, coquina was a unique material found in Floridian cemeteries.

Jews were always a minority in the New World. Following their expulsion from Spain in 1492, some relocated to the Netherlands or to Recife in Brazil. When the Portuguese captured Recife, the Jewish settlers relocated to the Dutch island of Curacao, and ultimately some came to Nieuw Amsterdam (New York). These Jewish pioneers were primarily Sephardic Jews, but over the course of the eighteenth and nineteenth centuries, Ashkenazim from Germany, Poland, Russia, and Lithuania also came to the New World (Seeman 2010a: 234). Jews established communities in port towns in North America and the Caribbean, especially Newport, Charleston, New York, and Philadelphia. Maintaining Jewish traditions meant having a Jewish burial ground. According to Talmudic injunctions, the burial ground needed to be enclosed, to provide protection "against incursions made by rooting animals and disrespectful gentiles" (Seeman 2010a: 238). Sadly, life for Jews in colonial America was not without persecution, as a notice in the 1751 *Pennsylvania Gazette* indicates: "Whereas, many unthinking people have been in the habit of . . . firing several shots against the fence of the Jews' burying ground, which not only destroyed said fence, but also a tombstone; there being a brick wall now erected, I must desire the sportsmen to forbear . . . firing against said wall. Nathan Levy, President of the Congregation" (Pool 1952: 67).

Jewish burial grounds appeared to be much like those in Europe. Indeed, perhaps more so than for other groups, Jewish immigrants were likely to import professionally carved gravemarkers from London and Holland (Seeman 2010a: 253). Some of these markers show incredibly elaborate carving, in contradistinction to the "Second Commandment's stricture against graven images" (Seeman 2010a: 253). Both men's and women's markers spoke to their personal character and hopes for eternal glory.

David Mayer Gradwohl has documented and published on many aspects of Jewish commemoration, including the historic cemetery in Newport, Rhode Island (Gradwohl 2007), and the broader topic of Sephardic Jewish cemeteries in North America and the Caribbean (Gradwohl 1998). Their markers are generally large tablets, sometimes richly illustrated despite religious prohibitions observed by many of the Jewish faith against human imagery. Mortality images and cherubs are found on some of their eighteenth-century markers. These well-traveled, cosmopolitan individuals often have markers inscribed with epitaphs in several different languages, including English, Dutch, Portuguese, Hebrew, and sometimes Ladino, sometimes called Jewish-Spanish, a language derived from Spanish but containing elements of Hebrew and Arabic. Some of their Caribbean gravemarkers were apparently imported from the Netherlands and other locations where professional carvers were active. In North America, early Sephardic burial grounds survive in Newport, Rhode Island; Savannah, Georgia; New York City; and Philadelphia (Halporn 1993: 133, 139).

The most extensively studied of North America's colonial Jewish burial grounds is the Newport, Rhode Island, burying ground associated with the Congregation Yeshuat Israel and Touro Synagogue. It is the oldest extant Jewish cemetery in North America (Gradwohl 2007: 1). Gradwohl's work is important for providing material evidence for the Sephardic background of Newport's early Jewish settlers and also highlighting the extensive trade networks they participated in. Furthermore, he highlights the iconography of the gravemarkers. In 1997 Gradwohl and his wife, Hanna Rosenberg Gradwohl, began a detailed documentation of the burial ground. The burial ground contains forty-two gravestones dating from

1761 to 1866, but this chapter focuses on the stones from the eighteenth and early nineteenth century (pre–War of 1812). Earlier burials are quite likely to be present as well, given the areas of open space still present in the burial ground. Initial Jewish settlement in Newport occurred in the mid-seventeenth century with Spanish-Portuguese Jews moving to New England from the Caribbean (Gradwohl 2007: 20). Rather curiously, the oldest extant gravemarkers date from the 1760s. Whether individuals who died before this date were buried elsewhere or reside in unmarked graves is unclear, though archival sources seem to indicate the latter. Ledgers, commonly used by Sephardic Jews, were particularly popular during the eighteenth century. Ledger stones were also considerably more expensive than headstones and may be seen as status symbols. In contrast, the colonial headstones are similar to those found in other colonial New England burial grounds. Curiously, all of these markers bear some form of decoration, whether human faces with wings or cherubs, which are present on five. A gravemarker for Jacob Lopez dating from 1822 has a crudely carved skull that is quite late for a skull motif to be found on New England gravestones (Gradwohl 2007: 36). The markers' inscriptions also speak to the nature of early American Judaism. Inscriptions in Hebrew, Spanish, Portuguese, Latin, and English are all present. Gradwohl (2007: 54) notes that Latin was perhaps the least obvious of these languages, and he concludes that it may have been seen as a mark of real or aspirational social status.

The language used on gravemarkers in Christian cemeteries may also provide insights into the lives and experiences of men and women in early America. A particularly fine example of this is Joy Giguere's work on gravemarkers in Cumberland County, Maine. Giguere's work focused on epitaphs and inscriptions rather than the iconography of the markers. Through painstaking analysis of gravemarker epitaphs from Cumberland County, Maine, she examines how epitaphs were used in the construction of gender roles. For her study she examined 1,150 gravestones dating from 1720 to 1820 (Giguere 2007: 2). The markers were almost evenly split between men and women. Giguere notes several differences between the number of men and women and also between the number of boys and girls represented in the burial ground. Although populations rose over time, there are more gravemarkers for boys than for girls and more surviving gravestones for women than for men. She also examined the use of titles on the gravemarkers. These may indicate the individual's kin relations, such as *wife, mother, son,* and *husband,* or use the archaic terms *consort* or *relict.* Indeed, the later term seems to have been used primarily for women with high-status husbands (Giguere 2007: 6). For men, title categories included military occupations, religious occupations, and the titles *Esquire, Mr.,* and *Captain* (Giguere 2007: 7). Giguere (2007: 12) also found that the most elaborate and laudatory inscriptions were for men who held religious offices—pastors, ministers, and the like. Moreover, different descriptive terms were used for men and for women, reflecting "whether that person had lived according to prescribed codes of behavior." For instance, while women were sweet, lovely, and happy, men were honest, useful, and wise. Moreover, while men were expected to exhibit public virtue, or self-sacrifice for the public good, virtue for women related to "temperance, prudence, faith, [and] charity," and to some extent also the growing cult of Republican Motherhood, which stressed having women show not only their Christian virtue but also a sense of patriotism and political awareness (Giguere 2007: 15). Giguere also finds interesting evidence for the creation of gender identities in childhood, in that both boys' and girls' adjectives had much less to do with virtue, wisdom, or piety, all associated with age; rather, they were characterized as flowers or "paragons of purity" (Giguere 2007: 20). Her careful reading of these early gravemarkers highlights the varied types of information that gravemarkers may provide.

Very few gravemarkers of Native Americans survive from the colonial period, but excavations of some of these sites are discussed in chapter 3, and the nineteenth-century markers that survive are discussed in chapter 6. In 1924, Harry Shapiro, then a graduate student at Harvard, excavated an eighteenth-century Native American burial ground. All aboveground material and most belowground material were removed through either Shapiro's excavation or farming activities. Shapiro did note that in 1924 the Christianized Wampanoag graves had plain fieldstone for headstones and footstones, indicating that the Wampanoags may have been influenced by their Quaker neighbors (Hodge 2005: 79).

African American gravemarkers in early America are also of great interest to scholars (Krüger-Kahloula 1989; Little 1989; Veit 1992; Garman 1994; Blouet 2010). Only a few professionally carved gravemarkers for African Americans survive from the eighteenth and early nineteenth centuries, though fieldstone markers are quite common. Those professionally produced markers that survive are fascinating, and they raise interesting questions about who was commemorated and why. Here eighteenth-century markers employed by African Americans are briefly discussed.

Nineteenth-century African American markers are more extensively examined in chapter 6.

An important study of early African American gravemarkers is James Garman's research on the Common Burial Ground in Newport, Rhode Island. Garman provides a fascinating glimpse of commemorative practices in a distinctive and often-overlooked early American community. Newport, Rhode Island, is perhaps best known for its Gilded Age mansions. It is also the home of the Touro Synagogue (America's oldest synagogue), an unparalleled collection of early American gravemarkers, and the John Stevens Shop, a gravestone carving business that has been in continuous operation since 1705. Garman's work, which builds on earlier research on New England gravemarkers, is unusual and important in that it focuses on the race or, to quote W. E. B. Du Bois, the color line or dual consciousness of African Americans (Garman 1994: 74). Garman's article examines what gravemarkers can tell us about attitudes toward race in colonial Newport, how the symbolic meanings of these artifacts can be read, and how "reception theory enables historical archaeologists to link African American pasts with the sociopolitics of practicing historical archaeology in the present" by focusing on how people read and understood the stones when they were erected (Garman 1994: 75). More than 10 percent of the population of colonial Newport was enslaved, and many slaves lived in urban white households. Some authors have seen this as evidence of a "kinder, gentler, Northern slavery" (Mason 1884: 104). In contrast, others have noted that household slavery of this form would have resulted in a very high degree of surveillance and perhaps heightened tension.

Garman's study focuses on the African American section of Newport's Common Burying Ground, a segregated space within a larger burial ground. Garman examines the size, placement, cost, and inscriptions of the markers and probes what these markers might have meant to the individuals interred there, the carvers who produced the stones, and the slaveholders who purchased them. In 1807 the U.S. Congress passed the Act Prohibiting the Importation of Slaves. This, in concert with new state laws enacted in the late eighteenth and early nineteenth centuries in the Northern states emancipating slaves, resulted in a confusing system of free and enslaved. During this period, markers for African American men and women grew larger and became less distinctive from those of their European American contemporaries. Garman's work is important as expanding the vision of archaeologists studying the lives of enslaved African Americans; it helps create a more inclusive view of the past while at the same time looking at the distinctive and shifting position African Americans held in early Rhode Island and the insights gravemarkers can provide into their lives and times, especially as witnessed by their contemporaries.

Several of the markers display fine portraits of the deceased. Generally speaking, the images of cherubs seen on early American gravemarkers were not depictions of the deceased but rather stylized depictions, generally of bewigged men (see figure 4.9, *right*), reflecting the carver's skill and idiosyncrasies rather than the physical appearance of the deceased (see figure 4.6, *right*). For the African American gravestones, the opposite seems true: several of the markers do seem to be portraits. This is especially interesting because African Americans were involved in the operation of the Stevens Shop where many of these markers were carved.

Beyond issues of religion and ethnicity, I (Veit 2009) have examined the increasingly competitive nature of the stone-cutting industry during the late eighteenth century. This was a period when more and more gravestone carvers signed their markers and decorated their products with monograms. Gravemarkers also became much more common. I argue that the growth of a consumer's republic in late eighteenth-century America seems to have had a large effect on marker design. Carvers started to advertise by inscribing their names onto the gravestones. Carver's names are found on gravestones in cemeteries in New England, as well as New York City, northern New Jersey, Long Island, and the Hudson River valley (Levine 1978b; Veit 1996; Wasserman 1972; Welch 1983). Moreover, family relationships seem to have helped drive purchases of gravestones from particular carvers (Heinrich 2003: 12). In studying the work of colonial New York carver John Zuricher, we found that ethnic and socioeconomic connections seem to have played an important role in determining the carver's clients (Baugher and Veit 2013). For example, elite individuals (of both Dutch and English heritage) buried in New York City's most prestigious burial place, Trinity Churchyard, purchased tombstones carved by John Zuricher (Baugher and Veit 2013). Zuricher carved stones with lettering in English for clients with Dutch surnames; perhaps these were families who for economic or social reasons wanted to assimilate into English culture. Cultural change is complex with individuals and families making choices about their identity, and the gravestones also reflect those choices.

Materials Employed for Gravemarkers in the Colonial Period

Although most researchers have focused their attention on formally carved stone markers, the earliest gravemarkers in much of eastern North America were probably made from wood rather than stone. According to historian Richard Welch, "At the time of the first large-scale English migrations to the New World (1620–60), there was no widespread method of identifying graves in England by means of stone markers. During this period, English graves, with the exception of those of the nobility and gentry, were identified by wooden markers constructed like a section of fence with two posts anchored in the ground and a plank fitted between them" (Welch 1983: 2; see also Mytum 2004: 26). These grave boards or grave rails could be carved, painted, and ornamented. A record of costs associated with the burial of John Hand from Cape May County, New Jersey, who died in 1736, lists "Items by Moneys pd for the Coffin and Grave Posts" (Crowell 1983: 94).

In other sections of the colonies, where stone was common it was almost immediately employed for gravemarkers. Sometimes simple fieldstones with crudely scratched inscriptions served as memorials, such as the seventeenth-century fieldstones in the Hudson River valley of New York and New Jersey. Other stones were shaped before carving.

Although the Greeks and Romans had used gravemarkers that resembled headstones, not until the end of the Middle Ages were headstones extensively used in Great Britain (Mytum 2004: 27; Little 1998: 12). In Virginia the earliest surviving colonial gravemarker is a tombstone bearing the outlines of a now-missing monumental brass relief in the form of a knight, probably marking the grave of Sir George Yeardley, governor of Virginia, who died in 1627 (Hudson 1967: 760–61) (figure 4.12). The earliest surviving examples of headstones in the Northeast date from the mid-seventeenth century; in Massachusetts a pair marks the graves of Bernard and Joan Capen, who died in 1638 and 1653, respectively (Chase and Gabel 1997: 5). New York City's oldest surviving headstone is for Richard Churcher, who is buried in Trinity Churchyard. His marker is dated 1681.

Headstones were often accompanied by footstones, often bearing only the initials of the deceased. The paired headstones and footstones were, in a sense, permanent physical metaphors of the bed of rest. Sadly, many footstones were removed in the nineteenth century as new standards of

Figure 4.12. Tombstone with insets for brass decorations, now lost, believed to be for Sir George Yeardley, governor of Virginia (d. 1627), Jamestown, Virginia. Photograph by Richard Veit.

burial ground maintenance came to the fore and footstones proved cumbersome to mow around (Veit and Nonestied 2008: 24).

Often the top front-facing portion of the headstone was decorated with a carving. This portion of the marker, like the head of a drum, is known as the tympanum. It was the carvings of the death's heads, cherubs, and urns and willows on the tympanum that attracted scholars like Deetz and Dethlefsen. In the eighteenth century, the forms of the headstones and footstones often resembled the form of doorways from the same time period (Veit and Nonestied 2008: 22). This was intentional. Gravemarkers, like doors, functioned as portals from one state of being to another: outdoor versus indoor and living versus dead (St. George 1988: 345). Moreover, gravemarkers shaped like doors played with the concept of materiality, with wood resembling stone or flowers or stone looking like wood, trees, or vines (St. George 1988: 345).

Wealthier individuals throughout the colonies had their graves marked with horizontal slabs called tombstones or ledgers. Ledgers are found marking elite graves of Protestants, Catholics, and Jews (Veit and Nonestied 2008; Gradwohl 2007; Kerr 2009). These ledgers are occasionally found inside churches, where they cover the graves of elite individuals and are common in colonial Tidewater Virginia (Crowell and Mackie 1990: 118). Raised on stone or brick legs or boxes, they became box or table tombs and marked elite graves in churchyards. Some even bore lead plaques or occasionally armorial crests for particularly noteworthy individuals (Gabel 2009).

While colonial stone markers were made primarily of sandstone, slate, or fieldstone, occasionally other materials were used. Iron does not seem like a good material for a permanent gravemarker, because it rusts and decays. Nevertheless, iron has a long history of use for gravemarkers, particularly in England (Willats 1987; Mytum 2004: 61). Perhaps the oldest surviving example of an iron gravestone in the United States is the gravemarker of Nathaniel Irish, who was born in the West Indies about 1680 and died in Hunterdon County, New Jersey, in 1747 (Veit and Nonestied 2008: 197). Originally buried in a cemetery near Union Furnace in Hunterdon County, his burial was later moved to Pittsburgh, a city famous for manufacturing iron (Veit and Nonestied 2008: 197).

Areas for Additional Research

This chapter highlights some of the major patterns and research in colonial gravestones, but there are still many areas of research to be undertaken in terms of ethnicity, religion, class, and consumer choice. For example, art historians and folklorists have recorded gravemarkers of Pennsylvania Germans, colloquially called the Pennsylvania Dutch (Barba 1954; Farber and Farber 1988; Graves 1988; Hardy 2003). Given the richness of Pennsylvania's early gravemarkers—carved from slate, sandstone, and soapstone and inscribed in English, German, and Welsh—it is surprising that archaeologists have not yet studied them. For example, in the colonial cemeteries of southeastern Pennsylvania, particularly Northampton Bucks, Lehigh, Montgomery, Berks, Schuykill, Lebanon, and Lancaster counties, numerous German-language gravemarkers are found. Dating from the eighteenth century, they are decorated with tulips, hearts, flowers, waning moons, hourglasses, and occasionally cherubs and mortality images (Barba 1954; Lichten 1946: 126–33; Farber and Farber 1988; Graves 1988). In some cases, both faces of the markers were carved in an elaborate folk-baroque style (see again figure 4.9, *left* and *right*). The equally ornate lettering on these markers was often carried out in a style known colloquially as *Fraktur* or *Gebrochene Schrift*, which translates into English as "broken writing" because of its angular forms (Hardy 2003: 12). Many are inscribed with biblical verses. Similar German-language markers are found in parts of Virginia and North Carolina (Little 1998: 89–99, 156). We are aware of no studies that have attempted to seriate these markers or link them to broader issues of cultural and religious change.

Portraits are sometimes found on colonial stones in cemeteries from the North to the South. Art historians, folklorists, and historians have noted the presence of portrait stones throughout New England, even in the heart of Deetz and Dethlefsen's study areas (Benes 1977; Forbes 1927; Ludwig 1966). The portrait stones are also found in New Jersey, in New York, and even as far south as Charleston, South Carolina (Duval and Rigby 1978; Wasserman 1972; Combs 1986; Mould and Loewe 2006). The portraits are distinctive and seem to represent individuals rather than being a cookie-cutter style used by carvers (figure 4.13).

Suzanne Spencer-Wood (1996) in testing Deetz and Dethlefsen's seriation pattern in one cemetery in Lexington, Massachusetts, used five-year rather than ten-year intervals and surprisingly found that portrait stones

Figure 4.13. Gravemarker for Mrs. Anna D'Harriette (d. 1754), carved by William Codner. This is an outstanding portrait stone in St. Philip's West Burial Ground, Charlestown, South Carolina. Farber Collection, reproduced courtesy of the American Antiquarian Society.

were actually more prevalent than cherubs during 1770–74. Other than Spencer-Wood's multiscalar seriation study, archaeologists have not examined portrait stones. What were the economic, social, ethnic, or class factors influencing the decision to purchase a portrait stone or even for the carvers to produce these unique stones?

Why are individual headstones so common in the Northeast but uncommon in the Southeast? Does this relate to different regional economies, which allowed a larger middle class, with the disposable income to purchase gravemarkers, to flourish in the Northeast, which seems to have been largely missing in the Southeast? How could broader trends in art and cultural sensibilities beyond religion have shaped commemorative trends? These are just a few of the questions future scholars might investigate using early American gravemarkers.

Conclusions

Early American gravemarkers are some of the most evocative and informative artifacts available to historical archaeologists. They combine aspects of the documentary record through inscriptions and epitaphs and carry symbolic and stylistic information in their forms, iconography, and even the material carvers selected for them. Often they are dated and retain their integrity of setting. Although most of early America's wooden gravemarkers have been lost, substantial numbers of stone markers survive despite attrition due to vandalism, the elements, and in some cases the destruction or redevelopment of urban burial grounds. In the 1960s, following years of study by genealogists and art historians, James Deetz and Edwin Dethlefsen, as well as contemporary historians, art historians, literary scholars, and other gravestone aficionados, discovered their value for studying early American life and for reflecting the American experience. James Deetz (1977) described gravestones as aboveground artifacts that can be analyzed for their iconographic and textual information. Beyond the theological issues, archaeologists started to analyze gravestones for evidence of patterns of ethnicity, class, consumer behavior, ideology, and trade networks. However, a word of caution is in order. To quote James Hijiya (1983: 340), "Interpreting gravestones is not as easy as it seems. Gravestone carvers and purchasers, unlike makers and buyers in more esteemed arts such as painting and architecture, almost never explained their commodity. They left behind virtually no written record of their motivations or intentions, no explanation of why they carved or ordered a particular design." At a glance this would seem like a rather depressing situation; however, through careful contextual analysis, researchers can elicit considerable information from these silent stones.

In colonial cemeteries, many of the graves contained wooden markers. Indeed, historical records indicate that wooden markers were widespread across the entire United States, and they continue to be used today by some religious groups, particularly Ukrainian and Russian Orthodox immigrants (Veit and Nonestied 2008: 191, 250). The cost of gravestones placed them within the reach of only the upper and middle classes. For example, in the early eighteenth century, a gravestone would have cost between two and three pounds sterling and a large flat ledger stone would have been ten pounds or more; this was at a time when laborers were paid one to two shillings a day (Veit 1996: 77). Twenty shillings is equal to one pound, so a laborer earning a shilling a day would have to work for sixty days (and use all of those earnings) to be able to purchase a gravestone. The ledger stone at ten pounds would translate into the total wages for two hundred days of work. However, the cost of food, clothing, and shelter on such a meager income would have made gravestones and ledgers unaffordable to laborers. Our study of colonial gravestones, while looking at socioeconomic, ethnic, religious, and gender issues, is necessarily limited to the stones purchased by the middle- and upper-class customers. Time and the elements have largely eliminated the wooden markers from colonial burial grounds, providing modern visitors with a distorted view of how many early American burial grounds appeared and the material culture they once contained. However, as discussed in chapter 3, belowground archaeology has unearthed information on the burial practices of the laborers and the poor.

5

Transformations in the Design of Nineteenth- and Twentieth-Century Cemeteries

The nineteenth century saw the transformation of disordered burying grounds into planned cemeteries, the replacement of markers with monuments, a fading away of regional folk carving traditions (which were replaced by new national and indeed international memorial trends), new ideas about commemoration, and new ways of treating the deceased, including embalming and cremation. Nineteenth-century cemeteries were built in response to the pressures of expanding urban populations at a time when urban land values were increasing. Cemeteries were constructed in areas that at that time were less expensive rural suburbs and were not part of the city proper. These large "rural," "romantic," or "garden" cemeteries were usually nonsectarian and were sometimes designed by landscape architects. Because of the wealth spent on these cemeteries, they also became outdoor museums of sculpture, arboretums, and forerunners of public parks. Nineteenth-century America was a consumer culture. American industries provided more affordable goods. Transportation improved with canals and railroads quickly shipping goods throughout the country. The emergent middle class, like the upper class, sought to display their material success. This display of wealth and status is also evident in their cemeteries. Class differences are quite apparent in these cemeteries in terms of gravestones, monuments, statues, fences, and mausoleums.

By the beginning of the twentieth century, the American frontier was closed. Americans were extending their political and economic influence beyond the Americas and into the Pacific and Asia. By midcentury, Americans had suffered through two world wars, the Korean War, and the Great

Depression. These changes altered Americans' views of death and cemeteries. The grand rural/garden centers were no longer popular. Cemetery tourism was a thing of the past. But Americans still had to bury their dead.

This chapter examines the evolution of the American burial place from the nineteenth through the twentieth century. The transition from burial grounds to cemeteries reflected changes in national attitudes toward materialism and conspicuous consumption, and these changes are seen in diverse cemeteries including rural cemeteries, lawn-park cemeteries, military cemeteries, churchyards, memorial parks, and pauper burial grounds. There was also a transformation in the markers found within these burial grounds. We provide an analysis of the diverse iconography found on markers, and a range of symbols found on the buildings and sculpture is discussed.

Treatment of the dead was also transformed. Bodies, which had been hurriedly buried in the eighteenth century, were preserved for increasingly long periods of time, at first using ice and then, especially in the years after the Civil War, through embalming. Cremation, long eschewed by major religions, began to make inroads in the late nineteenth century, and in 1876 Francis Julius Le Moyne constructed America's first crematorium in Washington, Pennsylvania (Veit and Nonestied 2008: 229). In the twentieth century, crematoriums and cemetery columbaria in which families place the ashes of their loved ones have become an increasingly important part of the cemetery landscape. In discussing these two centuries of changes in burial practices, we pay particular attention to issues of socioeconomic class and capitalism and their impact on the cemetery landscape.

The Development of Nineteenth-Century Cemeteries

Much of the research on the transformation of the American burial place has been the work of historians (Sloane 1991; Seeman 2010a), art historians (Linden-Ward 1989a, 1989b; Keister 2004), geographers (Francaviglia 1971; Jordan 1982), and scholars in English and folklore (Meyer 1989, 1993; Richman 1998) rather than archaeologists; nevertheless, their interdisciplinary research remains relevant for understanding this period.

The American Revolution changed the political, economic, and cultural landscape of the former British colonies. The new country struggled to develop a workable political system. With the paternalistic yoke of mercantilism removed, American industry blossomed. In the nineteenth century,

America moved from a primarily agricultural economy to an industrial economy, and a wide range of new jobs emerged with the new industries. With the development of the Erie Canal and other canals, the transportation of factory-made goods brought a wide range of inexpensive goods to the American consumer, providing Americans with more material possessions, including a variety of gravestones. But the transformation from eighteenth-century church and synagogue burial grounds to private, secular cemeteries was a slow process.

The early nineteenth century was a time of burial reform. Previously, burials had occurred on family property or in community, church, or synagogue burial grounds. By the early nineteenth century, urban church graveyards were filled to capacity. For example, scholars have estimated that New York City's Trinity Churchyard contained as many as 100,000 burials in a few acres, most in unmarked graves (Yalom 2008: 95). Health concerns also drove burial reform. Epidemics such as cholera and yellow fever in the 1790s and in the first two decades of the nineteenth century devastated urban populations and overwhelmed churchyards (Sloane 1991: 35). Although the germ theory of disease was a thing of the future, crowded burial grounds were increasingly seen as linked to outbreaks of disease. Forward-thinking citizens worked to solve the problems of overcrowded, unsightly, and unsanitary burial places by designing new burial places, organized and incorporated as businesses and managed by a board of trustees.

This was not an entirely homegrown transformation. Similar issues of cemetery overcrowding in Europe, known as the burial crisis, led to a cemetery reform movement and the rise of the first modern cemeteries. The word *cemetery*, derived from the Greek word for "sleeping chamber," became a widely employed term in the early nineteenth century and was linked to the idea of death as sleep, and a transition from life to eternal life, rather than death and decay (Sloane 1991: 55). As early as the late seventeenth century, John Evelyn and Sir Christopher Wren were arguing that large cemeteries should be established outside of cities. According to cemetery historian James Steven Curl (1993: 136), "Wren visualized cemeteries outside towns where fine monuments could be erected to designs by the best architects and sculptors of the period, subject to certain safeguards as to dimensions and basic forms. Wren also argued that architects should inspect the designs for individual's tombs to ensure a harmonious whole."

New Orleans, famous for its aboveground burials (constructed not so

Figure 5.1. St. Louis Cemetery Number 1, New Orleans. Detroit Publishing Company, c. 1900, courtesy Library of Congress, LC-D4-5748 DLC.

much because of a high water table as episodes of flooding), had a cemetery outside the city by 1725, and the famous St. Louis Cemetery Number 1 was established in 1788, in response to twin catastrophes: a fire and an epidemic (Curl 1993: 146) (figure 5.1). In the early nineteenth century, rural cemeteries were established in England with landscape features such as trees, shrubs, winding paths, ponds, and lawns (Richman 1998: 5). However, the most famous and arguably the most influential private, secular cemetery of the nineteenth century was Père-Lachaise, established in 1804 by the order of Napoleon Bonaparte on the former estate of Baron Desfontaines at Mont-Louis (Curl 1993: 154). That same year, France banned burial inside or immediately outside churches. During the French Revolution, the government also sought to dismantle the power of the Catholic Church and take away church property, including cemeteries. Père-Lachaise was one of four secular burial grounds established to serve the four sections of Paris. Many of the tombs in the cemetery followed neoclassical motifs and were widely imitated.

In North America, New Haven, Connecticut, was on the cutting edge of burial reform. That city's growth, yellow fever epidemics, and an increasingly taxed burial ground on the town green led James Hillhouse and others to argue for a new form of burial ground. The resulting New Haven Burying Ground (chartered by the state of Connecticut) was laid out on a grid, with a central roadway at the entrance, family plots, and plantings, particularly poplars and weeping willows; it opened in 1796 (Sloane 1991: 32–33). Other communities were investing in underground burial vaults that could hold large numbers of graves. For example, New York City experimented with secular cemeteries. In 1823, the private New York Marble Cemetery was established on a half acre with 156 underground vaults to be sold to wealthy New Yorkers (Bergman 1995: 196). Vaults filled up rapidly and proved to be only a short-term solution. In 1830, the investors built a second cemetery, New York City Marble, which also catered to the wealthy (Bergman 1995: 196). These early private cemeteries were relatively small, and they were often located too close to city centers in areas that were rapidly developing. Their developers underestimated the population growth that would occur in the nineteenth century, and initially, there was some resistance to being buried in these new and curious burial places.

This would change in the 1830s, with the rise of the rural cemetery movement. The first American rural cemetery was Mount Auburn in Cambridge, Massachusetts; it was established in 1831 by the Massachusetts Horticultural Society and was designed as a picturesque landscape, a style in vogue in England (Simon 1980: 53) (figure 5.2). Mount Auburn can be seen as the next step in burial place evolution, after the New Haven Burying Ground. It reflected both European antecedents in cemeteries and nineteenth-century English landscape design, but in the words of David Charles Sloane, "Mount Auburn was an American original" (1991: 44). The rural location of Mount Auburn was driven by concerns about hygiene in a rapidly growing Boston. There were also questions "as to whether vault burial was discriminatory within a democratic society" (Sloane 1991: 44). The scale of the proposed cemetery was unprecedented for North America, covering seventy-two acres. The site was named after Sweet Auburn, a location mentioned in Oliver Goldsmith's poem "Deserted Village" (Sloane 1991: 45). In an important and precedent-setting move, the Massachusetts Horticultural Society partnered with local businessmen, particularly Jacob Bigelow, in developing the site (Simon 1980: 53). The landscape plan itself was the work of Henry Alexander, Scammel Dearborn, and Alexander

Figure 5.2. Bartlett print of Mount Auburn Cemetery, Cambridge, Massachusetts. Note the man-made lake and picturesque setting. Courtesy of Mount Auburn Cemetery.

Wadsworth (Sloan 1991: 46). The combination of horticulture and burial interests was not random. This was a conscious reaction to the growing industrialization of America and its perceived woes. The landscape of the garden or rural cemetery drew from the picturesque gardens then popular in England, a concept that balanced nature and art. In the words of a contemporary commentator, the cemetery should be "in places lonely, but not deserted, where the beauty of nature is heightened by the care of man, where the gloom of death cannot sadden the hearts of the living" (Sloane 1991: 46). Of course, the term *rural cemetery* is something of a misnomer; these cemeteries were typically located on the edges of cities in what were relatively undeveloped areas. Today, many are fully within the cities they served.

Mount Auburn also saw increasingly regimentation in the use of the cemetery, a model that others would follow. The lots were relatively expensive and typically purchased by families, who erected family monuments, while single graves were offered to those unable to afford larger lots, and the markers were limited by regulation (Sloane 1991: 54). Many family lots were fenced, using ornate cast iron fences, most of which have been lost to time and scrap drives. Despite the restrictions, some of the monuments were quite elaborate; plantings on private lots reflected the individual family's financial investment in the property. This new model spawned many imitators.

In 1836 Laurel Hill Cemetery in Philadelphia was founded, and two years later, in 1838, Green-Wood opened in Brooklyn (Stannard 1980: 23). The motivation behind establishing these cemeteries is well represented in an 1835 diary entry by John Jay Smith, a Philadelphia Quaker, librarian of Philadelphia's Library Company and a passionate amateur horticulturist, who noted, "The City of Philadelphia has been increasing so rapidly of late years that the living population has multiplied beyond the means of accommodation for the dead. . . . [O]n recently visiting Friends grave yard in Cherry Street I found it impossible to designate the resting place of a darling daughter, [which] determined me to endeavor to procure for the citizens a suitable, neat and orderly location for a rural cemetery (*Laurel Hill Cemetery*)." Smith proposed a site well out of town, with spectacular vistas of the Schuylkill River (Brooks and Waskie n.d.: 2).

In 1838, Green-Wood Cemetery was in a rural area near the city of Brooklyn and within a ferry ride from New York City (then only Manhattan). The designers of Green-Wood chose land that contained hills, forests, glacial ponds, streams, dells, and valleys that could be improved upon to make it look more "natural" and picturesque (Richman 1998: 10). Because of the varied landscape, the cemetery contained diverse views, from very private secluded locations in the valleys to majestic views of New York City and New York Harbor from the tops of the hills. Just as in the real estate industry today, location and property size determined the price of the burial lots, from modest locations to spectacular settings. Families could purchase individual or family lots or even larger lots for mausoleums.

Green-Wood Cemetery was established during the economic depression of the 1830s. In an attempt to attract customers, the cemetery board sold grave lots to churches that wanted to relocate their graveyards and sell off their cemeteries within the city (Simon 1980: 53–54). In fact, in Green-Wood there are small clusters of colonial gravestones from these relocated graveyards. Green-Wood, however, remained a secular cemetery. In an attempt to market the cemetery, the graves of famous individuals, including former New York governor DeWitt Clinton, were relocated to Green-Wood, and the marketing ploy worked (Richman 1998: 13). Green-Wood, Mount Auburn, and Laurel Hill became models for other rural cemeteries around the country (Sears 1989: 99).

Figure 5.3. A fine example of Victorian sentimentality, the marker for Lina Reiss is in Der Stadt Freidhoff (The City Cemetery) in Fredericksburg, Texas. It shows an angelic child, presumably Lina, kneeling on a pillow and praying. Note the numerous hand-made iron fences. Photograph by Richard Veit.

By the mid-nineteenth century, nearly every sizeable American city had its rural cemetery. The garden/rural cemeteries were private corporations that sold permanent plots. In most European cities, burial plots were rented not purchased, and after the rental ended the "remains were removed to the charnel house" (Sloane 1991: 3). In America's colonial churchyards, people were generally buried as members of the congregation rather than in a family plot. One of the appeals of nineteenth-century

American private cemeteries was that families could purchase family plots to ensure that they would remain together in death in perpetuity. The nineteenth-century family plots were often bordered with cast iron fences and gates. With the growth of the iron industry in the nineteenth century, the middle class could afford cast iron fences (Linden-Ward 1990: 39). Victorian cemeteries display cast iron fences ranging from the simple to the ornate (figure 5.3). Within the fenced-in cemetery lot, families purchased cast iron benches, trellises, and planters (Linden-Ward 1990: 41). The furniture and the fencing were just two of the many ways families could assert their material success in this world and, mimicking the increasingly class-segregated neighborhoods of the time, created permanent monumental addresses for deceased family members.

Materialism and Class Distinctions within the Rural Cemeteries

With the emergence of the middle class, nineteenth-century class distinctions became more apparent. There was a belief that success was attainable through an individual's hard work, intelligence, and sobriety. Randall McGuire (1991: 104) notes that in the nineteenth century "the 'gospel of wealth' proclaimed that wealth was the emblem of success, the reward of the good life, and personal ability." Material possessions could be used to distinguish between those who had succeeded and those who had failed. The use of material possessions to display wealth was not limited to homes, furnishings, and clothing; the display of wealth was extended into cemeteries.

In the nineteenth century, class distinctions were apparent in both secular and religious burial grounds. The rural cemeteries, such as Mount Auburn (Boston), Laurel Hill (Philadelphia), and Green-Wood (Brooklyn), contained vivid displays of the materialism and consumer culture of the nineteenth century. With my colleagues in the New York City Archaeology Program, I (Baugher) surveyed nineteenth-century cemeteries in the five boroughs of New York City. We found that both secular and religious cemeteries had monuments and markers that conveyed marked economic differences among families within the cemeteries (New York City Landmarks Preservation Commission 1984). The most dramatic differences in wealth were apparent in cemeteries with mausoleums and elaborately landscaped property. Just as in property values for homes, the final resting place within a cemetery was determined by the location of plot. Property values were determined not only by size of the plot but also by majestic views, by waterfront locations on ponds, or by a location on hilltops or in secluded valleys. John Sears (1989: 114–15) notes that the nineteenth-century cemeteries "were monuments to the materialism of American culture" and that these American cemeteries both "intensified and reflected back the emerging, fashion-conscious, status-oriented, property-owning culture."

These cemeteries were burial places for the dead and gathering places for the living. They tended to have elaborate memorials, fenced family plots, and beautiful landscaping and were overseen by a board of trustees under a charter of incorporation. They also tended to be profit-making institutions. In an attempt to ensure that the public would accept these new secular burial grounds and to increase their prestige, the remains of major American historical figures were often reinterred in these so-called rural cemeteries. For example, buried at Laurel Hill are Charles Thompson, a signer of the Declaration of Independence; David Rittenhouse, the fist director of the U.S. Mint; and Hugh Mercer, a Revolutionary War hero (Brooks and Waskie n.d.: 5). Prominent architects and landscape architects often designed these cemeteries: John Notman designed the first twenty acres of Laurel Hill in Philadelphia, and David Bates Douglas, a civil engineer and landscape architect, designed Green-Wood Cemetery in Brooklyn, as well as Albany Rural Cemetery in Albany, New York (Richman 1998: 11).

Moreover, in an effort to draw both visitors and permanent residents, cemeteries sometimes invested in monumental gates and buildings. Often they drew inspiration from historical antecedents, such as the monumental Egyptian Revival gates of the Grove Street Cemetery in New Haven and Boston's Mount Auburn Cemetery (figure 5.4, *top*). The famous architectural firm of Richard Upjohn and Son designed the elaborate Gothic entrance gates for Green-Wood (Richman 1998: 20) (figure 5.4, *bottom*). In addition to the decorative gateways, rural cemeteries had chapels, receiving vaults, living quarters for the superintendent, office space, and equipment storage buildings. The styles for gatehouses, chapels, and mausoleums reflected popular architectural styles. For example, Laurel Hill Cemetery in Philadelphia has a classical-style gatehouse with Doric columns. Rural cemeteries also had receiving vaults; these were freestanding buildings that housed the remains of the dead during the cold winter months when digging graves by hand was impossible. Some vaults also incorporated chapels. The vaults were often built into hillsides within the

Figure 5.4. Gates to cemeteries, separating the land of the living from the land of the dead. *Top*, Egyptian Revival gates to the Grove Street Cemetery, New Haven, Connecticut. *Bottom*, the grand Gothic entrance gate to Green-Wood Cemetery in Brooklyn, New York. Photographs by Richard Veit.

cemetery, rather than being located at the entrance. Again, classical-style architecture was common. Within the receiving vault, coffins could be placed on shelves or stacked. It was not unusual to incorporate a bell to toll during the funeral procession in either the receiving vault or the cemetery gate.

Figure 5.5. A group of nineteenth-century mausoleums on "millionaire's row" in Phila-delphia's Laurel Hill Cemetery. Photograph by Richard Veit.

Besides the gatehouses, chapels, and vaults, the large, secular nine-teenth-century cemeteries had mausoleums for the wealthy. In the early nineteenth century, wealthy families began investing in semisubterranean vaults. These were later transformed into elaborate mausoleums. The mau-soleums were designed in the popular architectural styles of the day such as Egyptian and Gothic Revival. Some of the mid-nineteenth-century mau-soleums were modest and built into hillsides. In 1878, the body of Alexan-der T. Stewart (owner of a department store plus mills and factories) was stolen for ransom from his grave in a New York City churchyard, which led members of more-wealthy families to choose to be buried in mausoleums rather than in graves (Sloane 1991: 122). The late nineteenth century was the age of the grandiose mausoleums (Sloane 1991: 122). Conspicuous con-sumption reached new heights with the late nineteenth-century mausole-ums (figure 5.5). Besides being large, elaborately decorated buildings, they often had expensive Tiffany windows and sometimes decorated interiors, with marble fittings and terrazzo floors.

Transformations in Gravestone Iconography

Gravemarkers evolved from the headstones, footstones, table tombs, and tombstones of the eighteenth century to incorporate a much wider variety of gravemarker forms. Marble markers became the new national norm, rather than the earlier sandstone, slate, and fieldstone markers. Though widely employed in eighteenth-century Philadelphia and surrounding regions, they saw their popularity mushroom in the nineteenth century, perhaps helped by the reinterment of George and Martha Washington in 1837, with new marble sarcophagi carved by John Struthers of Philadelphia (McDowell and Meyer 1994: 5). The influence of Philadelphia as an American cultural center in the late eighteenth and early nineteenth century and the resonance of marble with the classically inspired architecture of Federal Period America are noteworthy.

These new monuments took a variety of forms, almost all of which were inspired by ancient antecedents. Soon America's cemeteries were filled with a hodgepodge of pyramids and obelisks, miniature Greek temples, and Gothic memorials (figure 5.6). Stylistic boundaries grew fuzzy as

Figure 5.6. A pyramid-shaped mausoleum commemorates Egyptologist Albert Parsons (d. 1933) in Green-Wood Cemetery, Brooklyn, New York. It is augmented by a sphinx as well as statues of Joseph, Mary, and Jesus. The door is covered with zodiac symbols. Mr. Parsons seems to have been hedging his bets about the afterworld. Photograph by Richard Veit.

America's monument makers pulled out all the stops in their efforts to create grander and more enduring memorials (McDowell and Meyer 1994).

These markers were replete with symbolism. Americans were very visually oriented and recognized the meanings of diverse symbols—symbols that have lost their meanings to twenty-first-century Americans. Floral emblems are found on gravestones, and today we might recognize the flower or the leaf without understanding the meaning of the symbol. For example, a chrysanthemum is a symbol of longevity, a pansy is a symbol of remembrance, and a daisy symbolizes the innocence of youth (Keister 2004: 44, 46, 52). Motifs including broken flower stems (life cut off in bloom), inverted torches (death), anchors (hope), lambs (innocence, Christ, sacrifice), and sheaves of wheat (bounty of the earth, a full life) all became common (Baugher et al. 1989: 2). Major shifts included the use of neoclassical forms in early nineteenth-century burial grounds. Archaeological excavations at Pompeii and Herculaneum led to a rebirth of interest in all things classical. Americans used imagery from the ancient world in their art, architecture, and ceramics, and also on their gravestones. For example, Doric, Ionic, and Corinthian columns are found on mausoleums. The obelisk is the most common monument found in nineteenth-century cemeteries. In ancient Egypt it denoted Ra, the ray of the sun, and served as a phallic symbol of fertility and male generative power (Cooper 1978: 121). It also symbolizes eternal life, making it an appropriate symbol for use in a cemetery (de Vries 1974: 348).

Captains of industry and distinguished professionals were sometimes commemorated with carvings reflecting their occupations: ships on captains' markers and military equipment on the gravestones of Civil War soldiers. Masonic emblems, which were found on colonial gravestones, were still used by Masons in the nineteenth century. Crosses eschewed by New England's Puritan settlers became commonplace. In the nineteenth century, people could and did individualize their stones with carvings of their loved ones, including the last image of their loved one. A very dramatic marker is the Jane Griffith stone (1857) in Green-Wood Cemetery (figure 5.7, *left*). The marble stone, carved by Patrizio Piatti, shows a well-dressed man saying goodbye to his wife, who stands on the steps of their brownstone house; the scene depicts the last image Charles Griffith had of his wife, who died of a sudden heart attack that day (Richman 1998: 29). Some markers have elaborate sculpture attached, such as weeping angels draped over the top of the gravestone or sleeping children on top of the

Figure 5.7. Two extraordinary Victorian memorials from Green-Wood Cemetery. *Above*, the Griffith memorial shows Mr. Griffith departing for work; his wife would pass away that day. The memorial was carved by Patrizio Piatti. *Left*, the "Precious Georgie" memorial shows George Cuyler, who died at the age of four. Photographs by Carl Foster.

gravestone. Others have portraits carved in stone of the face of a loved one. For example, in Green-Wood Cemetery in Brooklyn, "Precious Georgie" is a large marble cameo (protected by glass) of George Cuyler, who died at age four of scarlet fever (Richman 1998: 102) (figure 5.7, *right*). The lasting image of these nineteenth-century cemeteries is the tremendous diversity in the symbols, images, and sizes of the stones. Markers were available in all shapes and sizes to appeal to different tastes and pocketbooks. In fact, some gravestone companies produced catalogues of the wide range of symbols that could be reproduced on gravestones (Keister 2004: 11).

Some symbols had multiple meanings—such as a lamb, which in Christian art from the Middle Ages through the nineteenth century symbolized sacrifice, innocence, purity, or Jesus Christ, as in the phrase "the lamb of God" (Murray and Murray 1996: 267–68). In Victorian cemeteries, the carving of a lamb on the top of a tombstone was primarily used on the graves of children (Keister 2004: 84). In fact, this symbol of the lamb on children's graves transcends religion in that it is also found on graves of Jewish children in Jewish cemeteries and represents innocence (Segal 2005: 2008).

LouAnn Wurst (1991) studied urban and rural cemeteries in Broom County in central New York State looking for iconography associated with the Second Great Awakening. In the 1980s when Wurst began her research, she was working at a time when most archaeologists were still focused on colonial gravestones. Wurst asked ideological questions about the impact of the Second Great Awakening on nineteenth-century cemetery material culture. The symbols Wurst associated with the Second Great Awakening were the index finger pointing upward, clasped hands, the laurel wreath, the anchor, the Bible, and a hand holding a broken rose or a broken chain (Wurst 1991: 131–33). However, all of these symbols had multiple meanings beyond a specific religious symbol. For example, the image of the index finger pointing upward can symbolize the number one, the best, or that Christ is the way to salvation (Olderr 1986: 48). Some of the symbols Wurst associated with the Second Great Awakening had been used since Roman times, such as a laurel wreath for victory and triumph (Cirlot 1971: 181). The laurel wreath, because of its military association with victory, can also be found on numerous nineteenth-century graves and memorials to fallen soldiers. Because these symbols had multiple meanings, Wurst used the epitaphs on the stones, such as "gone to heaven" and "at rest in heaven," to further associate these symbols with the Second Great Awakening religious movements. After examining 1,644 gravestones, she found the Great Awakening symbols (with associated epitaphs) on only 119 stones, or just 7.24 percent of the total stones. The overwhelming majority of these "Great Awakening" stones were associated with the rural elite (Wurst 1991: 127, 139). Curiously, none of the symbols Wurst associated with the Second Great Awakening were found in the urban cemeteries she studied. Wurst (1991: 145–46) concluded that with these modest Second Great Awakening stones, the rural elite sought to minimize class differences while "the urban elite strove to accentuate those differences." It would be interesting to further test this hypothesis in other regions of the United States.

In these nineteenth-century cemeteries, some symbols reflected religious images, such as crosses or Stars of David, while other images reflected general cultural symbols. Some religious images could also reflect ethnicity, such as the Celtic cross, a cross with a circle where the bars meet. With the waves of immigrants from western, eastern, and southern Europe, there was also ethnic diversity in some cemeteries and ethnic exclusiveness in other cemeteries.

Gravemarkers were also transformed in terms of their shape. Instead of thin slabs of stone set vertically in the ground, tablets supported by a series of bases, keyed in place by stone tenons or metal dowels, became commonplace. Improved transportation routes, thanks to canals and railroads, and steam-powered carving tools made it faster, easier, and less expensive to shape and transport gravemarkers. Monuments increasingly replaced the old memorials. With increasingly larger monuments, bases and foundations of brick or stone became the norm. These bases were topped by a horizontal slab, then placed over the slab was a block known as a pedestal, base, or die. The entire monument would be surmounted by a capstone, sometimes topped by an obelisk, column, or draped urn. A broken column symbolized frustrated hope, unfinished work, and death (Olderr 1986: 28). The draped urn signified death (Cooper 1978: 184).

Some of the earliest monuments were erected in Congressional Cemetery in Washington, D.C. Designed by Benjamin Henry Latrobe as cenotaphs for congressmen, they consisted of square stones set on a stepped base, resembling Roman altar tombs (Veit and Nonestied 2008: 117) (figure 5.8). Increasingly, cemeteries came to look like outdoor sculpture museums, with Egyptian Revival, classical, and Gothic revival designs predominating. Sarcophagi, imitations of medieval canopy graves, and graves shaped like beds and cradles were all employed.

Artists also designed monuments for the rural cemeteries. In fact, some rural cemeteries, such as Green-Wood, encouraged the plot owners to express their individuality in the choice of gravestones and monuments, thus encouraging variety within the cemeteries (Richman 1998: 16). Thus, these cemeteries became outdoor museums. By the mid-nineteenth century, Green-Wood was recognized as having the finest collection of outdoor sculpture in America (Richman 1998: 15). Other rural cemeteries

Figure 5.8. Congressional cenotaphs designed by Benjamin Henry Latrobe in Congressional Cemetery, Washington, D.C. Most do not have burials beneath them. Photograph by Richard Veit.

were likewise proud of their statues. For example, a sculpture group called *Old Mortality*, based on a novel of the same name by Sir Walter Scott, greets visitors to Laurel Hill (figure 5.9). In the image, Sir Walter Scott, on the left, is seen leaning on a headstone as he converses with the stonecutter Old Mortality, on the right, who has been interrupted at his work. The bust in the right rear corner is James Thom, the artist who created this sculptural group. Old Mortality was a traveling sculptor who was reputed to have traveled across Scotland, recarving the inscriptions on the tombstones of Scotch Presbyterian martyrs. The founders of Laurel Hill, who were astute businessmen rather than peripatetic sculptors, saw their charge, much like that of Scott's Old Mortality, to be preserving the past through gravemarkers.

These rural cemeteries were developing at the same time as America was focusing on its unique heritage and natural resources. By the 1820s, a new type of tourism had developed in America—a tourism centered on visiting majestic landscapes, not cities. The new scenic tourism, dubbed the "Fashionable Tour" by tour promoters, developed in the Northeast with a focus on Niagara Falls, the Hudson River, the Catskills, and the springs at Saratoga (Brown 1995: 23–25). This tourism was made possible

Figure 5.9. *Old Mortality,* a sculpture that greets visitors at the entrance of Laurel Hill Cemetery in Philadelphia. The close-up image (*bottom*) shows a figure from Sir Walter Scott's tale, Old Mortality, an individual who traveled the Scottish countryside on horseback, preserving the memories of Presbyterian martyrs by recarving the inscriptions on their gravestones. The sculpture shows Old Mortality recarving a stone. In the background, Old Mortality's horse is seen. Both images courtesy of Laurel Hill Cemetery.

with new technological inventions such as the steamboat and transportation improvements such as the Erie Canal in 1825 and railroads in the 1830s (Sears 1989: 4). The design of rural cemeteries with their curved pathways and lovely winding carriage drives encouraged tourism (Sears 1989: 100). As the rural cemeteries grew, they became popular picturesque and sublime landscapes to visit while on a scenic tour. Guidebooks to rural cemeteries provide routes for visitors with information on famous grave sites with appropriate poetry and stories about the cemeteries (Sloane 1991: 56). The cemeteries became more than burial grounds; by mid-century they were tourist destinations. By 1860, a half a million tourists were visiting Green-Wood every year (Richman 1998: 16). The rural cemeteries with their emphasis on the picturesque and on native plantings reflected the growing American pride in the natural beauty of the nation (Sears 1989: 102; Sloane 1991: 56).

Lawn-Park Cemeteries

In 1855, Adolph Strauch advocated for a new type of cemetery that was still a pastoral landscape but emphasized open spaces, dispersed trees and plantings, small gravemarkers close to the ground, and a limited number of monuments in a narrower range of sizes and styles (Sloane 1991: 99, 101). The result was a new design, called the lawn-park cemetery, built at Spring Grove Cemetery in Cincinnati, Ohio. Strauch lengthened and widened the cemetery roads and looked for ways to more consciously and tastefully link monuments with landscape features. While some people, such as landscape architect Frederick Law Olmsted, the designer of major public parks throughout America, admired Strauch's ideas and vision, it took several decades before they gained acceptance (Sloane 1991: 107–8).

Strauch advocated taking the maintenance away from the survivors of the deceased and hiring professional landscapers. In rural cemeteries, lot holders were generally responsible for plantings and maintenance. With an increasingly mobile nineteenth-century society, the results were unpredictable: some plots were well maintained, while others were abandoned. In 1887, the American Association of Cemetery Superintendents was formed to help manage and design cemeteries (Veit and Nonestied 2008: 99).

Historian David Sloane (1991: 119) saw the development and popularity of public parks in the late nineteenth century as diminishing the need for

rural cemeteries to serve as parks, thus returning the cemeteries to function just as elaborate burial grounds; he also felt that park designs helped
to make people more receptive to the look of the lawn-park cemeteries.
Lawn-park cemeteries gained some acceptance by the end of the nineteenth century. Restrictions were commonly placed on the size of monuments in an effort to reduce what was seen as the clutter that had become
evident in many prime examples of the rural cemetery movement (Veit
and Nonestied 2008: 98). But because Americans still wanted their cemeteries to have elaborate monuments and mausoleums, most of the new
cemeteries incorporated Strauch's vision of an open lawn but ignored most
of his ideas regarding small markers and a limited number of modest uniform monuments (Sloane 1991: 122). The lawn-park cemeteries continued
to reflect class inequalities.

During the Gilded Age of the 1880s and 1890s, mausoleums reflected
the height of conspicuous consumption. Famous architects were hired by
the upper-class families to design grandiose mausoleums. For example, in
1882 William H. Vanderbilt purchased twenty-two acres of land next to a
large rural cemetery in Staten Island, New York, to build his own private
cemetery, designed by Frederick Law Olmsted, with a massive mausoleum
designed by Richard Morris Hunt (Salmon 2006: 187–88). Olmsted was
the designer of numerous famous urban parks, including Central Park in
New York City. Hunt designed many well-known buildings, including the
Metropolitan Museum of Art in New York City and the Breakers Mansion
in Newport, Rhode Island. The Vanderbilt cemetery was a landscape of
gender and power, with the mausoleum reserved only for males; females
were buried on the grounds with gravestones as markers. The Vanderbilt
Neo-Romanesque mausoleum was designed to be the permanent resting
place only for direct male descendants, with ample room on the grounds
surrounding the mausoleum for the burial of wives, daughters, sons of
daughters, and other Vanderbilt relatives (Salmon 2006: 189, 198).

In the late nineteenth century, the lawn-park cemeteries increased in
popularity, or, to be more exact, the new cemeteries combined features
of both the rural cemeteries and Adolph Strauch's original vision for the
design of lawn-park cemeteries. Americans still wanted to display their
wealth and their material success in their cemeteries, and the open lawns
enabled them to highlight their grand mausoleums and their statues. In
the lawn-park cemeteries, the individual gravestones were replaced with
granite family monuments. While the lawn-park cemeteries replaced the

clutter of rural cemeteries with their open lawns and rows of similar granite monuments, they lacked artistic diversity except for the elaborate mausoleums (Sloane 1991: 126).

But not everyone wanted to be buried in the lawn-park cemeteries.
Some Americans still wanted to be buried in rural cemeteries. Some rural
cemeteries made adaptations to the changing times and styles, and these
cemeteries survived. For example, Boston's Mount Auburn Cemetery
expanded by adding sections with more open lawn space and flowering
shrubs more in the style of lawn-park cemeteries (Linden-Ward 1990: 54).
With the development of lawnmowers, lawn-park cemeteries were easier
to maintain, but in rural cemeteries the elaborate nineteenth-century cast
iron fencing and curbs made maintenance more difficult and more costly.
By the late nineteenth century and into the twentieth century, some cemetery superintendents encouraged but did not require families to remove
their cast iron fences (Linden-Ward 1990: 55). During the scrap-metal
drives in World War II, many rural cemeteries, including Green-Wood,
removed most of their metal fences (Richman 1998: 21–23). The removal
of fencing opened up vistas in the older cemeteries and perhaps removed
some of the perceived clutter. However, in the late twentieth century, pres-
ervationists worked with the staff of some historic rural cemeteries to save
and repair the remaining decorative nineteenth-century cast iron fencing.

The Development of Military Cemeteries

The overwhelming number of dead during the Civil War had a massive
impact on American society. As Bruce Elliott (2011: 15) has noted, "The war
also occasioned the government's acknowledgement of the necessity to recognize the democracy of sacrifice by marking the graves of all who fought
for the Union, regardless of wealth or status. It was no longer acceptable to
leave the dead strewn on the field of battle or to bury them anonymously
in trenches or common graves, and erect public monuments merely to
the generals." In 1862, Congress passed legislation purchasing cemetery
grounds "for soldiers who shall have died in the service of the county"
(Yalom 2008: 256). By the end of the war, seventeen national military cemeteries had been established, a number that had increased to seventy-three
by 1870 (Yalom 2008: 256). The number of dead is mind-boggling, and the

need to create 300,000 lasting memorials tested the limits of what had, to that point, been largely a craft industry (Elliott 2011: 16).

Initially wooden markers were employed, but other ideas were soon proposed, including zinc-coated iron markers. Another idea that was briefly floated was to have small granite markers placed flush with the ground and the gravemarkers inscribed simply with identification numbers. This idea was also rejected (Elliott 2011: 17). In 1872, a competition was held to develop Civil War headstones. Although there were many respondents, none were satisfactory, and a second competition was held in 1873 calling for markers "of durable stone" (Elliott 2011: 23). Ultimately, distinctive markers for individual remains and for unidentified individuals were developed. The introduction of sandblasting, an innovative new technology, allowed for the efficient production of the monuments (Elliott 2011: 31). Although many questions were raised about the contracts for producing the markers, the project was ultimately a success (figure 5.10, *top*).

The new government-issued markers also provided African Americans, who had served in the Union forces in substantial numbers, with access to permanent gravemarkers provided free by the government. Thanks to these markers, African American burial grounds became much more visible than they previously had been.

In contrast to the Union dead, deceased Confederate soldiers were buried in mass graves and often minimally marked (figure 5.10, *bottom*). However, communities and individuals stepped forward to honor the Confederate dead. In addition, both Union and Confederate soldiers were buried in family cemeteries, churchyards, and grand rural cemeteries. Also, towns throughout the North and South erected monuments and memorials in town squares and parks to honor the fallen soldiers and remember their heroic deeds.

In 1906, as part of the effort toward reconciliation, Congress approved funds for tombstones to mark the graves of Confederate soldiers and sailors who died in Northern prisons and were still buried near those prisons (Gray 2001: 162). Congress authorized the same size and material for Confederate headstones as the headstones for other deceased military men, but they wanted the design for the Confederates to be slightly different, so the top was pointed instead of rounded and a military shield was omitted (U.S. Department of Veterans Affairs 2012). In 1930, the War Department

Figure 5.10. *Top*, gravemarkers for Union soldiers at Gettysburg National Cemetery in Gettysburg National Military Park. Photograph by Sherene Baugher. *Bottom*, Confederate prisoner of war gravemarkers c. 1880 in Woodlawn National Cemetery in Elmira, New York. Note that the markers are wooden and are decorated with laurel wreaths. Photograph courtesy of the Chemung County Historical Society.

implemented regulations for Confederate headstones that also authorized the inscription of the Confederate Cross of Honor in a small circle on the front face of the stone above the standard inscription of the soldier's name, rank, company, and regiment (U.S. Department of Veterans Affairs 2012).

Changes in Twentieth-Century Cemetery Design

In the twentieth century, the design debate was not simply over lawn-park cemeteries versus modifications to rural cemeteries; new designs and approaches to burials slowly gained public acceptance. Forest Lawn Cemetery was founded in 1906 in Tropico (today's Glendale), California (Yalom 2008). In many ways, it was an unassuming local cemetery that would be transformed by the vision of Hubert Eaton, a businessman from Missouri who relocated to California. In 1917, Eaton established the first American memorial park, Forest Lawn Memorial-Parks in Glendale, California (Sloane 1991: 157). Eaton's goal for the cemetery is enshrined on a stone tablet at Forest Lawn that reads, "I believe in a happy eternal life . . . I therefore prayerfully resolve on this New Year's Day 1917 that I shall endeavor to build Forest Lawn as different, as unlike other cemeteries as sunshine is unlike darkness. It is to be filled with towering trees, sweeping lawns, splashing fountains, singing birds, beautiful statuary, cheerful flowers, in contrast to traditional cemeteries containing misshapen monuments and other customary signs of earthly death" (Yalom 2008: 225). Death was not part of Eaton's vocabulary. He replaced it with less harsh terms such as *leave-taking*. In his conscious reaction against rural cemeteries and lawn-park cemeteries, ostentatious gravemarkers were not permitted; instead, flush-with-the-ground bronze or granite tablets were the norm. There were also strategically placed statuary and fountains and community mausoleums. Families could erect statuary, providing they had the approval of the cemetery association (Sloane 1991: 167; Mitford 2000: 103). Eaton also re-created churches and chapels modeled on European antecedents within the cemetery. Indeed, Eaton promoted Forest Lawn as a place not just for the dead but also for the living. He encouraged individuals to get married in his chapels, and tens of thousands of Americans obliged.

Twentieth-century cemeteries also reflect a significant change in Americans' attitudes toward death. With improvements in medicine, there was a dramatic drop in the death rate, especially in infant mortality, and an increase in the average life span (Sloane 1991: 273). More Americans were dying in hospitals or nursing homes rather than at home. Death, once a focus of rituals of mourning and remembrance, was increasingly hidden away. No longer were there the overly dramatic statues of weeping angels from the Victorian period. Americans sought landscapes of death that were more peaceful and serene. The memorial park, with its minimalist uniform markers, careful plantings, and uplifting statuary, replaced the increasingly crowded cemeteries of the Victorian era.

While Forest Lawn and its imitators reflected a new view of death, even in the 1950s some Americans found it unappealing: it was disparagingly called a "Disneyland of Death" and, mocking Eaton's use of euphemism, as the "cemetery in which nobody called a spade a spade" (Yalom 2008: 227). The profit-driven memorial parks limited plots to middle- and upper-class families and individuals, and unlike nineteenth-century cemeteries, they did not sell plots to charitable organizations for the burial of poor people (Sloane 1991: 84, 187–88).

Despite the criticisms, memorial park cemeteries gained in popularity. With the flat markers and the uniform look, the memorial park cemetery designers rejected the individuality of the nineteenth-century cemeteries. As more memorial parks were built, some superintendents allowed for burial groupings based on ethnic background, religion, and social affiliations, such as a section for Masons. However, all over the country memorial parks were only for white Americans: people of color were denied lots, and African Americans, Native Americans, and Asian Americans were excluded (Sloane 1991: 187–88). With the uniform appearance of the gravemarkers, memorial parks evoked a look of equality, whereas in reality they were places of segregation and economic exclusivity.

New Materials for Nineteenth- and Twentieth-Century Gravemarkers

The nineteenth century saw the local traditions of slate and sandstone markers that were popular in the eighteenth century replaced with white marble and white limestone markers. In cemeteries throughout the United States, marble markers became the norm (Veit and Nonestied 2008: 75). However, with the intense industrial pollution of the nineteenth century, the marble and limestone markers started to erode.

In the mid-nineteenth century, granite, a heavy and hard-to-work material, once employed predominantly in a limited portion of New England where the stone was quarried, became common. More durable than marble or sandstone, it became the material of choice in the later nineteenth century. By the early twentieth century, it had become the material of choice for the upper classes desiring permanent commemoration. Quarries in Vermont, particularly at Barre, and also around Elberton, Georgia, in the Southeast supplied the raw material, which was cut using compressed-air drills and shipped by railroad. Monument carvers replaced their mallets and chisels with air compressors, pneumatic tools, and sandblasting equipment. Promotional literature about how to construct monuments and how to price them for consumers reflects the ongoing professionalization of the industry. A conglomerate of New England granite companies came together with the slogan "Rock of Ages." This trademark came to be used by a single corporation that grew out of many individual quarries. Increasingly, "monument dealers became middlemen, purchasing stock patterns from distant granite companies, and inscribing them with sandblasted designs and lettering" (Veit and Nonestied 2008: 160). Much of the granite employed in late nineteenth- and twentieth-century markers was gray in color; however, today a new palette of blacks, reds, and other granite colors is coming to the fore.

The nineteenth and twentieth centuries saw an evolution from markers to monuments and a revolution in gravestone materials. Innovative craftsmen made markers from iron, ceramics, concrete, and even glass. Cast iron was a popular material for gravemarkers in some parts of North America. New Jersey's Pine Barrens, a lightly populated region in the south of the state, was once home to numerous ironworks. The area has little workable stone, and gravemarkers had to be imported from a distance. Between 1810 and 1840, resourceful ironworkers cast simple iron markers shaped like gravestones and painted white to resemble marble markers (Veit 1993; Mounier 1988; Veit and Nonestied 2008).

In New England, and scattered across parts of the eastern United States, Gothic cast iron memorials, apparently cast using a widely distributed foundry pattern, have been found. Some even display small metal frames where daguerreotypes could have been attached (Lowenthal 2008: 114). They have been found from New Hampshire to Alabama (Veit and Nonestied 2008: 199–200).

Blacksmith- and foundry-produced iron crosses are also found in nineteenth-century burial grounds across the country (Horton 1997). Some of the most spectacular have been recorded on the northern Great Plains and

Figure 5.11. Two iron markers from St. Vincent DePaul Parish Cemetery, Crown Butte, North Dakota. *Left*, a hand-wrought iron monument, marking the grave of Anton Bernhard (d. 1914). *Right*, a cast iron monument, marking the grave of Joseph Miller (d. 1922), typical of those employed by German immigrants in the early twentieth century. Both types of markers were commonly employed by German immigrants. Photographs by Charles A. Bello.

in parts of the Southwest, including Texas, where German and German-Russian settlers re-created Old World traditions in a new setting. What have been called iron-cross cemeteries are found in the "Dakotas, eastern Montana, western Kansas, southeast Texas, and the Canadian prairie provinces of Alberta, Manitoba, and Saskatchewan" (Kloberdanz 2005: 161) (figure 5.11).

If the cast iron gravemarkers of New Jersey's Pine Barrens and the wrought iron markers of the Great Plains represent the folk/handmade end of the manufacturing continuum, the products of the Monumental Bronze Company of Bridgeport, Connecticut, represent their industrial antithesis. In 1873, Mr. M. A. Richardson, unhappy with the condition of gravemarkers in his local burial ground, decided to find a more lasting and attractive material for monuments (Rotundo 1989: 264). With a business partner, C. J. Willard, he began manufacturing cast zinc gravemarkers under the trade name Monumental Bronze. These markers ranged in size from miniature obelisks and tablets to enormous statues. The company manufactured large numbers of commemorative statues in the years after the Civil War. Monumental Bronze markers were bluish gray in color and have lived up to the advertising about their longevity. Although the main manufacturer was located in Bridgeport, Connecticut, other subsidiaries were established in Chicago, Detroit, and Philadelphia (Rotundo 1989: 267). The markers, sold by salesmen from catalogs, varied in cost from as little as two dollars to as much as five thousand dollars and can be found in cemeteries in the Northeast and Midwest (Rotundo 1989: 275) (figure 5.12).

Ceramic gravemarkers also appear in nineteenth- and early twentieth-century cemeteries. In the southeastern United States, stoneware markers, which sometimes look like gravestones and sometimes resemble stoneware crocks, were produced with simple inscriptions (Oldshue 1987; Smith and Rogers 1979; Zug 1986). Ohio has incredible gravemarkers made from clay sewer tile. New Jersey and New York were home to exuberantly colorful terra-cotta gravemarkers. The latter date from the 1870s through the 1930s.

In the mid-nineteenth century, architect Andrew Jackson Downing introduced terra-cotta into the American architectural vocabulary. This is not the simple unglazed redware of flowerpots but a colorful, molded, sculpted, and glazed ceramic used as a substitute for stone in architecture. Scattered through the burial grounds of New Jersey's clay district are over one hundred terra-cotta gravemarkers, some quite colorful (Veit and Nonestied 2003). Many are found in and around Perth Amboy, New Jersey, once a center of the industry. The markers come in many different forms, including typical nineteenth-century styles: tablets, crosses, obelisks, pedestals surmounted by urns, and statues. Terra-cotta provided new immigrants (Danish, English, Italian, German, Hungarian, and Polish) with an inexpensive but beautiful way to memorialize their loved ones, while also displaying their incredible craftsmanship in a rapidly industrializing trade (Veit 1997) (figure 5.13).

Concrete was also widely used for gravemarkers and may be seen as a sort of poor man's marble. Concrete had many advantages as a grave-marking material. It was relatively inexpensive and could be worked with simple hand tools. Once set, it was long lasting. Concrete gravemarkers

Figure 5.12. *Our Drummer Boy*, a Monumental Bronze statue in Green-Wood Cemetery, Brooklyn. It commemorates Clarence D. McKenzie (d. 1861), a twelve-year-old drummer boy from Brooklyn, New York, who was accidentally shot in Annapolis, Maryland. The unfortunate Clarence was the first Brooklynite to die during the American Civil War. Photograph by Richard Veit.

Figure 5.13. The Bruno Grandelis (d. 1905) marker, Hillside Cemetery, Metuchen, New Jersey. Bruno's marker was made from terra-cotta by his father, Geremiah Grandelis, a prominent Italian sculptor. Photograph by Richard Veit.

were most common in the early twentieth century but continue to be made today. Many concrete gravemarkers were made by anonymous craftsmen. They range from simple slabs with scratched-in inscriptions to elaborate memorials. Rebar was often used to provide a sturdy core for the monuments. Some markers have coffin plates inset into their surfaces with the deceased's genealogical information. A few are painted. Others are decorated with insets of marbles, seashells, pebbles, watches, mirrors, and religious paraphernalia, such as rosaries. Scholars have only begun to study these fascinating folk markers (Rotundo 1997).

Metal, ceramic, and concrete markers are all examples of vernacular memorial traditions that coexisted with professionally carved markers. Many have suffered from vandalism, and most are in need of conservation. They provide a glimpse of populations living and working outside of the mainstream society and could be interpreted as material evidence of resistance to the hegemonic capitalist system that had engulfed nineteenth-century Americans. Produced at home or at the end of the day in the workplace, they deserve further study and documentation.

Cremation

The final change and challenge for all twentieth-century cemeteries was and continues to be the growing public interest in cremation over in-ground burials. Advocacy and discussion of cremation began in the previous century. Nineteenth-century advocates of cremation argued that cemeteries were contributing to the pollution of water sources and were breeding grounds for disease (Sloane 1991: 147–49). In 1876, Francis Julius LeMoyne, a doctor, constructed America's first crematorium on the outskirts of Washington, Pennsylvania (Veit and Nonestied 2008: 229). While cremation was successfully being advocated in Europe, it did not gain wide acceptance in the United States. Nineteenth-century Americans had several reasons to reject cremation, among them the facts that the shortage of crematories made cremation a very expensive option, different Protestant denominations believed that cremation ended an individual's hope of resurrection, and in 1886 the Vatican forbade cremation for Catholics (Sloane 1991: 144–45). In terms of cost, cremation technology improved. By the early twentieth century, cremation had become much more affordable; by 1921 there were seventy-four crematories in America (Sloane 1991: 155). Throughout the twentieth century, the opposition to cremation by religious leaders decreased, and in 1963 even the Catholic Church dropped its stand against cremation (Sloane 1991: 227). Social critics of the rising cost of funerals advocated cremation as an inexpensive alternative. Advocates of cremation believe that the dead can be memorialized and remembered in ways other than the expensive cemetery plots, monuments, and mausoleums of the nineteenth-century cemeteries. Because cremation is legally considered the final disposition of a body, cremated remains do not have to be buried, thus eliminating the need for a cemetery (Sloane 1991: 228). By the late twentieth century in some areas of the United States, cremation had become more popular than in-ground burials (Richman 1998: 24). Rather than take cremation as a threat to their financial survival, cemetery owners started building both crematoriums and cemetery columbaria with niches to hold the ashes of the deceased (Sloane 1991: 227–28). Some columbaria have niches with glass windows where urns and family memorabilia can be exhibited.

Conclusions

The nineteenth century was a period of intense changes in the country as America moved from a preindustrial to an industrial society and from a rural to an urban society. To promote the need for a large labor force, the government encouraged immigration. Cities became crowded and congested, as urban dwellers looked for places to escape the ills of the cities. The rural cemeteries offered that escape—a green space near the cities. The rural cemeteries offered a place of contemplation and recreation as well as a place of commemoration. These cemeteries were used as outdoor museums, public parks, and tourist destinations in addition to being cemeteries.

In the memorials of the nineteenth century we see reflected the emergence of the middle class. Both middle-class and upper-class families sought to display their material success not only in their homes but also in their burial plots. Cemeteries reflected the growing inequalities within the United States. The gravemarkers, monuments, sculpture, fencing, and mausoleums reflected the class differences.

During major nineteenth- and twentieth-century wars, there was a growth in military cemeteries. Since 1879, the U.S. government has paid and continues to pay for gravestones for all veterans, and the family can choose whether the marker will be placed in a military cemetery or in a private cemetery (Sloane 1991: 233). Since the 1970s, the Veterans

Administration has been responsible for all military cemeteries (Sloane 1991: 233).

With the twentieth century, world wars, depressions, and the rise of a postindustrial society changed Americans' view of death, dying, and cemeteries. Some archaeologists have analyzed the shifts that took place between the late nineteenth-century and twentieth-century cemeteries. The twentieth century saw the transformation of American burial places. The lawn-park cemetery, and later the memorial park, tried to correct the perceived shortcomings of the rural cemeteries, which like their earlier urban counterparts had become crowded and cluttered by the late nineteenth century. In the twentieth century, the language of death became more and more oblique as softer terms, like *passing* and *sleeping*, replaced harsh language like *died* and *struck down*. While the Victorians romanticized death and saw the cemetery as a bridge connecting the living and dead, this became distasteful in the twentieth century, and the emphasis shifted to socially inconspicuous ways of disposing of the dead (Jackson 1977: 147). The twentieth-century memorial parks had an increasing use of horizontal tablet markers installed flush to the ground with minimal information, emphasizing equality. However, in reality these cemeteries were not about equality, because nearly all memorial parks prohibited the burial of the poor and all people of color.

Memorial parks were not the only burial choice open to people. New immigrant groups persisted in traditional nineteenth-century forms of memorialization and rejected the minimalist memorial parks. In the twentieth century, Americans had a wide range of burial types and cemeteries to choose from. Their choices reflected their economic, ethnic, racial, and religious backgrounds. The choices also allowed the families to express their individuality and identity. Some families, and individuals, preferred individual headstones to family monuments; some families wanted plain markers while others wanted elaborately embellished monuments. By the mid-twentieth century, family mausoleums had declined in popularity while community mausoleums and cremation had grown more popular. By the late twentieth century, cremation had become an acceptable alternative to in-ground burial. In most states, cremation is legally considered the final disposition of the body, and the family of the deceased can decide what they want to do with the ashes—place them in a columbarium niche in a family grave site, keep them in an urn in the family home, or scatter the ashes on the landscape (Sloane 1991: 228). Cremation allows families to remember their loved ones in a private way without the cost of expensive funerary monuments for public display.

But not all Americans were willing to forgo the very public displays of funerary remembrance. By the 1980s, the Reagan presidency had ushered in a new era of conspicuous consumption and materialism. With this materialism came a renewed interest in flaunting wealth and achievements in life with the building of grand mausoleums, monuments, and very elaborate gravemarkers (Sloane 1991: 226–27). The end result was that despite the wishes of some cemetery superintendents for simple, flush-to-the-ground stones, which are easy to maintain, and perhaps falsely suggest equality and cultural uniformity, Americans continued to choose diversity in their cemetery memorials. Indeed, the introduction of relatively inexpensive, colorful imported granite, combined with new techniques of laser etching and hand stippling, allows photograph-like images to be carved on the stones. Today more options are available to Americans seeking commemoration than ever before: from a green burial, without embalming and markers, to having their ashes compressed into faux diamonds or mixed into concrete for undersea reefs (Cullen 2006). Something of the diversity of modern America is reflected in its increasingly individualized commemorative practices. The next chapter discusses how gravemarkers and mausoleums reflect ethnic, racial, and class diversity.

6

Ethnicity, Race, and Class within Nineteenth- and Twentieth-Century Cemeteries

For years relatively few archaeologists broke free of the siren songs of eighteenth-century cherubs and death's heads to study more-recent memorials. But in the twenty-first century, an increasing number of archaeologists are turning their attention to the wealth of ethnic data in nineteenth- and twentieth-century cemeteries. America's cultural landscape was transformed by the arrival of unprecedented numbers of immigrants. Revolutions in Europe and the Caribbean, famines, warfare, and persecution drove French, Irish, German, Italian, and eastern European immigrants to the Americas, while economic opportunities, democratic institutions, and religious freedom lured them. Facing prejudice and discrimination in both life and death, many of these new immigrants created their own burial places. In the period 1832–41 (the early years of the rural cemetery movement), more than three-quarters of a million people immigrated into the young nation's urban centers (Stannard 1980: 29). Some ethnic cemeteries looked similar to grand rural cemeteries but with less landscaping and less-elaborate monuments, while other immigrant cemeteries continued the grand rural cemetery practice of displaying wealth with expensive monuments. Other immigrant communities built cemeteries that evoked the look of cemeteries in eastern Europe rather than designing American rural or lawn-park cemeteries (Sloane 1991: 124). The waves of immigration continued throughout the twentieth century and indeed still continue today, albeit bringing different ethnic groups, including people from the Middle East, India, Latin America, the Caribbean, and Southeast Asia.

The focus in gravestone studies on ethnicity grows out of a broader interest in ethnicity among historical archaeologists. Charles Orser (2004:

251) notes that "ethnicity refers to the characteristics a group accepts as pertinent to them." Archaeologists have studied how material remains, such as pottery, clay smoking pipes, and even architecture, can reflect ethnic choices in consumer behavior (Deetz 1977; Upton 1987). Archaeologists have also looked at faunal remains to examine dietary preferences of different ethnic groups (Janowitz 1993). Ethnic affiliation can be a self-identification of an individual with a group or imposed from outside as a way to separate the new immigrants from the established community. For example, in the late nineteenth century, the educated and established German Jews in Boston wanted to separate themselves from the poorly educated Russian Jewish immigrants even though both groups shared the same religion (Spencer-Wood 2010: 190).

Although anthropologists and anthropological archaeologists generally agree that there is no biological foundation for race, it is an important sociological concept and is often deployed in a prejudicial manner. Indeed, the awful power of racism in American history cannot be ignored. Ethnicity and race have sometimes been connected and even conflated in American archaeology. For example, the Mohawk and the Navajo are distinct cultures with different religions, languages, economies, and social practices. However, the U.S. Census places all Indians within the racial category of Native Americans. Even anthropologists and archaeologists sometimes group individual American Indian nations within the larger category as Native Americans. In describing their burial practices, do we place them in an ethnic category or a racial category? Actually, they are both. European settlers used their cultural perception of racial differences and a belief in the "superior race" (the Europeans) and "inferior races" as a justification for taking lands from indigenous people or for enslaving Africans. Charles Orser (2007) has noted that the nineteenth-century dominant American perception of some of the new immigrants, such as the Irish, was that they were separate races.

In the past, archaeologists and physical anthropologists analyzed African American human remains and associated grave goods as if they were people from the same culture rather than as people from diverse cultures. For some scholars, race was the important factor, not ethnicity. However, as we note in chapter 2, Michael Blakey and the Howard University team tried to break new ground by focusing on culture and ethnicity, not race, in their analysis of the human remains and artifacts from the African Burial Ground in New York City. They have undertaken DNA testing to link individuals to members of distinct African cultures. Other scholars have emphasized the diversity of cultures within Africa and encouraged archaeologists to apply more-sophisticated analyses to African American archaeological sites (Posnansky 1999; DeCorse 1999). Scholars studying burial sites associated with the overseas Chinese in North America have often evaluated the material remains and gravestones of Chinese Americans in the broad ethnic category of Chinese Americans. Sometimes the material culture that has survived in the archaeological records does not enable archaeologists to link the artifacts with a specific Chinese ethnic group but archaeologists are able to associate the traits with the broader category of Chinese culture. However, as our knowledge of overseas Chinese burial practices grows, increasingly sophisticated analyses are becoming the norm (see Wegars 1993; Chung and Wegars 2005). Because of this overlap between race and ethnicity in the archaeological literature, we discuss both ethnicity and race in this chapter.

Within any discussion of ethnicity or race, one cannot discount the factor of class. Purchasing power can limit or open up an individual's consumer choices (Spencer-Wood 1987; Wurst and McGuire 1999). Status markers of the dominant culture can also cross ethnic and racial boundaries. The iconography on the marker may be a symbol of class and purchasing power rather than simply a reflection of one's ethnic or racial identity. Within diverse ethnic and racial groups, issues of class are intertwined. Charles Orser (2004: 258) notes that "class membership, gender roles, ethnic affiliation, and race are like strings of a net; they are interconnected and inseparable." For example, the upper-class members of a particular ethnic group often choose different memorials and symbolism than the iconography used by the working-class or middle-class members of the same ethnic group. Lynn Clark (1987: 394) found that the consumer choices of iconography on gravestones reflected the "individual's class standing, ethnicity, and the interaction between the two." With any study of markers and monuments, the graves of the poor and the homeless will often appear as unmarked graves. The poorest members of society regardless of ethnic or racial background could not afford tombstones. Their graves may have been marked only by wooden markers, which do not survive. More-affluent members of a community might purchase gravestones for servants, people in almshouses, or favorite slaves. These purchases are material statements not only about the deceased but also about the purchasers. Economics and purchasing power do impact what survives in a cemetery.

Within the ethnic/racial examples in this chapter, we also discuss the role class has played in consumer choices.

We present a selection of case studies relating to the aboveground archaeology of ethnic and racial burial places in the United States, including Native American, African American, overseas Chinese, Jewish, Spanish, Hispanic, Irish, Italian, and Romany/Gypsy burial places. This selection represents a cross section of case studies from across the United States, including Alaska and Hawaii. These certainly are not the only groups studied by archaeologists, but they were chosen to demonstrate geographical, chronological, and ethnic/racial diversity. It is worth noting that archaeologists are not the first or the only scholars to study ethnic burial places. Indeed, historians, geographers, and art historians, as well as archaeologists, have all investigated aspects of ethnic and racial commemoration (for example, Meyer 1989, 1993; Gosnell and Gott 1989; Cunningham 1989; Matturi 1993; Graves 1993; Mytum 2004). This chapter examines some of the traditions they have documented, with an emphasis on the work of historical archaeologists. In this chapter, we examine the material culture of the cemetery—the monuments and their placement on the landscape—and discuss how it reflects the identity of the deceased in terms of ethnicity, race, and class.

Native Americans

Native American burial practices were diverse across time and space. Here we present a few select examples of different cultures from the Northeast, Northwest, Southwest, and Aleutian Islands. Although this is not a comprehensive survey, it provides an overview of the approaches that historical archaeologists have taken to historic period Native American burial places.

As noted in chapter 2, the belowground burials of historic period Native Americans in the Northeast have seen considerable study by archaeologists. Only recently have their gravemarkers begun to garner the same attention. One particularly interesting study is Craig Cipolla's investigation of the markers employed by the Brothertown (also known as Brotherton) Indian community in the eighteenth and nineteenth centuries in upstate New York and in Wisconsin. Cipolla's work has focused on the concept of ethnogenesis, the creation of a new form of Native community, and how material culture, in this case gravemarkers, played an important role in the creation of that community, the shaping of memory, and evolving ideas about identity and community.

The Brothertown Indian community was formed by groups from several Algonquian-speaking northeastern tribes (primarily Christian Pequots and Mohegans) who, in the late eighteenth century, coalesced into a new community, based on a common Native American heritage, a shared belief in Christianity, and the practice of agriculture, as well as a desire to escape from what were perceived as the "corrupting influences of colonial culture on the East Coast" (Cipolla 2010: 5). They fled New England and received sanctuary from the Oneida Indians of New York, who allowed them to live on Oneida land. After settling first in New York, they relocated during the second quarter of the nineteenth century to Brothertown, Wisconsin. In a well-intentioned but ultimately problematic attempt to hold onto their lands, they petitioned for and received U.S. citizenship in 1839, but in doing so they gave up their tribal sovereignty (Cipolla 2010: 4). This has subsequently proven problematic as they have worked to have the federal government acknowledge their tribal status.

Cipolla's work is grounded in what might be termed collaborative historical archaeology, in that he has worked closely with and received the support of the modern Brothertown community. His work focuses on issues of identity, consumption, and discourse analysis (Cipolla 2010: 12). Scholars have proposed various theories of ethnicity. Historically many saw ethnicity as primordial, made up of ascribed inherited, unchanging characteristics (Cipolla 2010: 19). More recently, scholars following the lead of Fredrik Barth (1969) have highlighted the contingent, fluid, situational nature of ethnicity. In this view, ethnicity is seen as a form of self-classification (Cipolla 2010: 19). Cipolla is interested in how Native Americans refashioned their identities within colonial contexts, essentially the ethnogenesis of the Brothertown community. At the same time, he examines how the Brothertown monuments reveal historical memory.

The conclusions of this study are quite interesting. Although precontact Native Americans from diverse Algonquian cultures in the Northeast typically buried their dead without benefit of permanent gravemarkers, the Christian Brothertown Indians employed fieldstones as headstones. Fieldstones were also used in European American Christian cemeteries. Moreover, they oriented their deceased brethren's graves on an east-west axis. At the same time, like some Iroquoian groups they made small mounds over the graves (Cipolla 2010: 357). Their headstones were generally unmarked, which may relate to proscriptions against using the names of the dead by some Native American cultures. Over time the Brothertown Indians began using more purchased gravemarkers, and their burial grounds came to resemble those employed by their European American neighbors. This is particularly true of their burial grounds in Wisconsin, which are later than those in New York (Cipolla 2010: 359). Cipolla concludes that the earlier cemeteries emphasized communal histories, which downplayed distinctions between individuals, hence the unmarked stones and anonymous mounds. In contrast, the later cemeteries emphasized the family and individual relations, through inscribed (often professionally carved) markers and clusters of family monuments.

This fascinating study of aboveground markers might be followed up with by more work on the historic burial practices of other Native American tribes/nations. Because of the long negative legacy of archaeologists excavating Native Americans graves, on some reservations there is resistance to having archaeologists study burial practices. Occasionally scholars have found a few gravemarkers of Native Americans in European American Christian cemeteries, but there are very few studies on nineteenth-century Native American gravestones in the United States.

Canadian art historian Ronald Hawker (1990) did important research on Northwest Coast Indian designs appearing in Christian cemeteries (1880–1910) on Vancouver Island, British Columbia. Hawker found that some Christian Tsimshian Indians chose to incorporate traditional clan symbols such as beavers, bears, and birds onto their gravestones. Interestingly, Hawker found that that these traditional designs appeared when the Canadian government was both taking Indian land and trying to prevent potlatch ceremonies. Hawker (1990: 229) believed that the clan images on gravestones might have been a way for the Tsimshians to reaffirm their identity and their heritage in the face of adversity.

Native American Burial Grounds in the Southwest

In the Southwest, Native American, Mormon, and Mexican American burial places have seen some study. An excellent comparative study by Keith Cunningham (1989) examines twentieth-century Navajo, Anglo-American Mormon, and Zuni burial ways. Each of these cultures treat their dead in very different ways. Cunningham's study of the Ramah

Mormon cemetery in the Ramah, New Mexico, area provides a fascinating discussion of Navajo burial practices within an Anglo-Mormon burial ground. Traditionally the Navajos did not have cemeteries. Burials take place as quickly as possible, generally in a secluded spot outdoors. The Navajos consider death within one's home supremely unfortunate. Houses where a death occurred were abandoned to avoid the *ch'iidii*, the evil forces or spirits that remain after the good forces/spirits have left the dead body (Cunningham 1989: 210). To avoid the ch'iidii, Navajos avoid burial places. In modern burial grounds, such as the Ramah Cemetery, Navajo burials typically lack permanent markers, though sometimes temporary funeral home markers are used. The seventy-one Navajo graves are of Mormon Navajos, and they are buried in individual, not family, plots (Cunningham 1989: 202, 211).

In contrast, the Anglo-American Mormon portion of the cemetery includes crude native sandstone markers, commercial markers such as are found across much of North America, and a handful of handmade red sandstone markers. Unlike the Navajo burials, the Mormon graves are grouped by families, with joint stones for husband and wife. Moreover, the markers often provide information about the individual's life or kin relations. Anglo-Mormon markers have diverse carvings of floral motifs, lambs, and pictures of the deceased (all of these motifs appear on European American graves), but what is unique are the carvings of Mormon temples (Cunningham 1989: 204).

The Zunis have their own cemetery, the Vander Wagen Cemetery, some twenty-five miles east of Ramah. The Zunis had contact with Coronado and his soldiers in 1540 and later encountered Spanish missionaries (Cunningham 1992: 200). Zuni funeral practices were influenced by those of the Spanish, and in the historic period the Zunis buried their dead in mission courtyards and *camposantos*. In the twentieth century, the Zuni markers include government-issue markers, as well as folk markers made from sandstone and even cinder blocks and pavers. Some are beautifully painted. Wooden crosses are also common, and some graves are decorated with Zuni pots (Cunningham 1989: 200). Like Zuni villages, the burial place is set on the side of a hill. Cunningham interprets the different burial traditions as substantial reflections of the cultural practices of these three groups. Traditional and Mormon Navajos bury their dead separately, unlike the Anglo-Mormons and the Zunis. Cunningham (1989: 213) adds that "the Mormon is buried at Ramah Cemetery as a family member and a future god whose descendants shall call him blessed. The Zuni in death, as in life, is in a Zuni village surrounded by his people achieving the ultimate Zuni goal of being one with them."

Aleutian Islanders

A very different study of ethnic burial practices is Charles Bello's detailed recording and restoration of the Russian Orthodox and Native Aleut/public cemetery on the Island of Unalaska in the Aleutian chain. In 1998, Bello, a staff member at the Museum of the Aleutians, and his colleagues were asked to record a cemetery containing seven-hundred-plus graves dating from the late nineteenth century and perhaps earlier, in order to facilitate the continued use of the burial ground and avoid the unintentional disturbance of previous burials. In addition to numerous Native American graves, seamen from Revenue Cutters, the Coast Guard, fishermen, military personnel, and others were buried there (Bello 2007: 2).

The Aleutian Islands were colonized by Russia in the eighteenth century, and the Native population was converted to the Russian Orthodox faith. The Church of the Ascension, a National Historic Landmark, was constructed on the site of a major prehistoric village in what is today the community of Dutch Harbor on Unalaska (Bello 2007: 6). The islands remained part of Russian America until 1867. Here during the Second World War the frigid Aleutian campaign played out. More recently these islands have become famous as home to some of the world's richest and most dangerous fishing grounds.

Bello and his colleagues examined the public cemetery used as a burial place by both the local Aleut population and the many transient laborers, fishermen, factory workers, and others who live on the island. Although many gravemarkers survive in the burial ground, harsh weather conditions have led to the loss of many others, and unmarked burials are commonplace. As a result, each new burial in the historic cemetery ran the risk of disturbing an earlier grave or graves. Unsurprisingly, residents found this situation unacceptable and decided to employ archaeologists to map the cemetery and, wherever possible, identify unmarked graves. This represents a fruitful collaboration of Native leaders, church elders, civic officials, and residents (Bello 2007: 15). It is worth noting that archaeologists were not always welcome in the community, a situation that may be linked with the voracious excavations of early twentieth-century archaeologists such as Aleš Hrdlička, who is known to have pillaged sites in the region.

Bello's project began with an extensive surface survey of the site. The survey documented hummocks, depressions, coffin hardware, skeletal remains, animal burrows, gravemarkers, fragmentary markers, and any other potential indicators of former burials. Ultimately, 474 marked graves were recorded and 225 likely unmarked graves were mapped, with a total burial population estimated at roughly 1,000 individuals in an area of approximately one hectare (Bello 2007: 20).

Many of the markers are wooden three-bar crosses, sometimes painted white. Other markers were store-bought, presumably imported from the Lower 48. There were also several handmade markers commemorating sailors, which may have been made by ship's carpenters. Moreover, early twentieth-century Native leaders have well-marked graves complete with imported cast iron fences. Detailed information was recorded about each of the markers. This information was recorded using a database program. Digital photographs were taken of the markers, creating a permanent record. Select markers were identified for conservation. All told, the project is an exceptional example of applied archaeology, and the resulting map and new burial procedures have resulted in a less traumatic burial experience for the people of Unalaska while also recording a large quantity of information about what would otherwise be an intriguing but poorly understood cemetery.

African American Burial Grounds

African American gravemarkers from the nineteenth century are an important focus of archaeological research. A particularly good example of this work is Lynn Rainville's study of Virginia slave cemeteries. Rainville has documented over one hundred African American burial grounds in Virginia. She eloquently notes that

the antebellum cemeteries used by enslaved communities are more than just sacred memorials that mark the final resting place of African Americans; they are sepulchral museums of mortuary material culture and genealogical archives for enslaved families. Beyond genealogy, graveyards are important tools for reconstructing slave communities. They not only illustrate the distribution of enslaved families and individuals; they also provide rare above-ground clues to the possible location of slave communities, [and] serve as a beacon for archaeologists to locate domestic and agricultural remains. (Rainville 2009: 55)

Most of her research has focused on cemeteries in the Virginia Piedmont, an area where during the antebellum period roughly 50 percent of the population was enslaved. Although archaeologists employ a wide variety of techniques to identify human burials—including oral histories, historic maps, soil chemistry, ground-penetrating radar, magnetometry, and electrical resistivity—Rainville concludes that in many cases pedestrian survey, or simply walking the landscape, is the most effective way to find lost burial grounds. Various topographic clues may also help in the identification of forgotten African American burial grounds. Some are located adjacent to burial grounds for plantation owners; others are on hilltops; and a few may be marked by non-native plants, such as periwinkles, yuccas, daylilies, and cedar trees (Rainville 2009: 62).

Rainville has also created a typology of nineteenth-century slave burial grounds, which include burials within the owners' graveyard, burials adjacent to white cemeteries, and separate slave cemeteries. Rainville found that slave gravemarkers were commonly made of local fieldstones. These vary in size, shape, and placement. Moreover, in their irregular clusters of burials, she notes, "antebellum African-American cemetery landscapes more closely resemble the colonial pattern, rather than the manicured, Victorian style" (Rainville 2009: 69). Although many markers for former slaves are uninscribed, those that have inscriptions are of great value for researchers. Moreover, even uninscribed markers may be dated by their form or by association with other landscape features, such as trees that have grown around them.

African American burial grounds are also noteworthy for their grave decorations. These may include shells, ceramic vessels, and a variety of personal items (Bolton 1891; Vlach 1978: 142). In *Go Down Moses*, William Faulkner wrote of graves "marked off without order by shards of pottery and broken bottles and old brick and other objects insignificant to sight but actually of profound meaning and fatal to touch which no white man could have read" (Faulkner 1942: 135) (figure 6.1). Robert Farris Thompson explains that these grave goods reflect several different practices. Sometimes the last objects used by the deceased were placed on the grave (Thompson 1983: 134). Other items might serve metaphorically: for example, seashells for purity (Thompson 1983: 135). However, it is worth noting

Figure 6.1. Scraped, mounded, and decorated African American graves in Magnolia Colored Cemetery, Aiken, South Carolina, c. 1900. Detroit Publishing Company, Courtesy Library of Congress, LC-DIG-det-4a27273.

that in some cases, shells may also have different meanings. For instance, in nineteenth-century New Jersey, the graves of canal boat captains, both white and black, were sometimes decorated with the conch shells used to signal from boat to boat.

In African American burial grounds, the grave goods may, in some cases, have been the possessions of the deceased. In other instances, they appear to have served to keep the spirit of the deceased from wandering (Jamieson 1995: 50). They are found not only in the South but also, with less frequency, in the North. Sadly, individuals unfamiliar with the practice often overlook their significance.

Rainville was not the first scholar to study African American burial grounds (see Genovese 1972; Jordan 1982; Little 1989; Krüger-Kahloula 1989; Veit 1992). As noted in chapter 4, early gravemarkers for African Americans have been studied. As scholars have noted, "Memorials for slaves were a convenient medium for advertising ideal images of both servants and masters" (Krüger-Kahloula 1989: 36). Indeed, "erecting a tombstone authenticated the slave's existence and acknowledged him or her as a person in spite of his/her legal definition as chattel and the assertion of ownership in the epitaph" (Krüger-Kahloula 1989: 36). Moreover, memorials for slaves served to advertise ideal images of both servants and masters and were, for masters, a form of self-aggrandizement in a world where most individuals, regardless of race, failed to receive permanent memorials.

The inscriptions on the nineteenth-century gravestones have seen considerable study. Many emphasize the dedication and years of service of the deceased. Some note that individuals who were once enslaved became free. Others recount the African origins of the deceased. A few focus on heroic acts in which individuals saved their master's property (Krüger-Kahloula 1989: 50). Quite a few mention the respectability, moral qualities, and Christian faith of the deceased. At the same time, erecting gravemarkers for slaves could be seen as affirming a form of eternal ownership (Krüger-Kahloula 1989: 54).

The epitaphs for African American slaves often remind readers of the social conditions these individuals labored under, reading "slave of" or "faithful servant." Markers also speak of individuals as beloved members of the family, thereby reinforcing paternalistic relationships. Moreover, many epitaphs stress attachment to employers or masters but rarely to family, friends, or black institutions (Krüger-Kahloula 1989: 53). White masters purchased gravestones for their "faithful servants," but these tombstones account for only a small percentage of the entire slave population. Perhaps that suggests that most of the slaves were not "faithful and loyal" to their masters and resisted enslavement.

The organization of burial grounds is also of interest. African American slaves were sometimes buried on the edges of cemeteries. On one hand, this might be seen as indicating segregation in death that paralleled their segregation in life. On the other hand, Krüger-Kahloula (1989: 57) indicates that many slaves were reluctant to be buried near their masters for fear that they would continue to be tormented in death!

One of the authors (Veit 1992), in studying African American gravemarkers from New Jersey, found that only a handful of early nineteenth-century professionally carved markers survived. New Jersey has the ignominious distinction of being the last Northern state to abolish slavery. This occurred in 1804 with a half-hearted gradual emancipation act, which stated that the children of slaves born after the fourth of July were to be freed at the age of twenty-five if male and twenty-one if female, while those born before 1804 remained enslaved unless benevolent masters choose to

Figure 6.2. Gravemarkers for African Americans in New Jersey. *Left,* This granite marker is a close reproduction of the original red sandstone memorial for "Caesar, an African." Located in the Scotch Plains Baptist Churchyard, it commemorates an individual who overcame prejudice and racism and whose life story is still a relevant event today. *Right,* The marker for Ambo, a servant in the Terrill family of Scotch Plains, New Jersey. Born of African parents, she died at the age of one hundred years. Her marker notes her long service. Photographs by Richard Veit.

emancipate them. A small number of African Americans in New Jersey were still enslaved at the outbreak of the Civil War (Hodges 1997).

Two particularly interesting New Jersey markers commemorate Caesar and Ambo. Caesar is buried in the churchyard of the Scotch Plains Baptist Church (figure 6.2, *left*). His large sandstone marker was carved by the local stonecutter Jonathan Hand Osborn. The original marker is snapped near the base, but the inscription is legible:

Here rest the remains of
Caesar, an African,

Who died February 7th 1806
Aged 104 years
He was more than half a century
A worthy member of the Church in
This place and closed his life in the confidence of a
Christian
His numerous friends have erected this stone as a tribute
Of respect to his eminent
Virtues and Piety
[The gravestone is broken at this point]
When the last trump shall bid the dead Arise
When flames shall roll away the earth and skies
While Atheists, Kings, and infidels turn pale . . .
Caesar will soar from Nature's funeral pile
To bask forever in his Savior's smile.

The marker for Caesar is decorated with the single letter *C* employed like a monogram at the top of the stone, and chain link sidebars. One wonders whether this is a coincidence or there is symbolism here too. The inscription describes an extraordinary individual who had lived to a great age and won the respect of his primarily white congregation. Historical research shows that Caesar was a slave of Nathaniel Drake, a deacon in the Baptist Church (Veit and Nonestied 2008: 172–73). He served as a teamster during the American Revolution and was freed after the war. Recently, his original marker, which had broken and was exfoliating, was replaced with a near replica in granite.

Another extraordinary New Jersey marker commemorates a woman named Ambo (d. 1847) and is located in the Rahway Cemetery (figure 6.2, *right*). Ambo, like Caesar, lived to an extraordinarily advanced age (although their exact ages may have been unknown). She too was enslaved and then freed. She remained with the Terrill family after freedom and is buried with other members of the family. Her epitaph reads, in part,

Born of African parents
In the family of Abraham Terrill
She remained a faithful
Servant to him, his children
And grand children until
Her death

Ambo's name is in itself quite interesting, as it is of African derivation and remained with her despite her decades of servitude. The names employed on the some of the other markers are also noteworthy. While some, such as Caesar, Pompey, Titus, and Cato, were derived from the classics and may reflect an ironic streak on the part of the slave owners, who used the names of powerful figures from ancient Rome for subaltern figures in early nineteenth-century America, others are traditional day names, in which individuals were named after the day on which they were born—such as Jack, an anglicized version of the West African day name Quaco, and the aforementioned Ambo, another day name. In New Jersey's early nineteenth-century burial grounds, there seems to be a distinction between markers erected by owners for slaves and those erected by free individuals for their family members. The former often note the race of the deceased, while the latter rarely mention it.

In contrast to markers erected by owners and friends for enslaved individuals, there are a handful of professionally carved gravestones associated with free African Americans. One, the Thomas Titus stone, is located in Woodlot Park in South Brunswick, New Jersey. The story of Thomas and his marker is a contrast to that of Ambo and other "faithful servants." The memorial was erected on land that was owned by the Titus family and appears to be the only marker located on the property. This is indicative of private family burial grounds found throughout New Jersey where property owners were buried on their land.

The inscription on the marker reads in part as follows:

In
Memory of
Thomas Titus
Died
July [illegible] 1849
In the 65 year
of his age

Thomas was born into slavery in 1784 but was manumitted by Gerardus Beekman in 1817 or 1818 (Veit and Nonestied 2012). Thomas went on to own property, and after his death in 1849 he was buried on his land. A rather simple marble memorial, presumably purchased by his family, was erected over his grave. The inscription on his stone makes no reference to Thomas's African heritage. To his family he was simply Thomas Titus.

Moreover, during a period of segregation when even the dead were segregated within burial grounds, Thomas was buried on the only piece of land that was not segregated—his own (Veit and Nonestied 2012).

Other scholars have studied nineteenth- and twentieth-century African American burial grounds in Texas (Jordan 1982: 17–18) and in North Carolina (Little 1989, 1998). Terry Jordan (1982: 47), a cultural geographer, has written about anthropomorphic markers, which have profiles like human beings, that were cut out of rock slabs by slave artisans. Jordan has also mapped the distribution of scraped-earth burials and shell decorations on burial mounds. Both of these traditions are seen in Old World African burial grounds and in African American burial grounds (Jordan 1982: 21).

Ruth Little (1998), writing about nineteenth- and twentieth-century North Carolina burial grounds, notes that African American burials are generally oriented east-west but may not be placed in even rows. Families are loosely grouped. She observes, "African American artisans create original gravemarker designs and are less influenced by commercial norms. They appropriate various building materials and actual objects that have symbolic meaning or aesthetic appeal, and incorporate them to create often startling original gravemarkers. They use ephemeral materials such as shells and bric-a-brac, commercial metal and plastic items intended for functional household use, concrete, or perishable materials such as sculpted earth and wood" (Little 1998: 237). North Carolina graves were often mounded and occasionally decorated with seashells and even eggshells. Wooden headboards and footboards were used well into the twentieth century. Cast concrete was very common and allowed attractive standardized monuments to be made inexpensively. Indeed, some local artisans continued to produce these markers in the South well into the twentieth century (Rotundo 1997). Moreover, these markers could be decorated with marbles and other decorative objects. Some of the artisans who made these markers were incredibly talented. Although many of these markers are exceptional examples of vernacular art and craftsmanship, their eclectic forms, use of common materials, and decorations have endangered their long-term existence. Sometimes cemeteries are "cleaned up" by well-intentioned but unwitting individuals, resulting in a significant loss of information.

African American burial grounds became much more visible after the Civil War. The Civil War is one of the watershed events in American history. It also led to a transformation of African American burial grounds.

Unprecedented in terms of its casualties, the Civil War transformed American ideas about mourning, commemoration, and treatment of the dead. Neither the Union nor the Confederacy was well equipped to handle the number of deceased soldiers. Many individuals were buried without the benefit of formal gravemarkers. However, as time went on, modest marble and occasionally granite markers came to replace the crude wooden headboards that were initially employed (Faust 2008). Embalming became more common, as families wanted their lost sons shipped home, and firms that produced cast iron coffins did a brisk business. African American soldiers had suffered and bled like their white compatriots and received government-issue gravemarkers. In many instances, these are the first formal markers one finds in Northern African American burial grounds. One site where they are found is the African Union Church Cemetery in Polktown, Delaware, which has been studied by David Orr. The site was rediscovered in 1990, when gravestones marked "USCT" (United States Colored Troops) were found in a nearby marsh (Orr 2012: 1). The burial ground was established in 1835 and serviced the community of Polktown, a small African American community, located across the canal from Delaware City, Delaware. It is small, containing only eleven formal gravemarkers, five of which mark the final resting places of soldiers who served in the USCT (Orr 2012: 7). There were likely quite a few graves that lacked formal markers. The burial ground seems to have gone out of use around the time of World War I.

As Orr points out, African American cemeteries reflect the cultural traditions of a distinct group, who experienced life differently from white inhabitants. They, or their ancestors, had experienced slavery, and they shared "customs, beliefs, values, and traditions, far different than their white masters, and later, fellow citizens" (Orr 2012: 8). Indeed, Orr notes that the Victorian romanticization of death likely made little impact in African American communities.

The USCT markers, like all government-issue markers from this period, contained only minimal information: the name of the deceased, his company, and his regiment. Orr uses the markers to tell the stories of the veterans. The minimalist information contained on the markers allowed him to trace the soldiers' participation in various campaigns. In some cases, such as that of Alexander Draper, of the Sixth USCT Regiment, Company C, they suffered debilitating injuries (Orr 2012: 18). For Orr, these simple white marble markers, forgotten in a Delaware marsh, provide a vehicle for remembering the roles of African American soldiers in the Civil War.

Chinese American Cemeteries

Another group of immigrants of great interest to historical archaeologists are Chinese Americans. According to Sue Fawn Chung and Priscilla Wegars (2005: 1), "Until recently, little has been known about Chinese American funerary rituals and practices that illustrate the weltanschauung of the people." Perhaps more than any other ethnic group, Chinese immigrants were seen as a people that clung to their traditions and were unlikely to assimilate. The Chinese experienced intense prejudice and faced a variety of legal exclusions, including limits on who could immigrate. For example, the Page Law of 1875 stopped female immigration temporarily, the Exclusion Act of 1882 prohibited the naturalization of Chinese, and the Scott Act of 1888 prevented Chinese laborers who had visited their homeland from reentering the United States (Greenwood 2010: 275). These laws disrupted Chinese families for decades and forced later generations to modify traditional beliefs to fit the American situation.

Because burial with one's ancestors was important to most Chinese immigrants, mutual aid societies proliferated to assist with the return of human remains to China. The goal in returning the bones of these sojourners to their homeland was so that they would not be forgotten and the remains would rest in their native soil. Proper respect included exhuming their bodies, returning them to China, and remembering the dead during yearly celebrations, which would be conducted by their relatives in China. Because the bones would someday be exhumed, more-simple gravemarkers were used with identifying names to make it easy to locate the bodies for exhumation. Terry Abraham and Priscilla Wegars (2005: 157) in studying late nineteenth-century Chinese cemeteries in the Pacific Northwest found that name-identifying gravemarkers could be made of wood, stone, marked bricks, and sometimes even bottles, with the name of the deceased placed on a linen or paper slip inside the bottle.

Chinese burial rituals were derived from ancient rituals, including geomancy and the three major religions of China, Confucianism, Buddhism, and Daoism (Rouse 2005b: 21). A variety of offerings were placed at graves. Archaeologists studying the Chinese graves in America noticed that the

Chinese used the principles of feng shui in the placement of the graves. Feng shui, also known as geomancy, is connected to Daoist philosophy with the concern for balance and harmony in nature, including the proper alignment of graves (Chung and Wegars 2005: 4–5). The location of a grave in relation to hills and water was critical in protecting a grave from evil spirits. A brief summary of feng shui beliefs is provided by archaeologist Wendy Rouse (2005b: 26): "Hills and mountains provide a barrier to dangerous winds that might carry evil spirits while allowing beneficial winds to pass. Water balanced the yang influence of the mountains and carried along yin energy with it. However, even these two elements, if improperly oriented could bring bad luck to the family."

The specific alignment of the grave could also take into consideration both the birth date and the death date of the deceased (Rouse 2005b: 25). Rouse (2005a) investigated two abandoned nineteenth-century Chinese cemeteries in Virginiatown, California, and found that the graves were sited using feng shui principles. Although the bodies had all been exhumed, Rouse was able to determine the position of the grave shafts in relation to the hills, a ravine, and the flow of water. In one of the cemeteries there was a European American section and a Chinese section. The European American graves were all arranged in neat rows facing east-west, whereas the Chinese burials followed the contours of the hillside and other feng shui ideas, so the Chinese burials appeared to be arranged in a more haphazard manner compared to the European American burials (Rouse 2005a: 84–86). Archaeologists also found that the burials in the Chinese Cemetery in Carlin, Nevada, were arranged using feng shui. The graves all followed the contours of a ridge, the graves faced a creek, and to their back were the mountains (Chung et al. 2005: 120). However, not all Chinese communities in America had a person skilled in feng shui (a geomancer), even if the Chinese wanted to bury their dead according to traditional practices. Terry Abraham and Priscilla Wegars (2005: 150–52) found that only some Chinese communities in Idaho and British Columbia used feng shui and that the Chinese in Philadelphia did not bury according to feng shui principles. Both availability of a geomancer and pressures to assimilate into mainstream European American culture may have influenced burial decisions.

This concern for reburial continued into the twentieth century. Chinese Americans continued to believe that the living, to ensure good fortune for themselves and their descendants, had to observe proper reverence for the dead (Chung and Wegars 2005: 3). Mutual aid societies proliferated to assist with the return of human remains to China. Terry Abraham and Priscilla Wegars (2005), in studying Chinese American cemeteries in the Pacific Northwest, found that exhumation continued into the 1930s, and in many locations these exhumed graves were not backfilled. Exhuming bodies and returning them to China was a costly process. Because China was a strongly patrilineal society, in exhuming the bodies the focus was on married men, with less attention paid to married women, unmarried individuals, or children (Rouse 2005b: 27). Abraham and Wegars (2005: 155–56) found in the Pacific Northwest that Chinese women were not exhumed and that these cemeteries may still contain the bodies of women in graves that once had wooden markers. In California it was rare to have the bodies of Chinese women, children, and victims of violence exhumed (Greenwood 2005: 246). In the early part of the twentieth century, bone houses were still used in Chinese cemeteries. The bone houses were buildings where urns and boxes of the exhumed bones were kept prior to shipment and reburial. Bone houses were found in Chinese cemeteries in the mainland United States and in Hawaii (Abraham and Wegars 2005: 158; Chung and Neizman 2005: 179).

More recently, World War II and the Communist takeover of China made it difficult to ship bones back to China. President Richard Nixon's visit to China in 1972 opened the door for Chinese Americans to bring their deceased relatives from China for reburial in the United States (Greenwood 2005: 247). Archaeologist Roberta Greenwood (2005: 241) has found that as a growing number of Chinese Americans see the United States as their permanent home, they are bringing the bones of their ancestors to the United States for reburial so that the living descendants can honor their ancestors during important religious rituals during the year. In both China and in the United States, Chinese remember their dead during three major celebrations: Qingming in the spring, Yulanpen in mid-August, and the Chinese New Year (Rouse 2005b: 29). The celebration of the Qingming festival includes remembering the ancestors and cleaning their graves. In the United States, families can place the exhumed remains from China in mausoleums, columbaria, or in-ground burials. But the burial urn, no matter where it is placed, always has the name of the deceased facing outward (Greenwood 2005: 253).

Markers on twentieth-century Chinese cemeteries in the United States were often made of wood both because of cost and because the grave site

Figure 6.3. Modern Chinese American gravemarkers at the Mansfield Cemetery, Washington Township, New Jersey. Photograph by Richard Veit.

was regarded as only a temporary resting place. By the 1930s the practice of exhumation had waned, as more Chinese opted to reside permanently in the United States (Rouse 2005b: 38). There also was a shift from temporary markers to permanent markers (figure 6.3). On Chinese gravestones, inscriptions are in Chinese, English, or a combination of both languages. In Hawaii there were generations of intermarriage of Chinese men with non-Chinese women, and the Hawaiian Chinese cemeteries reflect these inter-ethnic marriages (Chung and Neizman 2005: 176). The twentieth-century Hawaiian Chinese graves vary in size, shape, and form, with a variety of images on the stones including flowers, pictures of the deceased, and even the designs of favorite objects, such as cars (Chung and Neizman 2005: 181).

The final distinguishing feature of Chinese American cemeteries is the funerary structure known as "the burner." Terry Abraham and Priscilla Wegars (2005: 159) provide a description of the burner: "This brick or masonry structure, usually over seven feet tall, serves as a safe place for the ritual burning of spiritual tributes. Often paper and cardboard facsimiles of money, clothing, possessions, and even houses, these objects are to serve the deceased in the afterlife. Burning them passes them to the spirit realm for use by the deceased." Roberta Greenwood (2005: 251–52) noted that in California the Chinese practice of burning offerings for the deceased has continued throughout the late twentieth century and into the twenty-first century.

A Hawaiian Burial in Connecticut and Hawaii

A unique archaeological study that deals with a fascinating topic is the archaeological exhumation and reinterment of Opukaha'ia (Henry Obookiah) (Bellantoni et al. 2007). Opukaha'ia, born in 1792, was a native of Hawaii. Orphaned as a youth and a witness to the tragic killing of many family members, he fled to a sealing ship and asked to become a crew member (Bellantoni et al. 2007: 208). After extensive travels, he sailed to New York with Caleb Brintnall, the captain of the ship. Ultimately, Henry Obookiah, as he was now called, learned English and became a member of the household of the Reverend Timothy Dwight and later the family of Reverend Samuel Mills. Traveling and living with various families in New England, he experienced several religious awakenings. He was extensively tutored, and ultimately, he became a student at the Foreign Mission School in Cornwall, Connecticut. Passionate about his studies, he was a model student. Sadly, on February 17, 1818, he died of typhus (Bellantoni et al. 2007: 216). Obookiah was buried under a large tombstone, like those often employed for ministers and other notables, in Cornwall, Connecticut. His death inspired many missionaries to travel to Hawaii, including other Hawaiians, most notably his friend Thomas Hoopoo. His grave in Cornwall became a shrine for visiting Hawaiians (Bellantoni et al. 2007).

In 1993, at the request of descendants from Hawaii, Henry Obookiah was exhumed from his grave. Bellantoni, who led the team that carried out the excavation, noted that he was buried in a wooden coffin painted black, with a brass tack pattern forming a heart-shaped motif and containing the letters "H. O. AE 26" (Bellantoni et al. 2007: 217). The coffin had a viewing glass through which to observe the face of the deceased. The skeletal remains were in excellent condition.

The remains were transferred to the Kahikolu Congregational church in Kealakehua, Kona, Hawaii, after services at the First United Church of Christ Congregational in Cornwall, Connecticut, with Reverend Tomas Walter, a descendant of Obookiah, presiding (Bellantoni et al. 2007: 221). The body was returned to Hawaii, lovingly decorated with orange feather leis and other traditional trappings, and was reinterred, fulfilling Henry Obookiah's dying wish to once more see Hawaii. In many ways, this project is a model of fruitful and respectful collaboration between archaeologists and a descendant community.

Jewish Burial Grounds

Historical archaeologists have examined North America's nineteenth- and twentieth-century Jewish cemeteries. Jews were always a minority in the New World. Until the twentieth century, American white northern European Protestants viewed Jews as a separate race (Spencer-Wood 2010). Furthermore, within the Jewish community there are clear separations based on ethnicity and class. As mentioned in chapter 4, archaeologist David Mayer Gradwohl has done important work documenting many aspects of Jewish commemoration, including the historic Touro Synagogue cemetery in Newport, Rhode Island, and the broader topic of Sephardic Jewish cemeteries in North America and the Caribbean (Gradwohl 1998, 2007). Sephardic Jews are the descendants of Jews from the Iberian Peninsula and are distinct from the Ashkenazi Jews from Germany, Poland, and eastern Europe. This distinction reflects ethnic differences within the Jewish community. In North America, nineteenth-century Sephardic burial grounds survive in Newport, Rhode Island; Savannah, Georgia; New York City; and Philadelphia (Halporn 1993: 133, 139).

Jewish burial grounds resembled those in Europe. Indeed, perhaps more so than other groups, Jewish immigrants were likely to import professionally carved gravemarkers from London and Holland (Seeman 2010a: 253). Some of these markers show incredibly elaborate carving, in contradistinction to the "Second Commandment's stricture against graven images" (Seeman 2010a: 253). Both men's and women's markers spoke to their personal character and hopes for eternal glory. Nineteenth-century Sephardic burial grounds in the New York and New Jersey region employ an aesthetic that included images of the Lion of Judah, the Torah, and the Jahrzeit candle, or Eternal Light, richly embellishing upright and ledger stones, generally in gray granite. Women's markers may have the menorah, reflecting "the woman's role in lighting Sabbath and holiday lights" (Gradwohl 1998: 20). In addition to Hebrew and English, the Ladino language is found on some of the stones (Gradwohl 1998). Ladino is a Judeo-Spanish language used by Sephardic Jews (Segal 2005: 29).

Figure 6.4. Jewish markers in the Beth Emeth section of Albany Rural Cemetery, Loudonville, New York. Note that the obelisks and family monuments here look quite similar to those seen in predominantly Christian cemeteries from the same time period. The gravemarkers in the foreground have pebbles on them as a traditional Jewish sign of remembrance left by visitors. Photograph by Sherene Baugher.

In evaluating seventeen nineteenth-century markers at Touro Cemetery in Newport, Rhode Island, Gradwohl (2007) found that during the period 1800–1854, there was a shift from brownstone, red sandstone, slate, and occasional marble markers in the eighteenth century to marble and granite markers in the nineteenth century. This shift to marble and granite stones is typical of all secular and religious cemeteries in the nineteenth century. While ledger stones continued to be used up to 1820, 79 percent of the ledgers were erected before 1800 (Gradwohl 2007: 26). Between 1814 and 1854, the new forms were obelisks or piers made out of marble or granite (Gradwohl 2007: 43). Obelisks were a monument style found in all North American cemeteries (figure 6.4). The obelisk was found in cemeteries of people of diverse ethnic, racial, and religious backgrounds. Because of cost, obelisks were a class marker. Perhaps the use of the obelisks suggests choices that reflect some assimilation into mainstream middle-class American culture. Secular symbols such as flowers, fruits, leaves, wreaths, garlands, and animals, including lambs, do appear on Jewish gravemarkers (Segal 2005: 205–11).

In contrast to the early Sephardic immigrants, "the German Jews quickly learned to dress, speak, and act like the successful Christian models around them. . . . It is no wonder that their gravemarkers and cemeteries became almost indistinguishable from their Christian neighbors. . . . [B]oth in Germany and in the United States, they commissioned Victorian urns, Greek columns and Roman catafalques to create pagan-inspired marble wonderlands" (Halporn 1993: 141). In my (Baugher) survey of nineteenth-century cemeteries in New York City, I found that the symbols on the markers and mausoleums in the upper- and middle-class German Jewish cemetery of Salem Fields in Brooklyn looked very similar to the iconography used in secular grand rural cemeteries such as Green-Wood Cemetery, also in Brooklyn (New York City Landmark Preservation Commission 1984). The upper-class and upper-middle-class German Jewish families buried in Salem Fields were displaying their material success through monuments and sculpture in the same way as their Christian neighbors did in other New York City cemeteries. The one difference I noticed was the use of Hebrew along with English on some of the inscriptions in Salem Fields, thus affirming a family's religious background.

Eastern European Jews, who came to the United States in great numbers in the late nineteenth and early twentieth centuries, emigrated from a broad area, including not just Russia but also Poland, Ukraine, Czechoslovakia, Bulgaria, Yugoslavia, and Turkey. These new immigrants, like the German Jews who preceded them, were Ashkenazic Jews. The Sephardic Jews from Spain, Portugal, and the Dutch Caribbean islands immigrated primarily in the colonial period (see chapter 4), but immigration of Sephardic Jews from North Africa and the eastern and western Mediterranean continued through the twentieth century. Most American Jews are from an Ashkenazic background (Segal 2005: 5). By the late nineteenth century, the German and the Spanish Jews had become established and were economically successful, especially in northeastern cities. Upper-class and middle-class Jewish women's organizations worked to aid the new Jewish immigrants. For example, in Boston, elite German Jewish women helped establish hospitals, schools, playgrounds, and settlement houses for the eastern European Jewish immigrants (Spencer-Wood 2010). In the late twentieth century, there has been a new wave of Jewish immigrants from Russia and other countries in the former Soviet Union.

There are three major divisions within Judaism: Reformed, Conservative, and Orthodox: Reformed Jews came primarily from Germany, Aus-
tria, and France, whereas Orthodox Jews were primarily from eastern Europe, and Conservative Judaism essentially developed in the United States
(Gradwohl 1993: 121, 124–25). The intragroup diversity within Judaism is
reflected in their gravestones and choice of cemeteries. For example, many
of the eastern European immigrants joined benevolent associations and,
perhaps because of traditions brought from eastern European ghettoes,
buried their dead in close proximity to each other.

Archaeologist David Gradwohl has investigated many Jewish cemeteries in the American Northeast and Midwest as well as in the Caribbean.
Gradwohl (1998: 18–19; 1993: 142) found that Sephardic Jews in both the
Caribbean and the United States preferred to use ledger stones. Gravestone
scholar Rabbi Joshua Segal (2005: 5) notes that in cemeteries, Jews have
adapted to local customs, with Sephardic Jews often choosing horizontal
markers and ledgers while the northern and eastern European Jews (Ashkenazic) chose vertical markers. Language choice on markers also continues to reflect this intragroup diversity. Ladino (Spanish and Hebrew)
continues to be found on Sephardic gravestones (Gradwohl 1998: 21; Segal
2005: 29). Yiddish, "the language spoken by much of the Ashkenazic European Jewish community," can be found on some Ashkenazic gravestones
(Segal 2005: 30). Reformed Jewish gravemarkers have inscriptions in English and occasionally may have a phrase in Hebrew (Gradwohl 1993: 133).
Conservative and Orthodox Ashkenazic markers may have inscriptions in
both Hebrew and English (Gradwohl 1993: 135, 142).

In David Gradwohl's (1993) research in Reformed, Conservative, and
Orthodox Jewish cemeteries in Louisville, Kentucky, he found patterns
that also were in Jewish cemeteries he studied in Lincoln, Nebraska, and
Des Moines, Iowa. On the gravestones for Reformed Jews, religious symbols were usually missing, whereas on Orthodox graves, Judaic symbols
such as the Star of David, a menorah, the Lion of Judah, and the Torah
were found on the gravestones (Gradwohl 1993: 136). Conservative families chose many of the same symbols as Orthodox families but were not
bound by some of the restrictions of the Orthodox (Gradwohl 1993: 127).
Reflecting gender roles, there are distinct symbols that can be used for
men and women in Judaism. For example, the image of two hands in the
position of a priestly blessing is found on graves of Orthodox and Conservative men with the last name of Cohen, Kagan, Kahn, Kaplan, or Katz

indicating that they are descended from the priests, the Kohanim (Segal 2005: 51). On the graves of Orthodox and Conservative men with the last name of Levine, Levy, or Segal is often an image of a hand holding a pitcher, indicating that this is a descendant of the Levites, the assistants to the priests (Segal 2005: 51). Other symbols are common, such as a candle or lamp as a symbol of light, a bunch of grapes indicating ritual wine, or a ram's horn indicating the Shofar that is sounded on high holy days (Gradwohl 1993: 136–37). Monuments in Reformed Jewish cemeteries often look similar to monuments found in non-Jewish cemeteries, including the presence of mausoleums (Gradwohl 1993: 131). Orthodox cemeteries prohibit mausoleums because Jews must be buried in the ground; this requirement has sometimes been circumvented by first burying the deceased in the ground and then building the mausoleum-like structure over the burial (Segal 2005: 12). Gradwohl (1993: 140) noticed in the Orthodox and Conservative cemeteries in Louisville and elsewhere that pictures of the deceased are found on gravestones throughout the twentieth century, even though this is discouraged and some religious authorities maintain that pictures are prohibited on graves. I (Baugher) also found pictures of the deceased on Jewish gravestones in New York City. Roberta Halporn (1993: 147) notes that late twentieth-century markers for Russian Jews are often carved on black granite and display photoengravings. Pictures of the deceased are also found on Christian gravestones, especially on the gravestones of Italian American and eastern European immigrants (Veit and Nonestied 2008: 193). This suggests that the broad cultural use of photoengravings is not a reflection of one specific ethnic group. Gradwohl (1993: 140) suggests that in regard to the use of pictures on Jewish gravestones, "the force of folk tradition seems to outweigh rabbinic proscription." One last feature that is unique to Jewish gravestones is the presence of pebbles on monuments. The pebble indicates that someone has visited the grave site. Rabbi Joshua Segal (2005: 22) notes that "Judaism teaches that the guarantee of immortality to the deceased is how they are remembered by the living," and thus the leaving of a pebble at a grave site demonstrates that the deceased has not been forgotten. Jewish cemeteries indicate the complexity in looking at ethnicity within a cemetery because intragroup patterns do occur. The Jewish identity depicted on a gravestone overlaps with country of origin, gender, class, and the religious subset of Judaism.

Spanish Catholic Cemeteries

Although many mission sites in the southeastern and southwestern United States have associated cemeteries, few had permanent markers and most are present only as belowground archaeological sites. Wooden gravemarkers were common—and still are in parts of the Southwest (Warren 1987). A noteworthy exception to this rule is Tolomato Cemetery, the oldest extant Spanish Catholic cemetery in the city of St. Augustine, Florida. It was established in 1777, but most of the markers date to the nineteenth century (Kerr 2009: 6). Tolomato Cemetery contained ledgers, cradles (raised tablets on a ledger), gravestones, obelisks, aboveground vaults, and box tombs.

The box tombs contain a marble ledger placed on top of a brick or coquina box that sits over a closed grave. There are twenty-four brick or coquina vaults that date from the 1850s through the 1880s (Kerr 2009: 56). The majority of the markers were marble gravestones with a cross. A few stones had inscribed "I.H.S."; these letters are usually found on Catholic gravestones and can have multiple meanings, including representing "the first three letters of Jesus in Greek" or "In Hoc Signo," or "In His Service," plus other meanings (Mytum 2004:139–40). Some stones in Tolomato Cemetery have floral motifs, and other religious symbols such as an open Bible or a dove. Historic pictures of Tolomato Cemetery show numerous large wooden crosses that have long since decomposed. With Tolomato Cemetery, the question is whether the choice of markers reflects ethnicity, religious beliefs, socioeconomic status, or some combination of all three. The use of brick vaults is common in the Spanish colonies (Zucchi 1997). However, archaeologists have also excavated similar brick vault tombs in an English nondenominational cemetery, the Colonial Park Cemetery, dating to the late eighteenth to mid-nineteenth century in Savannah, Georgia (Trinkley and Hackler 1999). Therefore, even though brick vaults are found within Spanish colonies, the brick vaults may not be an ethnic marker but may be an indicator of socioeconomic status. In terms of the predominant symbols employed on the Tolomato gravestones, crosses and I.H.S. are not unique to Spanish Catholic cemeteries, they also appear frequently on Catholic gravemarkers in Ireland and England (Mytum 2004: 139–40). The choices made by the families at Tolomato reflect a combination of Spanish and Catholic burial practices.

Even in the small Tolomato Cemetery there is evidence of class stratification. The majority of the markers are modest marble gravestones, left by middle-class families. The ledgers, while more expensive, may have been the cultural preference of middle-class families. However, other families invested more funds in erecting obelisks, aboveground vaults, and box tombs that perhaps reflected their material success and status within the St. Augustine community.

Mexican American Gravemarkers

An important archaeological study of the aboveground remains of an ethnic cemetery is Russell J. Barber's (1993) investigation of Agua Mansa Cemetery in southern California. Today the cemetery is the only surviving reminder of the early Californian Mexican communities that once existed here, and most of the surviving gravemarkers are from the twentieth century. In the 1830s, Genizaro settlers (of Pueblo Indian and Mexican background) living in Abiquiu, New Mexico (near Santa Fe), were encouraged to settle in the San Bernardino Valley. Many of the New Mexicans (Genizaros) participated in a Catholicism practiced in New Mexico, in which there was a lack of clergy and lay societies, known as the Confradía de Nuestro Padre Jesus Nazareño (or, more commonly, Penitentes), dominated religious life. Barber (1993: 162) expected that because the New Mexicans considered themselves distinct from their Mexican neighbors (who came directly from Mexico), Agua Mansa Cemetery would display mortuary art unique to the New Mexicans. Initially, Christian burials in New Mexico took place below the floors of churches; however, as the population grew, burial in burying grounds, or *camposantos,* became the norm. The earliest markers were likely wooden crosses, but none have survived. Low fences around graves, or *cerquitas,* also developed, possibly as protection against wild animals. Barber compared the gravemarkers at Agua Mansa to those in five nearby Mexican cemeteries. There were no surviving markers from the early years in Agua Mansa Cemetery. Barber (1993: 170) found that between 1859 and World War II the style of gravemarkers reflected the same styles found in the five Mexican cemeteries. The styles included molded concrete crosses; wooden fences around graves; *relicaritos,* or recesses in gravemarkers, to hold holy objects; *nichos,* or shallow *relicaritos,* to hold pictures of the deceased or religious pictures; grave curbs made of concrete; and pot holders cast in concrete (Barber 1993: 163). After World War

II he found that both groups' cemeteries showed a greater similarity to Anglo burial places, but by the 1960s in the cemeteries of the Mexicans and New Mexicans there was a resurgence in ethnic pride with a return to traditional markers and the use of Spanish inscriptions (Barber 1993: 170). Although in some ways the results of this study are unexpected, they are nevertheless valuable in highlighting the fact that burial places and commemorative practices sometimes fail to show differences between communities that were indeed distinct.

Mexican American burial places are also noteworthy for their grave decorations, which provide a means of expressing grief and continuing love for family members. Lynn Gosnell and Suzanne Gott (1989) have studied the practices of tending twentieth-century graves in a cemetery in the Westside section of San Antonio, Texas, among an urban Mexican American community. The Westside community was composed only of working-class and poor Mexican Americans, with the professional, technical, and managerial Mexican Americans living in different parts of the city (Gosnell and Gott 1989: 219). Both commercial and homemade grave decorations were widely employed. Although most modern cemeteries trend toward visual conformity, San Fernando Cemetery, a Mexican American burial ground from the early twentieth century in San Antonio, Texas, does not. It is lavishly decorated on many holidays, including Halloween, Christmas, All Souls' Day, Mother's Day, and Father's Day. Indeed, it is crowded with individuals coming to decorate during these times of the year, and vendors come to sell mourners grave decorations (Gosnell and Gott 1989: 218). Although many scholars are familiar with the material trappings associated with All Saints' Day and All Souls' Day (the two-day holiday known as Dia de los Muertos), Gosnell and Gott (1989: 220) highlight the fact that decorations occur cyclically during much of the year for both recognized holidays and personal anniversaries. Many of the decorations are vibrant and colorful. Many of the grave goods are mass-produced. These decorations "suggest a particular desire to include deceased family members within major holiday observances" (Gosnell and Gott 1989: 230). There is also an element of imitation as individuals select ideas from one another's decorations. Gosnell and Gott (1989: 234) conclude that "the creation of highly visible, colorful grave decorations by grieving families . . . projects vibrant evidence of the continuing presence of the departed loved ones in the world of the living as well as in the hearts of their family." As the Hispanic population of the United States grows, it will be interesting to see whether these practices spread and persist or are rejected by the growing number of middle-class and upper-class Mexican Americans.

Romany/Gypsy Commemoration

Historical archaeologists have also studied the burial grounds of the Romany people, or Gypsies. I (Veit 2007) have studied their burial places in New Jersey. Romany markers follow the pattern noted by Randall McGuire and Lynn Clark, who argued that ethnic groups create their own social hierarchies of commemoration (Clark 1987; McGuire 1988). They have done so through the creation of elaborate memorials that highlight their beliefs regarding family, gender roles, their shared heritage, and occupation.

Since at least the late nineteenth century, the Gypsy (or Romany) people buried their dead in New Jersey. Descendants of roaming tribes of nomads who trace their origins back to India, they call themselves Rom, Roma, Romani, Romany, or, in some cases, Gypsies (Clébert 1963; Hancock 1988: xviii–xix). Today they are found around the world. Their common name, *Gypsies*, comes from the popular but erroneous belief that they originally came from Egypt. Although many modern scholars prefer the term *Romany*, New Jersey's Gypsy people persist in using the historic term *Gypsies*. The terms are used interchangeably here.

My research focused on documenting New Jersey's Romany or Gypsy burials and the use of those markers by the Romany to reinforce critical cultural beliefs (Veit 2007). I paid particular attention to two cemeteries: Evergreen Cemetery on the border between Hillside and Elizabeth in Union County and Newark in Essex County and Rosedale Cemetery in Linden, New Jersey. Evergreen, established in 1853 as a rural cemetery for the cities of Newark and Elizabeth, covers 115 acres and contains over 100,000 monuments. There are reputed to be approximately 3,000 Gypsy burials in the cemetery (Turner 1996: 191–98).

Romany funerals and gravemarkers are noteworthy for their ostentation. One of the more impressive monuments is an arcade of black granite columns, marking the resting place of Big G (George) and Loveable Rose Nicholas (figure 6.5). A large gilt carving of the Madonna is in the center of the arcade, and enormous gilt letters "B" and "G" are set between the columns. Colored enamel portraits of the couple decorate the memorial.

Figure 6.5. The impressive Romany (Gypsy) monument for Big G (George) and Loveable Rose Nicholas in Evergreen Cemetery, Hillside, New Jersey, takes up five plots and is carved from black granite with gilt lettering and ceramic portraits. The marker is decorated for Christmas. Photograph by Richard Veit.

Northern New Jersey's other extraordinary Gypsy burial ground is Rosedale Cemetery in Linden. Established in 1900, it claims to be the largest burial ground in the state. Although a statistical study of the Romany gravemarkers in Linden is not possible, for the simple reason that it is often hard to tell when a gravemarker commemorates a Romany or someone with similar memorial taste in gravemarkers, there are certain characteristics common to many Romany memorials. Some employ colorful stone: red and black granite are quite common. Paul Erwin, researching Gypsy gravemarkers in Ohio, noted that the Scottish clans of Gypsies in the American Midwest prefer dark red granite monuments, a preference he attributes to the color of stone used in Scotland (Erwin 1993). Many Romany markers are carved from pink or red granite. Anne Sutherland (1975), in a discussion of color preferences among Gypsies, notes that red is considered a positive color, connoting good health, happiness, and protection from illness. Green is also viewed positively (Sutherland 1975: 284). Black, another common color for modern Romany gravemarkers, is a negative color associated with mourning, death, and funerals.

Since the 1950s, many Romany gravemarkers have been decorated with enamel portraits of the deceased. They range from locket-sized pictures to large photographs. Most of the pictures depict couples, and the typical gravemarker is for a married couple, sometimes accompanied by an unmarried adult child. The men tend to be shown wearing suits and hats. These may be fedoras, cowboy hats, or straw boaters. The women wear headscarves, bright sashes, earrings, and colorful dresses, showing an adherence to Romany custom that is less visible among the men. It is worth noting that headscarves were traditional attire for married women. In the most recent markers, those dating from the past few years, fewer photographs show this item of clothing.

Romany women are often the primary breadwinners, and many serve as fortunetellers (Anderson 1981). Men, in contrast, have much less prestige attached to their labor. Some markers note occupations, especially musicians. Markers for men note with pride that he was a "Man among Men" or "A Legend in His Own Time." One particularly lavish example for Mr. Mesa "Dino" Demetros notes, "He Used to Be a Big Shot, The World's Biggest Shot." Similarly, Jack Petro is described as a "Gentleman of Gentlemen."

Gambling is another theme seen in many gravemarkers, particularly those of men. The crypt of Larry "Beaver" Stevens notes that he would rather be in A.C. (that is, Atlantic City) playing keno. Similarly, the inscription on Robert Kaslov's marker (died 1986) notes with regret, "I'd rather be at O.T.B." (that is, off-track betting). Given the current locations of Beaver Stevens and Robert Kaslov, these longings seem reasonable. Other markers are inscribed with pithy sayings, such as the marker of T. J. Steve "Mr. Miami" Petro, which states, "You have to lose some to win."

Finally, some markers are humorous. Bingo and Sally Vlado have two swaying palm trees, two swaying hula dancers, and the words "Big Time" engraved on their marker. Perhaps tongue in cheek, the Joey Wallace marker (died 1989) noted that it "couldn't happen to a nicer guy." As though speaking to the reader about the afterlife, Mr. Mesa "Dino" Demetros's marker has carefully hidden in one corner a bit of carving that reads "It Sucks." Few other ethnic groups consistently show the sense of humor that is present in Romany markers (Veit 2007).

It is also worth noting that the markers show what might be interpreted as a fair degree of competition among Gypsies in terms of who can have the largest, most elaborate, or most colorful gravemarker. Some families erect entire compositions, complete with tables, chairs, shrubbery, and rosebushes as well as headstones. This fits well with how Carol Silverman presents the relationship of Gypsies to each other and to outsiders. According to Silverman (1991: 107), Gypsies will work to demonstrate wealth and status within their own community while at the same time concealing wealth and status from outsiders. This is certainly the case with the gravemarkers. These markers serve to set the Gypsies apart from their *gazhe* (outsider) neighbors, while at the same time reinforcing intragroup solidarity.

Italian American Burial Grounds

The early twentieth century saw the arrival of large numbers of Italian immigrants in the United States. Many lived in ethnic enclaves and continued their traditional funerary practices. Burials and monuments provided a way of demonstrating status within the community. This focus on material success resulted in a flowering of commemorative art, and in particular the widespread use of life-sized marble commemorative statues (figure 6.6). Moreover, Italian Americans are known for having created a distinctive cemetery aesthetic. Joseph Inguanti (2000: 10) has argued that among

Figure 6.6. The gravemarker of Mrs. Cutroneo in Oceanport, New Jersey, is a fine example of a twentieth-century Italian American marker. Commissioned by her sons so that she could watch over them in perpetuity, it shows Mrs. Cutroneo with her hand cupped to her ear, carefully listening. It serves as a reminder to all of us to listen to and learn from the stories that historic burial places have to tell. Photograph by Richard Veit.

Italian Americans the dead traditionally played a role similar to saints, and there was a continuing relationship between the living and the dead. This included tending the grave of the deceased, a form of duty or work, which is seen in the house, garden, and cemetery.

Catholic Calvary Cemetery in Queens, New York, is a particularly good example of Italian American commemorative behavior. It opened in 1848 and catered to the city's growing Roman Catholic population (Inguanti 2000: 12). Agricultural crises, high taxes, and overpopulation drove hundreds of thousands of southern Italians, particularly Sicilians, to migrate to the United States during the late nineteenth and early twentieth centuries. Today the cemetery is believed to contain several million graves (Inguanti 2000: 12).

Italian markers are commonly inscribed in Italian and often decorated with photo-ceramic portraits, depicting the deceased in a formal manner. Inguanti notes that similar formal portraits of the deceased were commonly displayed in houses of Italian Americans. Moreover, carefully landscaped gardens, fruit trees, and vegetables often surrounded these same houses. Inguanti notes that the headstones, like houses, are surrounded by plantings. Decorative shrubs are often planted symmetrically in front of the gravestones. Symmetry and cleanliness are stressed in the home, in the garden, and in the cemetery. Floral plantings, particularly of annuals, are also common. Behind the markers, tomato plants are sometimes planted.

Curiously, Italian cemeteries in Italy do not match what is seen in the eastern United States. In Italy, fresh flowers are common on graves. However, in Italy, there is no real evidence for the planting or cultivation of flowers, or even the tomatoes sometimes seen growing in Italian American cemeteries. Most graves in Italy have a large stone cover. As Inguanti (2000: 28) notes, "Stone, not earth, characterizes the texture of the contemporary Italian cemetery. . . . According to informants in Sicily, only the poorest members of the community are buried in the ground without the usual stone slab covering the burial site. Except for their extremely modest markers, such grass-covered burials look ordinary and familiar to American observers." In Italy, however, burials are not necessarily permanent, and bones may be removed to ossuaries. In New York's Calvary cemeteries, the graves are purchased just like houses, reflecting a very American landscape, but the grave tending reflects traditional ideals about the interaction of the living and the dead.

Class Studies of European Immigrant Burial Grounds

As noted throughout this book, class cannot be separated from the study of gravestones. Within ethnic, racial, and religious groups, a family's or individual's purchasing power impacts their choices of burial goods and memorial markers. Randall McGuire (1988) analyzed late nineteenth- and twentieth-century cemeteries in Broome County in central New York State. He provides a Marxist critique of commemorative practices. In the 1980s, when most historical archaeologists were studying colonial cemeteries, he was one of the first archaeologists to turn his attention to twentieth-century cemeteries, especially mid-twentieth-century cemeteries. His study highlighted the research potential of twentieth-century cemeteries. McGuire's study area is in the portion of central New York that borders on Pennsylvania. Settled in the early nineteenth century (it was Indian territory until after the Revolutionary War), Broome County was an agricultural county until the mid- to late nineteenth century. It first became a center for the manufacture of cigars, but by the beginning of the twentieth century shoe manufacturing had become the major industry, in turn replaced by IBM in the second half of the twentieth century (McGuire 1988: 441). As in many northeastern cities, there were waves of immigrants. In Broome County there was Irish immigration in the mid-nineteenth century, followed in the late nineteenth and early twentieth century by Italians, eastern European Jews, and both Catholic and Lutheran Slovaks (McGuire 1988: 442).

McGuire collected data from over two thousand gravestones in twenty-seven cemeteries, including urban and rural burial grounds, associated with Protestants, Catholics, and Jews. He and his colleagues also documented all of the family mausoleums in the Binghamton area. In his view, "the burial ritual is . . . an active part of the negotiation and struggle between the powerful and the powerless in society" (McGuire 1988: 436). McGuire hoped to see whether gravemarkers provided a direct reflection of social stratification in the community. He found that during some periods they did and in other periods they did not. Moreover, he sees the markers raised over the dead as reflecting "ideals concerning death, class and family . . . intended to establish and perpetuate a dialogue with the living" (McGuire 1988: 436). He believes that this shift in the dialogue reflects the changing nature of capitalism and a movement from "mystification based on naturalization to denial of inequalities and power relations" (Mc-Guire 1988: 436).

McGuire frames his work using a concept of ideology derived from Marxism, in which one class dominated another, but he also sees resistance as ethnically diverse workers disputed the dominant ideology. Ideology, according to McGuire, is necessary for a group to maintain political consciousness and is used by the ruling class to maintain its dominance and make it seem as though the interests of the ruling class are those of the whole society. Subordinate classes may accept the ideology or revolt against it (McGuire 1988: 439). Moreover, ideology has material manifestations. McGuire posits that the "uniform style and size of gravestones in early 19th-century Broome County cemeteries legitimated and affirmed an egalitarian ideology that denied inequalities in the community" (McGuire 1988: 440).

In Broome County, McGuire found the same general national nineteenth-century patterns that we describe in chapter 5. He found that from 1850 until the early twentieth century, the size and variety of gravemarkers increased as families invested more and more heavily in them. Prominent family memorials, often inscribed with only the family's name, came to be used in association with smaller markers for the individual family members (McGuire 1988: 447). Walls and fences, a pattern typical of grand rural cemeteries, surrounded many of these family plots. McGuire found that extremely well-to-do individuals, businessmen, and professionals in Broome County erected mausoleums before the 1920s. This reflects the national golden age for mausoleums, which was 1880–1920 (Sloane 1991: 225). Archaeological studies over the past twenty-five years have shown that what McGuire found in Broome County is a pattern repeated throughout the United States. Indeed, the cemetery patterns in Broome County seem to mirror patterns found by other archaeologists, that is, there was a direct relationship between mortuary investment and social position in the later nineteenth century.

The most interesting observances come from McGuire's twentieth-century data. He found that most of the burial grounds were lawn-park cemeteries. McGuire found that among different immigrant groups there were differences in how they approached cemetery memorialization depending on their economic class. He notes, "The Irish use of memorialization directly parallels [that of] the dominant group. . . . [T]he Irish never erected memorials distinctive in form from the dominant society, but rather depended on Catholic religious symbolism, and a separate cemetery to distinguish themselves" (McGuire 1988: 469). He notes that once the Irish Catholics entered the middle class their graves looked like those of Protestant middle- and upper-class graves, and after World War II the only thing to indicate that they might be Irish (other than their family name) was the use of the Celtic cross (McGuire 1988: 469). He also recognized that upper-class Jews of Germanic origin used markers very similar to those of upper-class Protestants, whereas eastern European working-class Jews used tall gray stones that were similar in form to those used by working-class eastern European Christians and Italians (McGuire 1988: 470). The eastern European Jews in Broome County did use Jewish symbols and Hebrew on their stones. The twentieth-century ethnic burial grounds in Broome County also show a sort of ethnic solidarity through their use of distinctive decorative motifs. According to McGuire, the presence of these ethnic markers shows a fracturing of the dominant ideology and highlights the varied meanings present in the gravemarkers (McGuire 1988: 471).

In analyzing the cemeteries in Broome County, McGuire claims that the early nineteenth-century gravemarkers created an "appearance of equality among the dead . . . that masked the relations of power among the living" (McGuire 1988: 458). Late nineteenth-century cemeteries, the product of capitalism and industrialization, emphasized inequalities rather than uniformity. McGuire found that late nineteenth- and early twentieth-century cemeteries reinforced the inequalities of life and preserved them through memorials. During the 1920s, he found, there was a redefinition of ideology, as mass production made markers and even mausoleums available to individuals besides the established elites. In discussing gravemarkers of northern European Protestants, McGuire (1988: 465) notes that "the competition in memorials lost meaning as more individuals could afford elaborate memorials." He noticed that after World War II their gravemarkers became increasingly uniform in size and shape and class distinctions were deemphasized. While he acknowledges that there are differences in iconography on these gravestones, he notes that the personal designs and inscriptions are visible from only a few yards away. However, McGuire does note that the graves of eastern Europeans and Italians did not follow the patterns he saw with northern European Protestants. In fact, for those groups, "contrary to Protestant trends, investment in memorials increases instead of decreasing" (McGuire 1988: 470). McGuire's examination of ideology and how it has played out in Broome County's cemeteries is widely applicable to other burial places through North America.

Like McGuire, Lynn Clark (1987) examined the intersection of ethnicity and class in Broome County burial grounds; she studied twelve cemeteries dating from the 1830s to 1980 and employed a statistical sample of 1,117 markers. Clark (1987: 384) argues that "class limits the number of choices a consumer can make and also provides more options to choose from." At the same time, she believes that ethnicity can either limit or expand consumer choices. Clark studied markers of twentieth-century Italians, Slovaks, and Jews. Clark found clear evidence that socioeconomic class impacted gravemarker choices. Not surprisingly, wealthier families erected mausoleums. Upwardly mobile families could emulate the elites in their choice of gravemarkers. Blue-collar workers employed a variety of memorials sometimes emulating monuments of the English American upper and middle classes and sometimes making ethnic choices. For example, the Italians and Slovaks made use of complex religious designs, photographs, and mausoleums. Jewish stones contained Hebrew epitaphs and other inscriptions as well as religious iconography, including the Star of David. Furthermore, some groups, such as Italian immigrants, persisted in using mausoleums, which had fallen from favor with the broader population, well into the 1960s, reflecting the prestige systems within their own ethnic group. Clark's study of twentieth-century markers shows the complex interplay of ethnicity and class in determining consumer choices in cemetery memorials.

Conclusions

One particular interest of archaeologists has been documenting and explaining the commemorative traditions of the diverse ethnic groups who make up America. The transformation of Native American burial places and their diversity has attracted the attention of some archaeologists. African American burial places, perhaps more than those of any other group, have seen extensive study, in both the Southeast and the Northeast. A handful of scholars, led by David Gradwohl (1993, 1998, 2007), have examined Jewish commemorative traditions. Gradwohl's studies of the diversity within a religion—as in the different choices made by Reformed, Conservative, and Orthodox Jews, as well as the regional differences in customs of Sephardic and Ashkenazic Jews—should serve as cautionary tales to prevent archaeologists from lumping an ethnic or religious group into one catch-all category. Gradwohl found that the range of diversity in consumer choices in Jewish gravemarkers reflected the individual's or family's class, ethnicity, and subset of Judaism (Reformed, Conservative, or Orthodox). We need to understand the subtle differences within a group in order to reach more-sophisticated and complex conclusions.

With the arrival of immigrants from Eastern and southern Europe and from China, ethnic diversity increased. The iconography of the gravestones reflects the diverse ethnic heritages of the interred families. Overseas Chinese, Irish, Italian, and Romany commemoration have begun to be studied by archaeologists, but much work remains to be done.

The study of the gravemarkers alone provides us with only one part of a very complex picture. Twenty-first-century archaeologists are challenged to take into consideration a wide range of factors, including inscriptions and iconography on gravestones or monuments, location of the graves within the cemetery, family plots, landscaping, and placement of gifts or remembrances on the graves (such as fresh flowers, potted plants, perennials, annuals, shrubs, pebbles, and even toys). As a result, archaeologists need to examine a range of variables when analyzing cemeteries in terms of consumer behavior and agency.

7

"He Being Dead Yet Speaketh" (Hebrews 14:4)

Conclusions

In the twenty-first century, most Americans die in hospitals and nursing homes, not at home with their families. The separation of death continues with the avoidance of cemeteries. Once a person dies and is buried, the burial site is often neglected by family members. So in our youth-oriented culture, why study cemeteries? As archaeologists and anthropologists, we are interested in all stages of life. In this book we demonstrate that cemeteries and burial places are important repositories of cultural information. They reflect and embody changing American ideas regarding commemoration and remembrance, as well as changing attitudes toward death and dying.

In the colonial period, infant mortality was high, many women died in childbirth, and young men died from accidents and in wars. Burial grounds were the stark reminders of the brevity of life. Protracted mourning and ostentatious displays in graveyard monuments and memorialization were considered an affront to God and a challenge to his divine Plan (Baugher et al. 1989: 1). The individual and the family were closely connected to their community. Compared to those of the nineteenth century, colonial-era burial grounds placed much less emphasis on the family and certainly had fewer ostentatious markers. Of course, the wooden markers of the poor and indigent have long since decomposed. Archaeologists have explored and analyzed the iconography of the markers—mortality images, cherubs, urns and willow trees, flowers, Masonic symbols, portraits, and monograms—and postulated what the emblems may have meant. These design trends reflected trade networks, artistic conventions, ethnic preferences, religious beliefs, the growth of a consumer culture, and sometimes even national cultural styles that transcended one religion or one region.

With the American Revolution and independence, a new social order emerged. America moved from an agrarian to an industrial economy. The middle class emerged in the nineteenth century, and the Industrial Revolution created a capitalist-based upper class that flaunted newly acquired wealth. Some believed that worldly success affirmed God's plan. Therefore, one could display one's material success in cemetery memorials—in the gravestones, statuary, monuments, and mausoleums. Even the design of the landscape and the location of the family plots (just as in the location of their homes) reflected real estate values and price tags. The nineteenth-century cemetery reflects the conspicuous consumption of the middle and upper classes, a consumer behavior that reflected one's status, class, ethnicity, and religion.

Twentieth-century cemeteries also reflect significant change in Americans' attitudes toward death. With improvements in medicine, there was a dramatic drop in the death rate, especially in infant mortality, and an increase in the average life span (Sloane 1991: 273). Americans were willing to mute death's presence with a change in the memorialization in cemeteries. No longer were there the overly dramatic statues of weeping angels from the nineteenth century. Americans sought landscapes of death that were more peaceful and serene. The memorial park, with its minimalist uniform markers, careful plantings, and uplifting statuary, replaced the increasingly crowded cemeteries of the Victorian era. Community mausoleums, providing aboveground resting places for the deceased, became popular. However, some ethnic groups marched to a different drummer and persisted in the erection of elaborate mausoleums. Other individuals, often of limited means, created their own folk markers of iron, ceramics, and concrete. Modern burial grounds reflect the incredible ethnic diversity of twenty-first-century America. Design choices, materials, and the inscription of languages reflect the family's or individual's ethnic, religious, and class backgrounds and in some cases just the individual's own unique personality.

Although memorial parks have seen almost no study by American historical archaeologists, their research potential is exceptional. What ethnic groups accepted them, what groups rejected them, how have they been modified, and will they persist into the future are all questions worth examining.

Focusing on the colonial period, archaeologists have looked at the differences in markers of English, Dutch, French, German, and Spanish;

however, compared to English-language and Dutch-language markers, those of the French, Germans, and Spanish have seen relatively little study. Archaeologists studying nineteenth- and twentieth-century cemeteries seem to have overlooked the ethnic diversity in markers of northern Europeans, treating them almost as if they were one group—"the dominant culture." There are still many questions that can be addressed in studying the ethnic markers of specific northern European groups. For example, what are the differences in the memorials of Americans of Scottish, Danish, Finnish, or Welch backgrounds? And within diverse northern European ethnic groups, what are the class differences in their choice of markers? Within all of the various ethnic groups, what role does gender play? Do men and women have different gravestones? All markers and forms of memorialization provide a fruitful proving ground for testing anthropological theories, they combine texts and material culture, and they are illustrative of America's cultural diversity. They deserve further attention.

Archaeologists studying late twentieth-century cemeteries, especially Chinese burial practices, have noted the role of music, prayers, funeral processions, and grave offerings, as well as the return to the grave with grave offerings made on ceremonial occasions during the year (Chance 2005; Rouse 2005b). What is the material evidence of any of these practices? The "burner" found in Chinese cemeteries is evidence of the continuing practice of burning grave offerings both during a funeral and during important yearly ceremonies. Using the same standard, how can colonial and nineteenth-century burial grounds reveal the complex practices of the funerals and postfuneral visits?

Furthermore, there is still much work to be done as America's immigrant populations continue to expand to include people from around the world, such as people from the Middle East, India, Pakistan, Southeast Asia, and Korea. These people will bring their own burial customs, traditions, and iconography to be memorialized on cemetery landscapes. Unlike many other artifacts, gravemarkers can often be linked to individuals of specific ethnicities. Markers also reflect socioeconomic class. Within any ethnic group, archaeologists study how consumer choices are reflections of class and ethnicity.

By the 1980s, mausoleums had regained popularity (Sloane 1991: 226). With a resurgence in materialism and conspicuous consumption to rival the Gilded Age of the 1880s, these late twentieth- and twenty-first-century mausoleums deserve study. Do they reflect contemporary architectural styles? What motifs are used? Are ethnic differences discernible on the mausoleums? How do community mausoleums compare to mausoleums for individuals? And in the gravemarker, is there more expression of individual identity beyond the restraints of ethnicity and religion? Clearly, modern cemeteries provide many opportunities for archaeological research.

The gravemarkers, monuments, and mausoleums found within cemeteries are only one way to memorialize the dead. Our historic battlefields contain statues and monuments to commemorate the heroic deeds of both individual soldiers and troops. In some cases, statues can reflect the valor of all of the soldiers from a specific state, such as the large Virginia Memorial at Gettysburg. Throughout American cities and towns, monuments and statues commemorate the soldiers who died in our many wars (especially in the Civil War, World War I, and World War II), and they also reflect the community's loss of a generation of young men. In some cases, the meanings of the monuments have changed as each generation views the memorials and reinterprets them in light of that generation's experiences, backgrounds, and time period. For example, Paul Shackel (2001) chronicles the changing and contrasting meanings of the Robert Gould Shaw Memorial on Boston Common, now referred to as the Fifty-Fourth Massachusetts Regiment Memorial. Over time, interpretation of the monument shifted from being seen as honoring the abolitionist Shaw to being considered racist, because Shaw was on a horse and the black soldiers were walking; more recently, it has been regarded as depicting the forgotten soldiers, the free black soldiers who fought bravely in the Civil War.

Contemporary memorialization of our wartime dead reflects changes in power in who controls the interpretation of history. In Washington, D.C., the Vietnam and Korean War memorials were controversial. It no longer was just a small select group of the rich and powerful who were determining the presentation of history; diverse stakeholders were exerting their rights and concerns. The growing power of diverse stakeholders can be seen in the memorialization at the African Burial Ground in New York City. The descendant community, with many different factions, debated and discussed appropriate memorials with the established power, in this case the U.S. General Services Administration, until an acceptable memorial was chosen.

The power of stakeholders can be vividly seen in the controversy over how to memorialize the site of the World Trade Center. The vocal stakeholders have been not only the families of the people who died at the Trade Center but also all New York City and greater metropolitan area residents who keenly felt the assault on their city. The pressure from the development community was to just rebuild the site, but the tragedy of September 11th had transformed the site from a vibrant financial center to a place of national mourning and remembrance. We believe that the issue of the memorialization is not only remembering the individuals who had died but also what this event means as a pivotal point in our nation's history, just as the Pearl Harbor memorial holds dual meaning for descendants and for all Americans.

The American burial place is also undergoing a major transformation that no doubt will provide ample research for future generations of archaeologists. Blanks for memorials are regularly shipped from China, India, and Brazil to the United States, adding color to American burial grounds. Laser- and hand-etched images decorate polished black granite markers. Inscriptions and ornaments detailed in polychrome colors are enlivening burial grounds. Web addresses engraved on markers provide cemetery visitors with the opportunity to learn more about the deceased.

Burial practices themselves have been transformed. Beautifully crafted Ghanaian coffins shaped like sneakers, cars, and cameras are exhibited in American art galleries. More-somber examples were used in reburial ceremonies at New York's African Burial Ground. Green cemeteries—where bodies are buried au naturel without tombstones, caskets, or embalming— are becoming increasingly popular. Some green burials have no permanent markers, but visitors can find them using Global Positioning System satellite technology, which in turn can be linked to Web content about the deceased (Cullen 2006: 54).

The complex patterns found in aboveground burials are also found in the archaeological excavations of burial sites. The human remains, grave goods, and positions of the graves have provided valuable information about the religious beliefs, socioeconomic status, and ethnic heritage of the deceased, as well as information about an individual's physiological characteristics: stature, sex, injuries suffered during life, and health. Perhaps more now than ever before, human remains can provide a wealth of information through scientific analysis. Nonetheless, archaeologists must consider the wishes of the descendant communities as they pursue their research. Ethical questions need to be addressed before any burial ground excavation is undertaken. What role should members of the descendant community play? Do we use oral histories? Whose history and culture is it? Whose past are we presenting and interpreting? Are we partnering and/or collaborating with descendant communities, or are we continuing an archaeological practice of totally independent research? And what happens to the bodies after the excavation and analysis are completed? Are the bodies reburied, as was the case with the African Burial Ground in New York City, or are they placed in boxes or drawers, like artifacts, in university or museum storage facilities? And who decides the ultimate fate of these bodies? Complex questions and ethical dilemmas should be addressed before burial grounds are excavated and human remains are displayed. These issues are not limited to Native Americans. Indeed, the placement of human remains at the new National September 11th Memorial Museum has raised some of these same issues (Colwell-Chanthaphonh and Thomas 2011: 4). As these cases demonstrate, consultation and respect are critical in the study of human skeletal remains.

Cremation is becoming increasingly accepted as an appropriate form of burial in the twenty-first century. Cremains (the term for the finely ground cremated remains) and their containers are part of a growing archaeological record of twenty-first-century life. Although cremains are commonly placed in columbaria or buried in small cemetery plots, sometimes they are transformed into synthetic diamonds (Cullen 2006: 67). Indeed, ashes have also been incorporated into artificial concrete reefs for at-sea burial (Cullen 2006: 88). Columbaria in cemeteries might be an area for future investigation. In columbarium niches, families are allowed to place memorabilia in addition to the urn with the ashes. Archaeologists can investigate questions such as, What memorabilia are exhibited? What ethnic groups use cremation? and Are there ethnic, religious, and socioeconomic differences within these columbaria?

So is there such a thing as an American cemetery, burial, or grave-marking tradition? The answer is yes. In this book we examine American burial places dating from the seventeenth century to today. Although our study is not exhaustive, some patterns are clear. American burial traditions derive from earlier practices: European, Native American, African, and Asian. Although never entirely separate from these earlier traditions, America's patterns of memorialization reflect a unique history. During the colonial period, vibrant regional gravestone carving traditions developed in New England, New York and New Jersey, Philadelphia, and the Southeast. These traditions, based on local materials, were influenced by regional consumption patterns, as well as religious, cultural, and ethnic traditions. In some areas lacking local stones, such as southern New Jersey, trade networks also impacted consumer choices. The slate and sandstone markers used in the colonial period were common well into the early nineteenth century, when they were replaced by marble markers, often carved in a neoclassical style, a trend noted throughout eastern North America. Later, granite and more recently bronze memorials placed flush with the ground to facilitate mowing have become commonplace.

The stark class differences in American culture are clearly evident in burial grounds. In the colonial period, only the upper and middle classes received permanent markers. Geography and geology also affected commemoration, and in many parts of the United States impermanent wooden markers were the norm. In the United States as in Great Britain (Tarlow 1999; Mytum 2004), the early nineteenth century saw a tremendous increase in the number of gravemarkers (Veit 2009). However, minority groups and the poor were often as disenfranchised in death as they had been in life, buried in less desirable locations without the benefit of professionally produced markers. The Civil War transformed American deathways with massive military cemeteries, government-issued markers, and an increasing acceptance of embalming. Later, Gilded Age robber barons erected mausoleums that are, as they say, to die for, while new immigrants brought traditions of iron markers, ceramic gravemarkers, and marble statuary to America's burial grounds. Overseas Chinese immigrants used principles from geomancy to lay out burials in auspicious locations and when possible exhumed and returned their ancestors' remains to China for final burial. Today, the raw material for gravemarkers, especially granite, is increasingly imported from overseas, where it can be quarried and cut more cheaply than here in the United States. This is introducing a richer palette of colors into the cemetery but also challenging local monument manufacturers.

America's history of religious freedom stands in marked contrast to European countries with state religions. The clear separation of church and state in the Constitution adds to the American religious experience reflected in the cemeteries. For example, in the nineteenth century some iconography on markers reflected religious views of Protestants, Catholics, Jews, and Mormons. Also, the placement of the Chinese American graves reflects the use of feng shui connected to Daoist philosophy.

The industrial growth of America and its devastating Civil War contributed to the need for rapid population growth. The waves of immigration brought together a mosaic of different cultures, creating a diversity of burial landscapes not seen elsewhere in Europe, where government edicts limited commemoration by certain groups of people (Sayer 2011: 132). The ethnic diversity in the markers also reflects the resistance of the immigrants to totally assimilate into the idealized American melting pot.

American cemetery design also has its own unique trajectory. The organization and design of places of burial in America drew on earlier European antecedents, including in-church burial and the creation of churchyards and later cemeteries. Some European practices, such as charnel houses and the reuse of space in graveyards, were uncommon in early America, likely reflecting the relative ease with which property could be obtained. Another by-product of the ready availability of land was the permanent family plot within the cemetery. American attitudes toward land and the availability of land shaped burial practices here.

In early America, graveyards, churchyards, family plots, and single graves, called frontier graves by David Sloane (1991: 4), were the norm. However, graveyards and churchyards, especially those located in urban areas, rapidly became overcrowded. They were seen as eyesores and believed to contribute to the ill health of neighbors. In urban areas, potter's fields for the burial of the indigent also became common. However, unlike in much of Europe where burial plots were rented or crypts were used and reused (Sloane 1991: 19), American burials were generally seen as permanent. With permanent grave sites, Americans may have been more willing to invest in family monuments and family plots that could have markers added in the future.

The urban demographic pressures that created the first cemeteries in Europe were also felt here, and architectural styles such as the Egyptian and Gothic revival styles were also international. Inspired by European antecedents, such as Paris's Père-Lachaise, and local pressures, Americans began to lay out cemeteries by the early nineteenth century. Grove Street Cemetery (1797) in New Haven, Connecticut, is generally recognized as the first, but others were also created. Most, unlike Grove Street, were modest in scale and soon became overcrowded. At Grove Street and its successors, there was a new focus on family burial plots. By the 1830s, the rural cemetery movement had begun, with an emphasis on carefully landscaped grounds interspersed with monumental memorials. Run by private corporations, Mount Auburn in Watertown and Cambridge, Massachusetts (1831), Laurel Hill in Philadelphia (1836), and Green-Wood in Brooklyn, New York (1838), are recognized as the first three American rural cemeteries. Again, the emphasis was on family lots, permanent commemoration, and beautiful landscaping. Often the founders of these cemeteries had an interest in horticulture as well as commemoration. Later still, Adolph Strauch in Spring Grove, Cincinnati, began a new style of cemetery, the lawn-park cemetery, which was simpler and more spacious. Strauch wanted to avoid the forests of monuments that had come to clutter the rural cemeteries (Sloane 1991: 104). Professional managers or superintendents were also the norm with these cemeteries, which were generally run by a board of directors.

In 1913, another visionary cemetarian, Hubert Eaton, transformed American burial practices with the creation of Forest Lawn Memorial Park in Glendale, California (Sloane 1991: 159). Instead of individual or family monuments, flush-to-the-ground markers became the norm, and community mausoleums were also installed. The property was beautifully landscaped and ornamented with uplifting and historically inspired statuary. This was a burial place for the twentieth century, and Eaton's ideas soon spread coast to coast. The American way of death had become big business (Mitford 1963, 2000).

Unlike European cemeteries, American burial places have followed their own trajectory, shaped by the availability of land, an emphasis on families, and a strong commercial streak. Today, memorial parks and cemeteries compete for business. There was and still is an emphasis on privately owned, entrepreneurial cemeteries, which operate as businesses (Sloane 1991: 6). Today's massive mausoleums and columbaria, the equivalent of permanent condominiums, inexpensively built but veneered in gleaming granite, are but the latest stage in the evolution of the American burial place.

Human remains also speak to the American experience, from the bones of early settlers who suffered from starvation at Jamestown Island to the wealthy but illness-wracked Calverts interred in extravagant lead coffins. The African Burial Ground in New York City and the Freedman's Cemetery in Dallas, Texas, provide insight into the lives and tribulations faced by African Americans in a world of intense prejudice and social injustice and have powerful messages for modern Americans. While the remains unearthed from the vaults of New York City's Spring Street Church show the range of ills that can befall the human body, here and elsewhere there is evidence of not only the diseases that afflicted early Americans and the injuries they suffered but also medical interventions (Crist 2010; Novak and Willoughby 2010). Recent remains bear witness to changing medical technologies that allow skillful surgeons to replace knees and hips and strengthen broken or failing bones (Owsley and Bruwelheide 2009).

Native American remains have long been an object of archaeological study. Their graves were all too often excavated with little regard for the concerns of descendant communities. This has begun to change thanks to the passage of NAGPRA, but challenges remain. It is our opinion that archaeologists must work collaboratively with all descendant groups if their work is to be accepted.

Today, Americans are incorporating new technology including engraving digital images on stones and sending cremains into low Earth orbit. Many historic burial places are celebrated through tours and workshops and as important public spaces. The Association for Gravestone Studies has a well-attended yearly conference, affectionately nicknamed Gravestone Camp by its participants, that features tours, workshops, and lectures on all things related to cemeteries. At the same time, however, many urban cemeteries are abandoned, vandalized, and sometimes home to vagrants and sites of prostitution and drug dealing. Rural cemeteries sometimes are neglected, overgrown, and plowed under. Americans, it seems, have mixed feelings about the dead. Nevertheless, American cemeteries reflect the cultural mosaic and historical trajectory of the nation. The cemeteries and their permanent residents provide an unparalleled historical record of American culture. They are worth studying.

References Cited

Abraham, Terry, and Priscilla Wegars
2005   Respecting the Dead: Chinese Cemeteries and Burial Practices in the Interior Pacific Northwest. In *Chinese American Death Rituals: Respecting the Ancestors*, edited by Sue Fawn Chung and Priscilla Wegars, 147–73. AltaMira Press, Lanham, Md.

Ahlstrom, Sydney E.
1972   *A Religious History of the American People.* Yale University Press, New Haven, Conn.

Alden, Timothy
1814   *A Collection of American Epitaphs and Inscriptions with Occasional Notes.* S. Marks, New York.

Allen, Peter
1968   An Investigation into the Validity of a Fundamental Assumption of Archaeology Utilizing Data from New England Gravestones. Master's thesis, Department of Anthropology, Brown University, Providence, R.I.

Ames, Kenneth L.
1981 Ideologies in Stone: Meanings in Victorian Gravestones. *Journal of Popular Culture* 14 (4): 641–56.

Anderson, Ruth E.
1981   Symbolism, Symbiosis, and Survival: Roles of Young Women of the Kalderaša in Philadelphia. In *The American Kalderaš Gypsies in the New World*, edited by Matt T. Salo, 11–29. Gypsy Lore Society, North American Chapter, Centenary College, Hackettstown, N.J.

Aries, Philippe
1974   *Western Attitudes towards Death from the Middle Ages to the Present.* Johns Hopkins University Press, Baltimore, Md.

Atalay, Sonya
2006   Indigenous Archaeology as Decolonizing Practice. *American Indian Quarterly* 30 (3–4): 280–310.

Audin, Michael, Sarah Hlubik, and Erol Kavountzis
2005   Phase III Cemetery Excavation of the Old First Presbyterian Church, Newark Downtown Core Redevelopment Project, Newark, Essex County, New Jersey. Prepared for the City of Newark by Langan Engineering and Environmental Services, Elmwood Park, N.J.

Audin, Michael, and Scott Warnasch
2011   Newark's Iron Coffins. Paper presented at the May 2011 meeting of the Archaeological Society of New Jersey, Roebling, N.J.

Barba, Preston A.
1954   *Pennsylvania German Tombstones: A Study in Folk Art.* Pennsylvania German Folklore Society, Allentown.

Barber, John Warner
1837   *Historical Collections, Being a General Collection of Interesting Facts, Traditions, Biographical Sketches, Anecdotes, & etc. Relating to the History and Antiquities of Every Town in Connecticut, with Geographical Descriptions.* Durie, Peck, and J. W. Barber, New Haven, Conn.
1848   *Historical Collections, Being a General Collection of Interesting Facts, Traditions, Biographical Sketches, Anecdotes, & etc. Relating to the History and Antiquities of Every Town in Massachusetts, with Geographical Descriptions.* Warren Lazell, Worcester, Mass.

Barber, John Warner, and Henry Howe
1844   *Historical Collections of the State of New Jersey: Containing a General Collection of the Most Interesting Facts, Traditions, Biographical Sketches, Anecdotes, etc., Relating to Its History and Antiquities, with Geographical Descriptions of Every Township in the State.* B. Olds, Newark, N.J.
1845   *Historical Collections of the State of New York: Containing a General Collection of the Most Interesting Facts, Traditions, Biographical Sketches, Anecdotes, etc., Relating to Its History and Antiquities, with Geographical Descriptions of Every Township in the State.* S. Tuttle, Chatham Square, New York.

Barber, Russell J.
1993   The Agua Mansa Cemetery: An Indicator of Ethnic Identification in a Mexican-American Community. In *Ethnicity and the American Cemetery*, edited by Richard E. Meyer, 156–72. Bowling Green State University Popular Press, Bowling Green, Ohio.

Barth, Fredrik (editor)
1969   *Ethnic Groups and Boundaries: The Social Organization of Cultural Difference.* Waveland Press, Long Grove, Ill.

Baugher, Sherene
2005   Sacredness, Sensitivity, and Significance: The Controversy over Native American Sacred Sites. In *Heritage of Value, Archaeology of Renown: Reshaping Archaeological Assessment and Significance*, edited by Clay Mathers, Tim Darvill, and Barbara Little, 248–75. University Press of Florida, Gainesville.
2009   The John Street Methodist Church: An Archaeological Excavation with Native American Cooperation. *Historical Archaeology* 43 (1): 46–64.

Baugher, Sherene, Judith Guston, Edward J. Lenik, Diane Dallal, Thomas Amorosi, Daniel Russell, and Bobbi Brickman
1991   The John Street United Methodist Church: An Archaeological Investigation. Prepared for the John Street Methodist Church, New York, by the Archaeology Program of New York City Landmarks Preservation Commission.

Baugher, Sherene, Gina Santucci, Robert W. Venables, and Gaynell Stone

1989   *Preserving Historic Cemeteries: New York City Landmarks Preservation Commission Gravestone Project.* Brochure. New York City Landmarks Preservation Commission, New York.

Baugher, Sherene, and Richard Veit

2013   John Zuricher, Stone Cutter, and His Imprint on the Religious Landscape of Colonial New York. In *Tales of Gotham: Historic Archaeology and Ethnohistory in New York,* edited by Meta Janowitz and Diane Dallal, 225–48. Springer, New York.

Baugher, Sherene, and Frederick A. Winter

1983   Early American Gravestones: Archaeological Perspectives on Three Cemeteries of Old New York. *Archaeology* 36 (5): 46–54.

Bell, Edward L.

1990   The Historical Archaeology of Mortuary Behavior: Coffin Hardware from Uxbridge, Massachusetts. *Historical Archaeology* 24 (3): 54–78.

1991   Artifacts from the Almshouse Burial Ground. In *Archaeological Excavations at the Uxbridge Almshouse, Burial Ground in Uxbridge, Massachusetts,* edited by Ricardo J. Elia and Al. B. Wesolowsky, 254–84. BAR International Series 564. British Archaeological Reports, Oxford.

1994   *Vestiges of Mortality and Remembrance: A Bibliography on the Historical Archaeology of Cemeteries.* Scarecrow Press, Metuchen, N.J.

Bellantoni, Nicholas F., and David A. Poirier (editors)

1997   *In Remembrance: Archaeology and Death.* Praeger, New York.

Bellantoni, Nicholas F., Paul S. Sledzik, and David A. Poirier

1997   Rescue, Research, and Reburial: Walton Family Cemetery, Griswold, Connecticut. In *In Remembrance: Archaeology and Death,* edited by David A. Poirier and Nicholas F. Bellantoni, 131–54. Bergin and Garvey, Westport, Conn.

Bellantoni, Nicholas, Roger Thompson, David Cooke, Michael Park, and Cynthia Trayling

2007   The Life, Death, Archaeological Exhumation, and Reinterment of Opukaha'ia (Henry Obookiah), 1792–1818. *Connecticut History* 46 (2): 206–26.

Bello, Charles A.

2007   Recording and Analysis of the Russian Orthodox (Native Aleut) and Public Cemetery, Unalaska, Alaska. Paper presented at the World Archaeological Conference, Kingston, Jamaica.

Benes, Peter

1977   *The Masks of Orthodoxy: Folk Gravestone Carvings in Plymouth County, Massachusetts, 1689–1805.* University of Massachusetts Press, Amherst.

Benrimo, Nancy

1966   *Camposantos: A Photographic Essay.* Amon Carter Museum of Western Art, Fort Worth, Tex.

Bergman, Edward F.

1995   Cemeteries. In *The Encyclopedia of New York City,* edited by Kenneth T. Jackson, 195–96. Yale University Press, New Haven, Conn.

Bianco, Barbara A., Christopher R. DeCorse, and Jean Howson
2009   Beads and Other Adornment. In *The New York African Burial Ground: Unearthing the African Presence in Colonial New York*, vol. 2, *The Archaeology of the New York African Burial Ground*, edited by Warren R. Perry, Jean Howson, and Barbara A Bianco, 321–47. Howard University Press, Washington, D.C.

Binford, Lewis R.
1971   Mortuary Practices: Their Study and Potential. In *Approaches to the Social Dimensions of Mortuary Practices*, edited by James A. Brown, 6–29. Memoirs of the Society for American Archaeology no. 25. Society for American Archaeology, Washington, D.C.

Binford, Sally R., and Lewis R. Binford
1968   *New Perspectives in Archaeology*. Aldine, Chicago.

Blakely, Robert L., and Judith M. Harrington (editors)
1997   *Bones in the Basement: Postmortem Racism in Nineteenth-Century Medical Training*. Smithsonian Institution Press, Washington, D.C.

Blakey, Michael L.
1992   Research Design for the Temporary Curation and Anthropological Analysis of the "Negro Burying Ground" (Foley Square) Archaeological Population at Howard University. In *Hearings before the Subcommittee on Public Buildings and Grounds of the Committee on the Public Works and Transportation, House of Representatives, One Hundred Second Congress, Second Session*. U.S. Government Printing Office, Washington, D.C.
2009   Introduction to *The New York African Burial Ground: Unearthing the African Presence in Colonial New York*, vol. 1, *The Skeletal Biology of the New York African Burial Ground*, edited by Michael L. Blakey and Lesley M. Rankin-Hill, 3–18. Howard University Press, Washington, D.C.

Blakey, M. L., L. M. Rankin-Hill, A. H. Hill, and F. L. C. Jackson
2009   Discussion. In *The New York African Burial Ground: Unearthing the African Presence in Colonial New York*, vol. 1, *The Skeletal Biology of the New York African Burial Ground*, edited by Michael L. Blakey and Lesley M. Rankin-Hill, 269–73. Howard University Press, Washington, D.C.

Blouet, Helen
2010   Marking Life and Death on St. John, Virgin Islands, 1718–1950: An Historical Archaeology of Commemoration through Objects, Space, and Transformation. Doctoral dissertation, Department of Anthropology, Syracuse University, Syracuse, New York.

Bolton, H. Carrington
1891   Decoration of Graves of Negroes in South Carolina. *Journal of American Folklore* 4: 214.

Bonomi, Patricia
1971   *A Fractious People: Politics and Society in Colonial New York*. Columbia University Press, New York.

Bradford, William, and Edward Winslow
1966 [1622] *Journall of the English Plantation at Plimoth*. Reprint of 1866 edition; University Microfilms, Ann Arbor, Mich.

Bragdon, Kathleen J.
1996 *Native People of Southern New England, 1500–1650*. University of Oklahoma Press, Norman.
1999 Ethnohistory, Historical Archaeology, and the Rise of Social Complexity in Native North America: Case Studies from Southern New England. In *Old and New Worlds*, edited by Geoff Egan and R. L. Michael, 84–95. Oxbow Books, Oxford, U.K.

Bray, Tamara L. (editor)
2001 *The Future of the Past: Archaeologists, Native Americans, and Repatriation*. Garland Publishing, New York.

Brenner, Elise M.
1988 Sociopolitical Implications of Mortuary Ritual Remains in Seventeenth-Century Native Southern New England. In *The Recovery of Meaning*, edited by Mark P. Leone and Parker B. Potter Jr., 147–81. Smithsonian Institution Press, Washington, D.C.

Bridenbaugh, Carl
1966 *Cities in the Wilderness: The First Century of Urban Life in America, 1625–1742*. Oxford University Press, London.

Bromberg, Francine W., and Steven J. Shephard
2006 The Quaker Burying Ground in Alexandria, Virginia: A Study of Burial Practices of the Religious Society of Friends. *Historical Archaeology* 40 (1): 57–88.

Brooks, Michael, and Andrew Waskie
N.d. *A Guide to the Famous and Blameless in Laurel Hill Cemetery*. Laurel Hill Cemetery, Philadelphia.

Brown, Dona
1995 *Inventing New England: Regional Tourism in the Nineteenth Century*. Smithsonian Institution Press, Washington, D.C.

Brown, Ian W.
1992 The Lamson-Carved Gravestones of Watertown, Massachusetts. In *The Art and Mystery of Historical Archaeology: Essays in Honor of James Deetz,* edited by Anne Elizabeth Yentsch and Mary C. Beaudry, 165–94. CRC Press, Boca Raton, Fla.
2007 Statements of Power: Cemeteries on Indian Mounds. Paper presented at the Association for Gravestone Studies Thirtieth National Conference and Meeting, Nashua, N.H., June 20–24, 2007.

Brown, James P.
1971 The Dimension of Status in the Burials at Spiro. In *Approaches to the Social Dimensions of Mortuary Practices*, edited by James A. Brown, 92–112. Society for American Archaeology Memoir 25. Society for American Archaeology, Washington, D.C.

Buikstra, Jane E.

1981   A Specialist in Ancient Cemetery Studies Looks at the Reburial Issue. *Early Man* 3 (3): 26–27.

2000   Summary and Conclusions. In *Never Anything So Solemn: An Archaeological, Biological, and Historical Investigation of the Nineteenth-Century Grafton Cemetery*, edited by Jane E. Buikstra, Jodie A. O'Gorman, and Cynthia Sutton, 142–45. Center for American Archaeology, Kampsville, Ill.

Burnston, Sharon Ann

1997a   The Invisible People: The Cemetery at Catoctin Furnace. In *In Remembrance: Archaeology and Death*, edited by David A. Poirier and Nicholas F. Bellantoni, 93–104. Bergin and Garvey, Westport, Conn.

1997b   Babies in the Well: An Insight into Deviant Behavior in Eighteenth-Century Philadelphia. In *In Remembrance: Archaeology and Death*, edited by David A. Poirier and Nicholas F. Bellantoni, 51–64. Bergin and Garvey, Westport, Conn.

Bushman, Richard L.

1971   The Great Awakening in Connecticut. In *Essays in Political and Social Development in Colonial America*, edited by Stanley N. Katz, 297–308. Little, Brown, Boston.

Cadzow, Donald A.

1936   *Archaeological Studies of the Susquehannock Indians of Pennsylvania*. Safe Harbor Report No. 2. Pennsylvania Historical Commission, Harrisburg.

Cannon, Aubrey

1989   The Historic Dimension in Mortuary Expressions of Status and Sentiment. *Current Anthropology* 30 (4): 437–58.

Cantwell, Anne-Marie, and Diana diZerega Wall

2001   *Unearthing Gotham: The Archaeology of New York City*. Yale University Press, New Haven, Conn.

Carr, Christopher

1995   Mortuary Practices: Their Social, Philosophical-Religious, Circumstantial, and Physical Determinants. *Journal of Archaeological Method and Theory* 2 (2): 105–200.

Chance, Paul C.

2005   On Dying American: Cantonese Rites for Death and Ghost-Spirits in an American City. In *Chinese American Death Rituals: Respecting the Ancestors*, edited by Sue Fawn Chung and Priscilla Wegars, 47–79. AltaMira Press, Lanham, Md.

Chapman, Robert, Ian Kinnes, and Kavs Randsborg (editors)

1981   *The Archaeology of Death*. Cambridge University Press, Cambridge.

Chase, T., and Laurel K. Gabel

1997   *Gravestone Chronicles*. 2 vols. 2nd ed. New England Historic Genealogical Society, Boston.

Childe, Vere Gordon

1945   Directional Changes in Funerary Practices during 50,000 Years. *Man* 45: 13–19.

Chung, Sue Fawn, Fred P. Frampton, and Timothy W. Murphy

2005   Venerate These Bones: Chinese American Funerary and Burial Practices as Seen in Carlin, Elko County, Nevada. In *Chinese American Death Rituals: Respecting the Ancestors*, edited by Sue Fawn Chung and Priscilla Wegars, 107–45. AltaMira Press, Lanham, Md.

Chung, Sue Fawn, and Reiko Neizman
2005   Remembering Ancestors in Hawai'i. In *Chinese American Death Rituals: Respecting the Ancestors*, edited by Sue Fawn Chung and Priscilla Wegars, 175–94. AltaMira Press, Lanham, Md.

Chung, Sue Fawn, and Priscilla Wegars
2005   Introduction to *Chinese American Death Rituals: Respecting the Ancestors*, edited by Sue Fawn Chung and Priscilla Wegars, 1–17. AltaMira Press, Lanham, Md.

Cipolla, Craig N.
2010   The Dualities of Endurance: A Collaborative Historical Archaeology of Ethnogenesis at Brothertown, 1780–1910. Publicly accessible University of Pennsylvania dissertations. Paper 162. http://repository.upenn.edu/edissertations/162.

Cirlot, Juan Eduardo
1971   *Dictionary of Symbols*. 2nd ed. Philosophical Library, New York.

Clark, Lynn
1987   Gravestones: Reflectors of Ethnicity or Class. In *Consumer Choice in Historical Archaeology*, edited by Suzanne M. Spencer-Wood, 383–96. Plenum Press, New York.

Clébert, Jean Paul
1963   *The Gypsies*. E. P. Dutton, New York.

Colwell-Chanthaphonh, Chip
2010   Opening America's skeleton closets. *Denver Post,* May 9, 2010. http://www.denverpost.com/opinion/ci_15034481 (accessed April 30, 2011).

Colwell-Chanthaphonh, Chip, and T. J. Ferguson (editors)
2008   *Collaboration in Archaeological Practice: Engaging Descendant Communities*. AltaMira Press, Lanham, Md.

Colwell-Chanthaphonh, Chip, and David Hurst Thomas
2011   Unidentified Human Remains and the 9/11 Museum. *Anthropology News* 52 (6): 4, 12.

Combs, Diana Williams
1986   *Early Gravestone Art in Georgia and South Carolina*. University of Georgia Press, Athens.

Cook, Lauren
1991   The Uxbridge Poor Farm in the Documentary Record. In *Archaeological Excavations at the Uxbridge Almshouse, Burial Ground in Uxbridge, Massachusetts*, edited by Ricardo J. Elia and Al B. Wesolowsky, 40–82. BAR International Series 564. British Archaeological Reports, Oxford.

Cooper, J. C.
1978   *An Illustrated Encyclopedia of Traditional Symbols*. Thames and Hudson, London.

Cordell, Linda S.
1992   Durango to Durango: An Overview of the Southwest Heartland. In *Columbian Consequences*, vol. 1, *Archaeological and Historical Perspectives on the Spanish*

Borderlands West, edited by David Hurst Thomas, 17–41. Smithsonian Institution Press, Washington, D.C.

Costello, Julia G., and David Hornbeck

1992   Alta California: An Overview. In *Columbian Consequences*, vol. 1, *Archaeological and Historical Perspectives on the Spanish Borderlands West*, edited by David Hurst Thomas, 303–33. Smithsonian Institution Press, Washington, D.C.

Cotter, John L.

1958   *New Discoveries at Jamestown: Site of the First Successful English Settlement in America*. U.S. Government Printing Office, Washington, D.C.

Crist, Thomas

2002   Empowerment, Ecology, and Evidence: The Relevance of Mortuary Archaeology to the Public. In *Public Benefits of Archaeology*, edited by Barbara J. Little, 101–17. University Press of Florida, Gainesville.

2010   "That Class of Persons Who Cannot Afford a Pew": Analysis of the Human Remains from the Spring Street Presbyterian Church Burial Vaults. *Northeast Historical Archaeology* 39: 65–97.

Crist, Thomas A. J., and Daniel G. Roberts

1996   An Archaeological Investigation of Washington Square, Philadelphia, Pennsylvania. Prepared for the Delta Group, Philadelphia, Penn., by John Milner Associates, West Chester, Penn. http://www.phillyarchaeology.org/reports/pdf/Washington-Square-1996.pdf (accessed August 8, 2011).

Crist, Thomas A. J., Daniel G. Roberts, Reginald H. Pitts, John P. McCarthy, and Michael Parrington

1997   The First African Baptist Church Cemeteries: African-American Mortality and Trauma in Antebellum Pennsylvania. In *In Remembrance: Archaeology and Death*, edited by David A. Poirier and Nicholas F. Bellantoni, 19–50. Bergin and Garvey, Westport, Conn.

Crosby, Constance A.

1988   From Myth to History, or Why King Philip's Ghost Walks Abroad. In *The Recovery of Meaning: Historical Archaeology in the Eastern United States*, edited by Mark P. Leone and Parker B. Potter Jr., 183–210. Smithsonian Institution Press, Washington, D.C.

Crowell, Elizabeth Anne

1981   Philadelphia Gravestones: 1740–1820. *Northeast Historical Archaeology* 10: 23–29.

1983   Migratory Monuments and Missing Motifs: Archaeology Analysis of Mortuary Art in Cape May County, New Jersey, 1740–1810. Doctoral dissertation, Department of Anthropology, University of Pennsylvania, Philadelphia.

Crowell, Elizabeth A., and Norman Vardney Mackie III

1990   The Funerary Monuments and Burial Patterns of Colonial Tidewater Virginia, 1607–1776. *Markers* 7: 103–38.

Cullen, Lisa Takeuchi

2006   *Remember Me: A Lively Tour of the New American Way of Death*. Collins, New York.

Cunningham, Keith

1989   Navajo, Mormon, Zuni Graves: Navajo, Mormon, Zuni Ways. In *Cemeteries and Gravemarkers: Voices of American Culture*, edited by Richard E. Meyer, 197–217. UMI Research Press, Ann Arbor, Mich.

Curl, James Stevens

1993   *A Celebration of Death: An Introduction to Some of the Buildings, Monuments, and Settings of Funerary Architecture in the Western European Tradition.* B. T. Batsford, London.

Curry, Dennis

1999   *Feast of the Dead: Aboriginal Ossuaries in Maryland.* Maryland Historical Trust Press, Crownsville.

Daehnke, Jon, and Amy Lonetree

2011   Repatriation in the United States: The Current State of the Native American Graves Protection and Repatriation Act. *American Indian Culture and Research Journal* 35 (1): 87–97.

Dally, Joseph W.

1873   *Woodbridge and Vicinity: The Story of a New Jersey Township.* A. E. Gordon, New Brunswick, N.J.

Davidson, James Michael

2004   Mediating Race and Class through the Death Experience: Power Relations and Resistance Strategies of an African-American Community, Dallas, Texas, 1869–1907. Doctoral dissertation, Department of Anthropology, University of Texas, Austin.

DeCorse, Christopher R.

1999   Oceans Apart: Africanist Perspectives on Diaspora Archaeology. In *"I, Too, Am America": Archaeological Studies of African-American Life*, edited by Theresa A. Singleton, 132–58. University of Virginia Press, Charlottesville.

Deetz, James

1965   *The Dynamics of Stylistic Change in Arikara Ceramics.* University of Illinois Press, Urbana.

1977   *In Small Things Forgotten.* Anchor Books, New York.

Deetz, James, and Patricia Scott Deetz

2000   *The Times of Their Lives: Life, Love, and Death in Plymouth Colony.* W. H. Freeman, New York.

Deetz, James, and Edwin Dethlefsen

1965   The Doppler Effect and Archaeology: A Consideration of the Spatial Aspects of Seriation. *Southwestern Journal of Anthropology* 21 (3): 196–206.

1967   Death's Head, Cherub, Urn and Willow. *Natural History* 76 (3): 29–37.

1971   Some Social Aspects of New England Colonial Mortuary Art. *American Antiquity* 36: 30–38.

Deloria, Vine, Jr.

1969   *Custer Died for Your Sins.* Macmillan, New York.

1994   *God Is Red: A Native View of Religion.* Fulcrum Publishing, Golden, Colo.

Dethlefsen, Edwin

1992 Strange Attractors and the Cemetery Set. In *The Art and Mystery of Historical Archaeology: Essays in Honor of James Deetz*, edited by Anne Elizabeth Yentsch and Mary Beaudry, 149–65. CRC Press, Boca Raton, Fla.

Dethlefsen, Edwin, and James Deetz

1966 Death's Heads, Cherubs and Willow Trees: Experimental Archaeology in Colonial Cemeteries. *American Antiquity* 31 (4): 502–10.

1967 Eighteenth Century Cemeteries: A Demographic View. *Historical Archaeology* 1: 40–42.

Dethlefsen, Edwin S., and Kenneth Jensen

1977 Social Commentary from the Cemetery. *Natural History* 86 (6): 32–39.

de Vries, Ad

1974 *Dictionary of Symbols and Imagery*. North Holland Publishing, Amsterdam, The Netherlands.

Diamond, Joseph

2006 Owned in Life, Owned in Death: The Pine Street African and African-American Burial Ground in Kingston, New York. *Northeast Historical Archaeology* 35: 47–62.

Dongoske, Kurt E., Mark Aldenderfer, and Karen Doehner (editors)

2000 *Working Together: Native Americans and Archaeologists*. Society for American Archaeology, Washington, D.C.

Douglas, Mary

1966 *Purity and Danger: An Analysis of Concepts of Pollution and Taboo*. Praeger, New York.

Duval, Francis Y., and Ivan B. Rigby

1978 *Early American Gravestone Art in Photos*. Dover Publications, New York.

Earle, Timothy

1963 Chatham, Massachusetts: A Study in Death. Paper prepared for Anthropology 112, Harvard University. Manuscript on file at Tozzer Library, Harvard University, Cambridge, Mass.

Echo-Hawk, Walter E., and Roger C. Echo-Hawk

1991 Repatriation, Reburial, and Religious Rights. In *Handbook of American Indian Religious Freedom*, edited by Christopher Vecsey, 63–80. Crossroad Publishing, New York.

Elia, Ricardo J.

1992 Silent Stones in a Potter's Field: Grave Markers at the Almshouse Burial Ground in Uxbridge, Massachusetts. *Markers* 9: 132–57.

Elia, Ricardo J., and Al B. Wesolowsky (editors)

1991 *Archaeological Excavations at the Uxbridge Almshouse, Burial Ground in Uxbridge, Massachusetts*. BAR International Series 564. British Archaeological Reports, Oxford.

Elliott, Bruce S.

2011 Memorializing the Civil War Dead: Modernity and Corruption under the Grant Administration. *Markers* 27: 14–55.

Ellis, Meredith A. B.

2010   The Children of Spring Street: Rickets in an Early Nineteenth-Century Congrega-
       tion. *Northeast Historical Archaeology* 39: 120–34.

Erwin, Paul F.

1993   Scottish, Irish, and Rom Gypsy Funeral Customs and Gravestones in Cincinnati
       Cemeteries. In *Ethnicity and the American Cemetery*, edited by Richard E. Meyer,
       104–30. Bowling Green State University Popular Press, Bowling Green, Ohio.

Fagan, Brian

2005   *A Brief History of Archaeology: Classical Times to the Twenty-First Century.* Pear-
       son Prentice Hall, New York.

Farber, Daniel

1975   Massachusetts Gravestones. *Antiques* 107 (6): 1122–29.

Farber, Daniel, and Jessie Lie Farber

1988   Early Pennsylvania Gravemarkers. *Markers* 5: 96–121.

Faulkner, William

1942   *Go Down Moses.* Random House, New York.

Faust, Drew Gilpin

2008   *This Republic of Suffering: Death and the American Civil War.* Random House,
       New York.

Ferguson, Leland

2011   *God's Fields: Landscape, Religion and Race in Moravian Wachovia.* University
       Press of Florida, Gainesville.

Ferguson, T. J.

2004   Academic, Legal, and Political Contexts of Social Identity and Cultural Affilia-
       tion Research in the Southwest. In *Identity, Feasting, and the Archaeology of the
       Greater Southwest*, edited by Barbara J. Mills, 27–41. University Press of Colorado,
       Boulder.

Fischer, David Hackett

1989   *Albion's Seed: Four British Folkways in America.* Oxford University Press, New
       York.

Fisher, Charles L.

2003   Trace Elements and Stable Isotope Analysis of the Human Remains from the Lu-
       theran Church Lot. In *People, Places, and Material Things: Historical Archaeology
       of Albany*, New York, edited by Charles L. Fisher, 63–68. New York State Museum
       Bulletin 499. University of the State of New York, New York State Education De-
       partment, Albany.

Fithian, Philip Vickers

1990   *The Beloved Cohansie of Philip Vickers Fithian.* Introduction and comments by F.
       Alan Palmer. Cumberland County Historical Society, Greenwich, N.J.

Fitts, Robert K.

1990   *Puritans, Yankees, and Gravestones: A Linguistic Analysis of New England Grave-
       stone Inscriptions.* Volumes in Historical Archaeology no. 15. South Carolina In-
       stitute of Archaeology and Anthropology, University of South Carolina, Colum-
       bia.

Foley, Vincent
1965   Bethlehem Pennsylvania—A Unique Historic Site. *Papers of the Fifth Annual Historic Sites Conference* 18 (3/2): 61–64.

Forbes, Harriette M.
1927   *Gravestones of Early New England and the Men Who Made Them, 1653–1800.* Houghton Mifflin, Boston.

Ford, James A.
1962   *A Quantitative Method for Deriving Cultural Chronology.* Pan-American Union, Washington, D.C.

Forman, Henry Chandlee
1938   *Jamestown and St. Mary's, Buried Cities of Romance.* Johns Hopkins University Press, Baltimore, Md.

Francaviglia, Richard V.
1971   The Cemetery as an Evolving Cultural Landscape. *Annals of the Association of American Geographers* 61 (3): 501–9.

Franklin, Benjamin
1987   *Benjamin Franklin: Essays, Articles, Bagatelles, Letters, Poor Richard's Almanack, and Autobiography.* Library of America, New York.

Fremmer, Ray
1973 Dishes in Colonial Graves: Evidence from Jamaica. *Historical Archaeology* 3: 58–62.

Gabel, Laurel
2009   Headstones, Hatchments, and Heraldry, 1650–1850. In *Markers* 26: 10–53.

Gallivan, Martin D.
2004   Reconnecting the Contact Period and Late Prehistory: Household and Community Dynamics in the James River Basin. In *Indian and European Contact in Context: The Mid-Atlantic Region,* edited by Dennis B. Blanton and Julia A. King, 22–46. University Press of Florida, Gainesville.

Gannon, Michael V.
1993   Introduction to *The Missions of La Florida,* edited by Bonnie G. McEwan, xxiii–xxvi. University Press of Florida, Gainesville.

Garman, James C.
1994   Viewing the Color Line through the Material Culture of Death. *Historical Archaeology* 28 (3): 74–92.

Genovese, Eugene
1972   *Roll Jordan Roll: The World the Slaves Made.* Pantheon, New York.

Gibson, Susan G. (editor)
1980   *Burr's Hill: A Seventeenth Century Wampanoag Burial Ground in Warren, Rhode Island.* Studies in Anthropology and Material Culture 2. Haffenreffer Museum of Anthropology, Providence, R.I.

Giguere, Joy M.
2007   Virtuous Women, Useful Men, and Lovely Children. *Markers* 24: 1–23.

Gillon, Edmund V.
1972   *Victorian Cemetery Art.* Dover Publications, New York.

Gilmore, William J.

1989   *Reading Becomes a Necessity of Life: Material and Cultural Life in Rural New England, 1780–1835.* University of Tennessee Press, Knoxville.

Glassie, Henry

1968   *Pattern in the Material Folk Culture of the Eastern United States.* University of Pennsylvania Press, Philadelphia.

Gluckman, Max

1937   Mortuary Customs and the Belief in Survival after Death among the South Eastern Bantu. *Bantu Studies* 11: 117–36.

Goodfriend, Joyce D.

1992   *Before the Melting Pot: Society and Culture in Colonial New York City, 1664–1730.* Princeton University Press, Princeton.

Goodwin, Conrad M.

1981   *Ethnicity in the Graveyard.* Master's thesis, Department of Anthropology, College of William and Mary, Williamsburg, Va.

Gorman, Frederick, and Michael DiBlasi

1976   Nonchronological Sources of Variation in the Seriation of Gravestone Motifs in the Northeast and Southeast Colonies. In *Puritan Gravestone Art*, edited by Peter Benes, 79–87. Boston University Press, Boston.

1981   Gravestone Iconography and Mortuary Ideology. *Ethnohistory* 28 (1): 79–98.

Gosnell, Lynn, and Suzanne Gott

1989   San Fernando Cemetery: Decorations of Love and Loss in a Mexican-American Community. In *Cemeteries and Gravemarkers, Voices of American Culture*, edited by Richard E. Meyer, 217–36. UMI Research Press, Ann Arbor, Mich.

Gradwohl, David Mayer

1993   The Jewish Cemeteries of Louisville, Kentucky: Mirrors of Historical Processes and Theological Diversity through 150 Years. *Markers* 10: 116–49.

1998   Benditcha Sea Vuestra Memoria: Sephardic Jewish Cemeteries in the Caribbean and Eastern North America. *Markers* 15: 1–29.

2007   *Like Tablets of the Law Thrown Down: The Colonial Jewish Burying Ground, Newport, Rhode Island.* Sigler Printing, Ames, Iowa.

Graves, Thomas

1988   Pennsylvania German Gravestones: An Introduction. *Markers* 5: 60–96.

1993   Keeping Ukraine Alive through Death: Ukrainian-American Gravestones as Cultural Markers. In *Ethnicity and the American Cemetery*, edited by Richard E. Meyer, 36–76. Bowling Green State University Popular Press, Bowling Green, Ohio.

Gray, Michael P.

2001   *The Business of Captivity: Elmira and Its Civil War Prison.* Kent State University Press, Kent, Ohio.

Greenwood, Roberta S.

2005   Old Rituals in New Lands: Bringing the Ancestors to America. In *Chinese American Death Rituals: Respecting the Ancestors*, edited by Sue Fawn Chung and Priscilla Wegars, 241–62. AltaMira Press, Lanham, Md.

2010   A Chinese Temple in California, Lost and Found. In *Archaeology and Preservation of Gendered Landscapes*, edited by Sherene Baugher and Suzanne M. Spencer-Wood, 273–90. Springer, New York.

Grumet, Robert S.

1995   *Historic Contact: Indian People and Colonists in Today's Northeastern United States in the Sixteenth through Eighteenth Centuries.* University of Oklahoma Press, Norman.

Habenstein, Robert W., and William M. Lamers

1981   *The History of American Funeral Directing.* 3rd ed. Bulfin Printers, Milwaukee, Wis.

Hacker-Norton, Debi, and Michael Trinkley

1984   *Remember Man Thou Art Dust: Coffin Hardware of the Early Twentieth Century.* Research Series 2. Chicora Foundation, Columbia, S.C.

Hall, David D.

1976   The Gravestone Image as a Puritan Cultural Code. In *Puritan Gravestone Art,* edited by Peter Benes, 23–32. Boston University Press, Boston.

Halporn, Roberta

1993   American Jewish Cemeteries: A Mirror of History. In *Ethnicity and the American Cemetery,* edited by Richard E. Meyer, 131–55. Bowling Green University Popular Press, Bowling Green, Ohio.

Hancock, Ian

1988   *We Are the Romani People.* University of Hertfordshire Press, Hertfordshire, U.K.

Hardy, Sandra J.

2003   *Pennsylvania German and German-American Gravestone Language and Symbol Guide.* Privately printed.

Harrington, Spencer P. M.

1993   Bones and Bureaucrats. *Archaeology* 46 (2): 28–38.

Harris, Gale, Jean Howson, and Betsey Bradley

1993   The African Burial Ground and the Commons Historic District Designation Report. Report on file at the New York City Landmarks Preservation Commission, New York.

Harris, William T.

1869   *Epitaphs from the Old Burying Ground in Watertown.* Privately printed, Boston.

Hawker, Ronald W.

1990   In the Way of the White Man's Totem Poles: Stone Monuments among Canada's Tsimshian Indians, 1879–1910. *Markers* 7: 213–31.

Heilen, Michael P.

2012   *Uncovering Identity in Mortuary Analysis: Community-Sensitive Methods for Identifying Group Affiliation in Historical Cemeteries.* Left Coast Press, Walnut Creek, Calif.

Heinrich, Adam

2003   "Remember Me . . ." but "Be Mindfull of Death": The Art of Commemoration in Eighteenth-Century Monmouth County, New Jersey. Manuscript on file with the author.

2012   Cherubs or *Putti*? Gravemarkers Demonstrating Conspicuous Consumption and the Rococo Fashion in the 18th Century. Paper presented at the annual conference of the Society for Historical Archaeology, Baltimore, Md.

Hertz, Robert

1960   *Death and the Right Hand*. Translated by Rodney and Claudia Needham. Free Press, Glencoe, Ill.

Hester, Thomas R.

1992   Texas and Northeastern Mexico: An Overview. In *Columbian Consequences*, vol. 1, *Archaeological and Historical Perspectives on the Spanish Borderlands West*, edited by David Hurst Thomas, 191–211. Smithsonian Institution Press, Washington, D.C.

Heye, George G., and George H. Pepper

1915   *Exploration of a Munsee Cemetery near Montague, New Jersey*. Contributions from the Museum of the American Indian, Heye Foundation, vol. 2, no. 1. Museum of the American Indian, Heye Foundation, New York.

Hijiya, James A.

1983   American Gravestones and Attitudes toward Death: A Brief History. *Proceedings of the American Philosophical Society* 127 (5): 339–63.

Hodder, Ian

1982a   Theoretical Archaeology: A Reactionary View. In *Symbolic and Structural Archaeology*, edited by Ian Hodder, 1–16. Cambridge University Press, Cambridge.

1982b   The Identification and Interpretation of Ranking in Prehistory: A Contextual Perspective. In *Ranking, Resource and Exchange: Aspects of the Archaeology of Early European Society*, edited by Colin Renfrew and Stephen Shennan, 150–54. Cambridge University Press, Cambridge.

Hodge, Christina J.

2005   Faith and Practice at an Early Eighteenth-Century Wampanoag Burial Ground: The Waldo Farm Site in Dartmouth, Massachusetts. *Historical Archaeology* 39 (4): 73–94.

Hodges, Graham Russell

1997   *Slavery and Freedom in the Rural North, African Americans in Monmouth County, New Jersey, 1665–1865*. Rowman and Littlefield, New York.

Horn, James, William Kelso, Douglas Owsley, and Beverly Straube

2013   *Jane: Starvation, Cannibalism, and Endurance at Jamestown*. Colonial Williamsburg Foundation and Preservation Virginia, Williamsburg.

Horton, Lauren N.

1997   The Remarkable Crosses of Charles Andera. *Markers* 14: 110–33.

Houdek, Diane, Jane E. Buikstra, and Christopher Stojanowski

2000   Osteological Analysis. In *Never Anything So Solemn: An Archaeological, Biological, and Historical Investigation of the Nineteenth-Century Grafton Cemetery*, edited by Jane E. Buikstra, Jodie A. O'Gorman, and Cynthia Sutton, 91–114. Center for American Archaeology, Kampsville, Ill.

Howard, Ronald W.

2001 The English Province (1664–1776). In *The Empire State: A History of New York*, edited by Milton M. Klein, 113–225. Cornell University Press, Ithaca, N.Y.

Howson, Jean, and Leonard G. Bianchi

2009 Coffins. In *The New York African Burial Ground: Unearthing the African Presence in Colonial New York*, vol. 2, *The Archaeology of the New York African Burial Ground*, edited by Warren R. Perry, Jean Howson, and Barbara A. Bianco, 213–45. Howard University Press, Washington, D.C.

Howson, Jean, Leonard G. Bianchi, and Warren R. Perry

2009 Introduction to *The New York African Burial Ground: Unearthing the African Presence in Colonial New York*, vol. 2, *The Archaeology of the New York African Burial Ground*, edited by Warren R. Perry, Jean Howson, and Barbara A. Bianco, 1–34. Howard University Press, Washington, D.C.

Howson, Jean, Barbara A. Bianco, and Steven Barto

2009 Documentary Evidence on the Origin and use of the African Burial Ground. In *The New York African Burial Ground: Unearthing the African Presence in Colonial New York*, vol. 2, *The Archaeology of the New York African Burial Ground*, edited by Warren R. Perry, Jean Howson, and Barbara A. Bianco, 35–66. Howard University Press, Washington, D.C.

Hrdklička, Aleš

1916 *Physical Anthropology of the Lenape or Delaware, and of the Eastern Indians in General.* Bulletin 62. Smithsonian Institution, Bureau of American Ethnology, Washington, D.C.

Hudson, J. Paul

1967 Knight's Tombstone at Jamestown, Virginia. *Antiques* 91 (June 1967): 760–61.

Huntington, Richard, and Peter Metcalf

1979 *Celebrations of Death: The Anthropology of Mortuary Ritual.* Cambridge University Press, Cambridge.

Inguanti, J. J.

2000 Domesticating the Grave: Italian American Memorial Practices at New York's Calvary Cemetery. *Markers* 17: 9–31.

Jackson, Charles O. (editor)

1977 *Passing: The Vision of Death in America.* Greenwood Press, Westport, Conn.

Jamieson, R. W.

1995 Material Culture and Social Death: African-American Burial Practices. *Historical Archaeology* 29 (4): 39–58.

Janowitz, Meta F.

1993 Indian Corn and Dutch Pots: Seventeenth-Century Foodways. In *New Amsterdam/New York: Health, Sanitation, and Foodways in Historical Archaeology*, edited by Joan H. Geismar and Meta F. Janowitz. Special issue, *Historical Archaeology* 27 (2): 6–24.

Jefferson, Thomas

1999 [1787] *Notes on the State of Virginia.* Edited with an introduction and notes by Frank Shuffelton. Penguin Books, New York.

Jemison, G. Peter
1997   Who Owns the Past? In *Native Americans and Archaeologists: Stepping Stones to Common Ground*, edited by Nina Swidler, Kurt E. Dongoske, Roger Anyon, and Alan S. Downer, 57–63. AltaMira Press, Walnut Creek, Calif.

Jordan, Terry G.
1982   *Texas Graveyards: A Cultural Legacy.* University of Texas Press, Austin.

Keegan, W. F.
1989   Stable Isotope Analysis of Prehistoric Diet. In *Reconstruction of Life from the Skeleton*, edited by M. Yasar Iscan and Kenneth A. R. Kennedy, 223–36. Alan R. Liss, New York.

Keister, Douglas
2004   *Stories in Stone: A Field Guide to Cemetery Symbolism and Iconography.* Gibbs Smith, Salt Lake City, Utah.

Kelso, William M.
2006   *Jamestown: The Buried Truth.* University of Virginia Press, Charlottesville.

Kelso, William M., J. Eric Deetz, Seth W. Mallios, and Beverly A. Straube
2001   *Jamestown Rediscovery VII.* Association for the Preservation of Virginia Antiquities, Richmond.

Kelso, William M., Nicholas M. Luccketti, and Beverly A. Straube
1998   *Jamestown Rediscovery IV.* Association for the Preservation of Virginia Antiquities, Richmond.

Kerr, Mathew
2009   In Reverence: A Plan for the Preservation of the Tolomato Cemetery, St. Augustine, Florida. Master's thesis, Department of City and Regional Planning, Cornell University, Ithaca, N.Y.

Killion, Thomas (editor)
2008   *Opening Archaeology: Repatriation's Impact on Contemporary Research and Practice.* School for Advanced Research Press, Santa Fe, N.Mex.

Klesert, Anthony L., and Shirley Powell
2000   A Perspective on Ethics and the Reburial Controversy. In *Repatriation Reader: Who Owns American Indian Remains?* edited by Devon A. Mihesuah, 200–210. University of Nebraska Press, Lincoln.

Kloberdanz, Timothy
2005   "Unser Lieber Gottesacker" (Our Dear God's Acre): An Iron-Cross Cemetery on the Northern Great Plains. *Markers* 22: 160–81.

Kniffen, Fred
1967   Necrogeography in the United States. *Geographical Review* 57: 426–27.

Kraft, Herbert C.
1993   The Minisink Site: A National Historical Landmark. *Bulletin of the Archaeological Society of New Jersey* 48: 73–81.

Kroeber, Alfred L.
1927   Disposal of the Dead. *American Anthropologist* 29: 308–15.

Krüger-Kahloula, Angelica
1989   Tributes in Stone and Lapidary Lapses: Commemorating Black People in Eighteenth- and Nineteenth-Century America. *Markers* 6: 33–102.

Lanphear, Kim M.
1988   Health and Mortality in a Nineteenth-Century Poorhouse Skeletal Sample. Doctoral dissertation, Department of Anthropology, State University of New York at Albany.

Larkin, Jack
1988   *The Reshaping of Everyday Life*. Harper and Row, New York.

LaRoche, Cheryl J., and Michael L. Blakey
1997   Seizing Intellectual Power: The Dialogue at the New York African Burial Ground. *Historical Archaeology* 31 (3): 84–106.

Larsen, Clark Spencer
1993   On the Frontier of Contact: Mission Bioarchaeology in La Florida. In *The Spanish Missions of La Florida*, edited by Bonnie G. McEwan, 322–56. University Press of Florida, Gainesville.
1997   *Bioarchaeology: Interpreting Behavior from the Human Skeleton*. Cambridge University Press, Cambridge.

Larsen, Clark Spencer
1993   On the Frontier of Contact: Mission Bioarchaeology in La Florida. In *The Missions of La Florida*, edited by Bonnie G. McEwan, 322–56. University Press of Florida, Gainesville.

Laurel Hill Cemetery
2011   http://www.thelaurelhillcemetery.org/index.php?m=1&p=1&s=1 (accessed September 28, 2011).

Lenik, Edward J.
1996   The Minisink Site as Sacred Space. *Bulletin of the Archaeological Society of New Jersey* 51: 53–63.

Levine, Gaynell Stone (also see Stone, Gaynell)
1978a   Colonial Long Island Grave Stones: Trade Network Indicators, 1670–1799. In *Puritan Gravestone Art II*, edited by Peter Benes, 46–58. Boston University Press, Boston.
1978b   Colonial Long Island Gravestones and Trade Networks. Master's thesis, Department of Anthropology, Stony Brook University, Stony Brook, New York.

Lichten, Frances
1946   *Folk Art of Rural Pennsylvania*. Charles Scribner's Sons, New York.

Limp, W. F., and J. Rose
1985   Introduction to *Gone to a Better Land*, edited by Jerome Rose, 1–5. Arkansas Archeological Survey Research Series no. 25. Arkansas Archeological Survey, Fayetteville.

Linden-Ward, Blanche
1989a   *Silent City on a Hill: Landscapes of Memory and Boston's Mount Auburn Cemetery*. Ohio State University Press, Columbus.
1989b   Strange but Genteel Pleasure Grounds: Tourist and Leisure Uses of Nineteenth

Century Rural Cemeteries. In *Cemeteries and Gravemarkers: Voices of American Culture*, edited by Richard Meyer, 293–328. UMI Research Press, Ann Arbor, Mich.

1990   "The Fencing Mania": The Rise and Fall of Nineteenth Century Funerary Enclosures. *Markers 7*: 34–58.

Little, M. Ruth

1989   Afro-American Gravemarkers in North Carolina. *Markers 6*: 103–36.

1998   *Sticks and Stones: Three Centuries of North Carolina Gravemarkers*. University of North Carolina Press, Chapel Hill.

Little, Barbara J., Kim M. Lanphear, and Douglas W. Owsley

1992   Mortuary Display and Status in a Nineteenth-Century Anglo-American Cemetery in Manassas, Virginia. *American Antiquity 57*: 397–418.

Loren, Diana DiPaolo

2008   *In Contact: Bodies and Spaces in the Sixteenth- and Seventeenth-Century Eastern Woodlands*. AltaMira Press, New York.

Lossing, Benson

1972 [1852]   *Field Book of the American Revolution: Illustrations, by Pen and Pencil, of the History, Biography, Scenery, Relics, and Traditions of the War for Independence; With Eleven Hundred Engravings on Wood, by Lossing and Barritt, Chiefly from Original Sketches by the Author*. Reprint; Polyanthos Press, Cottonport, La.

Lowenthal, William

2008   "Gothic" Cast-Iron Gravemarkers of New Hampshire (and Beyond). *Markers 25*: 94–121.

Ludwig, Allan

1966   *Graven Images*. Wesleyan University Press, Middletown, Conn.

1999   *Graven Images*. 3rd ed. Wesleyan University Press, Middletown, Conn.

Luti, Vincent

2002   *Mallet and Chisel: Gravestone Carvers of Newport, Rhode Island, in the 18th Century*. New England Historic Genealogical Society, Boston.

Lynott, Mark J., and Alison Wylie (editors)

2000   *Ethics in American Archaeology*. 2nd ed. Society for American Archaeology, Washington, D.C.

MAAR Associates

2000   Archaeological Investigations at the Mother UAME Church Cemetery (7NC-E-132), Wilmington, Delaware. Report authored by Ronald A. Thomas, Betty C. Zebooker, Christopher M. Hazel, and David L. Weinberg, with contributions by Arthur Washburn, Thomas A. J. Crist, and Megan Springate. MAAR Associates, Wilmington, Del.

Mack, Mark E., and Michael L. Blakey

2004   The New York African Burial Ground Project: Past Biases, Current Dilemmas, and Future Research Opportunities. *Historical Archaeology 38* (1): 10–17.

Mack, M. E., A. H. Goodman, M. L. Blakey, and A. Mayes

2009   Odontological Indicators of Disease, Diet, and Nutrition Inadequacy. In *The New York African Burial Ground: Unearthing the African Presence in Colonial New*

York, vol. 1, *The Skeletal Biology of the New York African Burial Ground*, edited by Michael L. Blakey and Lesley M. Rankin-Hill, 157–68. Howard University Press, Washington, D.C.

Mackie, Norman Vardney, III

1986   Funerary Treatment and Social Status: A Case Study of Colonial Tidewater Virginia. Master's thesis, Department of Anthropology, College of William and Mary, Williamsburg, Va.

Mainfort, Robert C., Jr.

1979   *Indian Social Dynamics in the Period of European Contact: Fletcher Site Cemetery, Bay County, Michigan.* Anthropological Series vol. 1, no. 4. Publications of the Museum, Michigan State University, East Lansing.

1985   Wealth, Space, and Status in a Historic Indian Cemetery. *American Antiquity* 50 (3): 555–79.

Maish, Amy, Jerome C. Rose, and Murray K. Marks

1997   Cedar Grove: African-American History in Rural Arkansas. In *In Remembrance: Archaeology and Death*, edited by David A. Poirier and Nicholas F. Bellantoni, 105–14. Bergin and Garvey, Westport, Conn.

Mallios, Seth, and David Caterino

2007   Transformations in San Diego County Gravestones and Cemeteries. *Historical Archaeology* 41 (4): 50–71.

Manucy, Albert

1992   *The Houses of St. Augustine, 1565–1821.* University Press of Florida, Gainesville.

Marrinan, Rochelle A.

1993   Archaeological Investigations at Mission Patale, 1984–1992. In *The Missions of La Florida*, edited by Bonnie G. McEwan, 244–94. University Press of Florida, Gainesville.

Mason, George Chapman

1884   *Reminiscences of Newport.* Charles E. Hammett Jr., Newport, R.I.

Mather, Cotton

1853   *Magnalia Christi Americana; or, The Ecclesiastical History of New-England, from Its First Planting, in the Year 1620, unto the Year of Our Lord 1698, in Seven Books.* Vol. 2. Silas Andrus and Son, Hartford, Conn. Originally published in 1702.

Matturi, John

1993   Windows in the Garden: Italian-American Memorialization and the American Cemetery. In *Ethnicity and the American Cemetery*, edited by Richard E. Meyer, 14–15. Bowling Green State University Popular Press, Bowling Green, Ohio.

McCarthy, John P.

1998   Plates in Graves: An Africanism? *African American Archaeology Newsletter*, Spring 1998.

McDowell, Peggy, and Richard E. Meyer

1994   *The Revival Style in American Memorial Art.* Bowling Green State University Popular Press, Bowling Green, Ohio.

McGuire, Randall

1988   Dialogues with the Dead: Ideology and the Cemetery. In *The Recovery of Mean-*

ing: *History Archaeology in the Eastern United States*, edited by Mark P. Leone and Parker B. Potter Jr., 435–80. Smithsonian Institution Press, Washington, D.C.

1991   Building Power in the Cultural Landscape of Broome County, New York, 1880 to 1940. In *The Archaeology of Inequality*, edited by Randall H. McGuire and Robert Paynter, 102–24. Basil Blackwell, Oxford, U.K.

1992   Archaeology and the First Americans. *American Anthropologist* 94 (4): 816–36.

McLeod, Paul Joseph

1979   *A Study of the Gravestones of Monmouth County, New Jersey, 1716–1835: Reflections of a Lifestyle*. Independent Research Project in Anthropology, College of William and Mary. Report on file with the Monmouth County Historical Association, Freehold, N.J.

McVarish, Douglas C., Rebecca Yamin, and Daniel G. Roberts

2005   An Archaeological Sensitivity Study of Franklin Square, Philadelphia. Prepared for Once Upon a Nation, by John Milner Associates, West Chester, Penn. http://www.phillyarchaeology.org/reports/pdf/Franklin-Square1.pdf (accessed August 11, 2011).

Meade, Elizabeth D.

2010   "A Free Church for the People": The History of the Spring Street Church and Its Burial Vaults. *Northeast Historical Archaeology* 39: 8–19.

Meighan, Clement W.

1984   Archaeology: Science or Sacrilege? In *Ethics and Values in Archaeology*, edited by E. L. Green, 208–33. Free Press, New York.

1996   Burying American Archaeology. In *Archaeological Ethics*, edited by Karen D. Vitelli, 209–13. AltaMira Press, Walnut Creek, Calif.

2000   Some Scholars' Views on Reburial. In *Repatriation Reader: Who Owns American Indian Remains?* edited by Devon A. Mihesuah, 190–99. University of Nebraska Press, Lincoln.

Meyer, Richard E. (editor)

1989   *Cemeteries and Gravemarkers: Voices of American Culture*. UMI Research Press, Ann Arbor, Mich.

1993   *Ethnicity and the American Cemetery*. Bowling Green State University Popular Press, Bowling Green, Ohio.

Mihesuah, Devon A. (editor)

2000   *Repatriation Reader: Who Owns American Indian Remains?* University of Nebraska Press, Lincoln.

Miller, Henry M., Silas D. Hurry, and Timothy B. Riordan

2004   The Lead Coffins of St. Mary's City: An Exploration of Life and Death in Early Maryland. *Maryland Historical Magazine* 99 (3): 351–73.

Miller, Perry

1971   Jonathan Edwards and the Great Awakening. In *Essays in Political and Social Development in Colonial America*, edited by Stanley N. Katz, 283–97. Little, Brown, Boston.

Mitford, Jessica

1963   *The American Way of Death*. Simon and Schuster, New York.

2000   *The American Way of Death Revisited*. Random House, New York.

Mooney, Douglas B.

2010   Lost within the Rubble: The Archaeological Findings from the Spring Street Presbyterian Church Burial Vaults. *Northeast Historical Archaeology* 39: 19–40.

Mooney, Douglas B., and Thomas A. J. Crist

2007   Archaeological Recovery and Investigation of Disturbed Human Remains, Washington Square, Philadelphia, Pennsylvania. Prepared for PECO Energy Company, Philadelphia, Penn., by URS Corporation, Burlington, N.J. http://www.phillyarchaeology.org/reports/pdf/Washington-Square-2007.pdf (accessed August 8, 2011).

Mooney, Douglas B, Edward M. Morin, Robert G. Wiencek, and Rebecca White

2007   Archaeological Investigations of the Spring Street Presbyterian Church Cemetery, 244–246 Spring Street, New York City, New York. Prepared for Bayrock/Sapir Organization, New York, by URS Corporation, Burlington, N.J.

Morin, Edward M.

2010   Introduction: Archaeological and Forensic Investigations of an Abolitionist Church in New York City. *Northeast Historical Archaeology* 39: 1–8.

Mould, David R., and Missy Loewe

2006   *Historic Gravestone Art of Charleston, South Carolina, 1695–1802*. McFarland, Jefferson, N.C.

Mounier, R. Alan

1988   A Stage II Archaeological Survey of Rosewood Condominiums, Town of Hammonton, Atlantic County, New Jersey. Report prepared for William Lamanna, Hammonton, N.J.

Murray, Peter, and Linda Murray

1996   *The Oxford Companion to Christian Art and Architecture*. Oxford University Press, Oxford, U.K.

Mytum, Harold

2000   *Recording and Analyzing Graveyards*. Council for British Archaeology Handbook 15. Council for British Archaeology, York, U.K.

2004   *Mortuary Monuments and Burial Grounds of the Historic Period*. Kluwer Academic Publishing, New York.

Nassaney, Michael S.

2000   Archaeology and Oral Tradition in Tandem: Interpreting Native American Ritual, Ideology and Gender Relations in Contact-Period Southeastern New England. In *Interpretations of Native North American Life: Material Contributions of Ethnohistory*, edited by Michael S. Nassaney and Eric S. Johnson, 412–32. University Press of Florida, Gainesville.

National Park Service

2011   *African Burial Ground*. Pamphlet. Department of the Interior, National Park Service, Washington, D.C.

Neal, Avon, and Ann Parker

1970   Graven Images: Sermons in Stone. *American Heritage* 21: 18–29.

Neely, Paula

2013   Jamestown Colonists Resorted to Cannibalism. *National Geographic Daily News,*
        May 1, 2013. http://news.nationalgeographic.com/news/2013/13/130501-james-
        town-cannibalism-archeology-science (accessed September 17, 2013).

New York City Landmarks Preservation Commission

1984   City Archaeology Program Gravestone Files (files of the survey of eighteenth-
        and nineteenth-century cemeteries in New York City). Files at the New York City
        Landmarks Preservation Commission, New York, New York.

Noël Hume, Ivor

1975   *Historical Archaeology.* W. W. Norton, New York.

1979   *Martin's Hundred.* University Press of Virginia, Charlottesville.

1983   *Discoveries in Martin's Hundred.* Colonial Williamsburg Archaeological Series
        no. 10. Colonial Williamsburg Foundation, Williamsburg, Va.

1996   *In Search of This and That: Tales from an Archaeologist's Quest.* Colonial Williams-
        burg Foundation, Williamsburg, Va.

Novak, Shannon A., and Wesley Willoughby

2010   Resurrectionists' Excursions: Evidence of Postmortem Dissection from the
        Spring Street Presbyterian Church. *Northeast Historical Archaeology* 39: 134–52.

Oakley, Rosalee

2003   *Analyzing Cemetery Data.* Association for Gravestone Studies Field Guide No. 1.
        Association for Gravestone Studies, Greenfield, Mass.

O'Gorman, Jodie

2000   Preface to *Never Anything So Solemn: An Archaeological, Biological, and Histori-
        cal Investigation of the Nineteenth-Century Grafton Cemetery,* edited by Jane E.
        Buikstra, Jodie A. O'Gorman, and Cynthia Sutton, xiv. Center for American Ar-
        chaeology, Kampsville, Ill.

Olderr, Steven

1986   *Symbolism: A Comprehensive Dictionary.* McFarland, Jefferson, N.C.

Oldshue, Jerry C.

1987   Ceramic Gravestones of Northeast Mississippi and Northeast Alabama. *Newslet-
        ter of the Association for Gravestone Studies* 11 (2): 17.

Orr, David

2012   The Federal United States Colored Troops Gravestone: Removing the Anonym-
        ity of the American Civil War Soldier. Paper presented at the annual confer-
        ence of the Association of Gravestone Studies, Monmouth University, West Long
        Branch, N.J.

Orser, Charles E.

2004   *Race and Practice in Archaeological Interpretation.* University of Pennsylvania,
        Philadelphia.

2007   *Archaeology of Race and Racialization in Historic America.* University Press of
        Florida, Gainesville.

O'Shea, John

1981   Social Configuration and the Archaeological Study of Mortuary Practices: A Case

Study. In *The Archaeology of Death*, edited by Robert Chapman, Ian Kinnes, and Klavs Randsborg, 39–52. Cambridge University Press, Cambridge.

Owsley, Douglas, and Karin Bruwelheide
2009   *Written in Bone*. Lean To Press, Minneapolis, Minn.

Owsley, Douglas W., Karin S. Bruwelheide, Larry W. Cartmell Sr., Laurie E. Burgess, Shelly J. Foote, Skye M. Chang, and Nick Fielder
2006   The Man in the Cast Iron Coffin: An Interdisciplinary Effort to Name the Past. *Historical Archaeology* 40 (3): 89–108.

Owsley, Douglas W., and Bertita E. Compton
1997   Preservation in Late Nineteenth-Century Iron Coffin Burials. In *Forensic Taphonomy: Post Mortem Fate of Human Remains*, edited by William D. Haglund and Marcella H. Sorg, 511–26. CRC Press, Boca Raton, Fla.

Owsley, Douglas W., and Robert W. Mann
1995   Multidisciplinary Investigation of Two Iron Coffin Burials. In *Proceedings of the First World Congress on Mummy Studies*, 2:605–14. Museo Arqueológico y Etnográfico de Tenerife, Organismo Autónomo de Museos y Centros, Cabildo de Tenerife, Tenerife, Canary Islands.

Parker, Ann, and Avon Neal
1963   The Art of New England Gravestones. *Art in America* 51 (3): 96–105.

Parker, Arthur C.
1922   *The Archaeological History of New York*. New York State Museum Bulletin, Nos. 235 and 236. University of the State of New York, Albany.

Parker Pearson, Michael
1982   Mortuary Practices, Sociology and Ideology: An Ethnoarchaeological Study. In *Symbolic and Structural Archaeology*, edited by Ian Hodder, 99–114. Cambridge University Press, Cambridge.
1999   *The Archaeology of Death and Burial*. Texas A and M University Press, Austin.

Patterson, Daniel W.
2012   *The True Image: Gravestone Art and the Culture of Scotch Irish Settlers in the Pennsylvania and Carolina Backcountry*. University of North Carolina Press, Chapel Hill.

Peebles, Christopher, and Susan Kus
1977   Some Archaeological Correlates of Ranked Societies. *American Antiquity* 42: 412–48.

Perry, Warren R., Jean Howson, and Barbara A. Bianco
2009a   *The New York African Burial Ground: Unearthing the African Presence in Colonial New York*, vol. 2, *The Archaeology of the New York African Burial Ground*. Howard University Press, Washington, D.C.

Perry, Warren R., Jean Howson, and Barbara A. Bianco
2009b   Summary and Conclusions. In *The New York African Burial Ground: Unearthing the African Presence in Colonial New York*, vol. 2, *The Archaeology of the New York African Burial Ground*, edited by Warren R. Perry, Jean Howson, and Barbara A. Bianco, 367–76. Howard University Press, Washington, D.C.

Perry, Warren R., and Janet L. Woodruff

2009 Burials with Coins, Shells, Pipes, and Other Items. In *The New York African Burial Ground: Unearthing the African Presence in Colonial New York*, vol. 2, *The Archaeology of the New York African Burial Ground*, edited by Warren R. Perry, Jean Howson, and Barbara A Bianco, 349–66. Howard University Press, Washington, D.C.

Phillips, Shawn M.

2003 Skeletal Analysis of the Human Remains from the Lutheran Church Lot, 1607–1816. In *People, Places, and Material Things: Historical Archaeology of Albany, New York*, edited by Charles L. Fisher, 57–62. New York State Museum Bulletin 499. New York State Education Department, Albany.

Poirier, David A., and Nicholas F. Bellantoni (editors)

1997a *In Remembrance: Archaeology and Death*. Praeger, New York.

Poirier, David A., and Nicholas F. Bellantoni

1997b In Partnership: Descendants, Friends-of-the-Dead, and Archaeologists. In *In Remembrance: Archaeology and Death*, edited by David A. Poirier and Nicholas F. Bellantoni, 231–35. Bergin and Garvey, Westport, Conn.

Pool, David deSola

1952 *Portraits Etched in Stone—Early Jewish Settlers, 1682–1831*. Columbia University Press, New York.

Posnansky, Merrick

1999 West Africanist Reflections on African-American Archaeology. In *"I, Too, Am America": Archaeological Studies of African-American Life*, edited by Theresa A. Singleton, 21–38. University of Virginia Press, Charlottesville.

Preucel, Robert W., Lucy F. Williams, Stacey O. Espenlaub, and Janet Monge

2006 Out of Heaviness, Enlightenment. In *Archaeological Ethics*, edited by Karen D. Vitelli and Chip Colwell-Chanthaphonh, 178–87. 2nd ed. Rowman and Littlefield, Lanham, Md.

Price, H. Marcus, III

1991 *Disputing the Dead: U.S. Law on Aboriginal Remains and Grave Goods*. University of Missouri Press, Columbia.

Prioli, Carmine E.

1979 Review Essay: Early New England Gravestone Scholarship. *Early American Literature* 14 (3): 328–36.

Project Lead Coffins

n.d. http://www.stmaryscity.org/Lead%20Coffins/project_lead_coffins.htm (accessed September 29, 2011).

Prown, Jules David

1982 Mind in Matter: An Introduction to Material Culture Theory and Method. *Winterthur Portfolio* 17 (1): 1–19.

Quick, Polly McW. (editor)

1985 *Proceedings: Conference on Reburial Issues*. Society for American Archaeology and Society of Professional Archeologists, Newberry Library, Chicago, June 14–15, 1985.

Quimby, George Irving

1966   *Indian Culture and European Trade Goods: The Archaeology of the Historic Period in the Western Great Lakes Region.* University of Wisconsin Press, Madison.

Rainville, Lynn

1999   Hanover Deathscapes: Mortuary Variability in New Hampshire, 1770–1920. *Ethnohistory* 46 (3): 541–97.

2009   Home at Last: Mortuary Commemoration in Virginian Slave Cemeteries. *Markers* 26: 54–83.

Rathje, William L.

1979   Modern Material Culture Studies. In *Advances in Archaeological Method and Theory,* vol. 2, edited by Michael B. Schiffer, 1–37. Academic Press, New York.

Rauschenberger, Bradford L.

1977   A Study of Baroque- and Gothic-Style Gravestones in Davidson County, North Carolina. *Journal of Early Southern Decorative Arts* 3 (2): 24–50.

Reps, John

1980   *Town Planning in Frontier America.* University of Missouri Press, Columbia.

Richards, Brandon

2007   New Netherland's Gravestone Legacy: An Introduction to Early Burial Markers of the Upper Mid-Atlantic States. *Markers* 25: 24–39.

Richman, Jeffrey I.

1998   *Brooklyn's Green-Wood Cemetery: New York's Buried Treasure.* Green-Wood Cemetery, Brooklyn, N.Y.

Riding In, James

2002   Our Dead Are Never Forgotten: American Indian Struggles for Burial Rights and Protections. In *"They Made Us Many Promises": The American Indian Experience, 1524 to the Present,* edited by Philip Weeks, 291–323. Harlan Davidson, Wheeling, Ill.

2005   Decolonizing NAGPRA. In *For Indigenous Eyes Only: A Decolonization Handbook,* edited by Waziyatawin Angela Wilson and Michael Yellow Bird, 53–66. School of American Research, Santa Fe, N.Mex.

Riordan, Timothy B.

1997   The 17th-Century Cemetery at St. Mary's City: Mortuary Practices in the Early Chesapeake. *Historical Archaeology* 31 (4): 28–40.

2000   *Dig a Grave Both Wide and Deep: An Archaeological Investigation of Mortuary Practices in the 17th-Century Cemetery at St. Mary's City, Maryland.* Historic St. Mary's City, St. Mary's City, Md.

2004   Philip Calvert: Patron of St. Mary's City. *Maryland Historical Magazine* 99 (3): 329–49.

2009   "Carry Me to Yon Kirk Yard": An Investigation of Changing Burial Practices in the Seventeenth-Century Cemetery at St. Mary's City, Maryland. *Historical Archaeology* 43 (1): 81–92.

Ritchie, William A.

1965   *The Archaeology of New York State.* Natural History Press, Garden City, N.Y.

Robinson, Paul A., Marc A. Kelly, and Patricia E. Rubertone
1985   Preliminary Biocultural Interpretations from a Seventeenth-Century Narragansett Indian Cemetery in Rhode Island. In *Cultures in Contact*, edited by William W. Fitzhugh, 107–30. Anthropological Society of Washington Series. Smithsonian Institution Press, Washington, D.C.

Rogers, Raynor R.
1984   *The Story of the Old John Street Church.* John Street Press, New York.

Rogers, S. T., Douglas W. Owsley, Robert W. Mann, and Shelly Foote
1997   The Man in the Cast Iron Coffin: A Tale of Historic and Forensic Investigation. *Tennessee Anthropologist* 22 (2): 95–119.

Romey, Kristin
2005   The Dead of Snake Hill: A Man's Search for His Grandfather Sparks an Unusually Moving Excavation along the New Jersey Turnpike. *Archaeology* 58 (3): 42. http://www.archaeology.org/0505/abstracts/njturnpike.html (accessed August 21, 2011).

Rose, Jerome C., Thomas J. Green, and Victoria D. Green
1996   NAGPRA Is Forever: Osteology and the Repatriation of Skeletons. *Annual Review of Anthropology* 25: 81–103.

Rothstein, Edward
2010   A Burial Ground and Its Dead Are Given New Life. *New York Times,* February 25, 2010. http://www.nytimes.com/2010/02/26/arts/design/26burial.html (accessed June 20, 2011).

Rotman, Deborah, John Adams-Graf, Kathryn Jakes, Marjorie Schroeder, and Christina Fulton
2000   The Material Culture of Mortuary Behavior: Artifacts from the Grafton Cemetery. In *Never Anything So Solemn: An Archaeological, Biological, and Historical Investigation of the Nineteenth-Century Grafton Cemetery*, edited by Jane E. Buikstra, Jodie A. O'Gorman, and Cynthia Sutton, 60–90. Center for American Archaeology, Kampsville, Ill.

Rotundo, Barbara
1989   Monumental Bronze: A Representative American Company. In *Cemeteries and Gravemarkers: Voices of American Culture*, edited by Richard E. Meyer, 263–92. UMI Research Press, Ann Arbor, Mich.
1997   A Modern Gravestone Marker: Some Lessons for Gravestone Historians. *Markers* 14: 86–110.

Rouse, Wendy
2005a   Archaeological Excavations at Virginiatown's Chinese Cemeteries. In *Chinese American Death Rituals: Respecting the Ancestors*, edited by Sue Fawn Chung and Priscilla Wegars, 81–106. AltaMira Press, Lanham, Md.
2005b   "What We Didn't Understand": A History of Chinese Death Ritual in China and California. In *Chinese American Death Rituals: Respecting the Ancestors*, edited by Sue Fawn Chung and Priscilla Wegars, 19–45. AltaMira Press, Lanham, Md.

Rubertone, Patricia E.
2001   *Grave Undertakings: An Archaeology of Roger Williams and the Narragansett Indians.* Smithsonian Institution Press, Washington, D.C.

Salmon, Patricia
2006   *Realms of History: Staten Island Cemeteries.* Staten Island Institute of Arts and Sciences, New York.

Sanborn, Laura Sue
1989   Camposantos: Sacred Places of the Southwest. *Markers* 6: 159–80.

Sandford, M. K.
1992   A Reconstruction of Trace Element Analysis in Prehistoric Bone. In *Skeletal Biology of Past Peoples: Research Methods*, edited by Shelley Rae Saunders and Mary Anne Katzenberg, 79–103. Wiley-Liss, John Wiley and Sons, New York.

Saunders, Rebecca
1993   Architecture of the Missions Santa Maria and Santa Catalina de Amelia. In *The Missions of La Florida*, edited by Bonnie G. McEwan, 35–61. University Press of Florida, Gainesville.

Saville, Foster
1920   *A Montauk Cemetery in Easthampton, Long Island.* Indian Notes and Monographs vol. 2, no. 3. Museum of the American Indian, Heye Foundation, New York.

Saxe, Arthur A.
1970   *The Social Dimensions of Mortuary Practices.* Doctoral dissertation, Department of Anthropology, University of Michigan, Ann Arbor. University Microfilms International, Ann Arbor, Mich.

Sayer, Duncan
2011   Death and the Dissenter: Group Identity and Stylistic Simplicity as Witnessed in Nineteenth-Century Nonconformist Gravestones. *Historical Archaeology* 45 (4): 115–34.

Scharfenberger, Gerard P.
2004   You Can't Take It with You, Or Can You? Grave Goods from the Potter's Field, Secaucus, New Jersey. Paper presented at the 2004 Society for American Archaeology Conference, Montreal, Quebec.

Sears, John F.
1989   *Sacred Places: American Tourist Attractions in the Nineteenth Century.* University of Massachusetts Press, Amherst.

Seeman, Eric R.
2010a   *Death in the New World: Cross-Cultural Encounters 1492–1800.* University of Pennsylvania Press, Philadelphia.
2010b   Reassessing the "Sankofa Symbol" in New York's African Burial Ground. *William and Mary Quarterly* 67 (1): 101–22.

Segal, Joshua L.
2005   *Field Guide to Visiting a Jewish Cemetery: A Spiritual Journey to the Past, Present and Future.* Jewish Cemetery Publishing, Nashua, N.H.

Shackel, Paul A.
2001   The Robert Gould Shaw Memorial: Redefining the Role of the Fifty-Fourth Massachusetts Volunteer Infantry. In *Myth, Memory, and the Making of the Ameri-*

can Landscape, edited by Paul A. Shackel, 141–53. University Press of Florida, Gainesville.

Shanks, Michael, and Christopher Tilley
1982   Ideology, Symbolic Power and Ritual Communication: A Reinterpretation of Neolithic Mortuary Practices. In *Symbolic and Structural Archaeology*, edited by Ian Hodder, 129–54. Cambridge University Press, Cambridge.

Silliman, Stephen
2005   Culture Contact or Colonialism? Challenges in the Archaeology of Native North America. *American Antiquity* 70 (1): 55–74.

Silverman, Carol
1991   Strategies of Ethnic Adaptation: The Case of Gypsies in the United States. In *Creative Ethnicity, Symbols and Strategies of Contemporary Ethnic Life*, edited by Stephen Stern and John Allan Cicala, 107–21. Utah State University Press, Logan.

Simmons, William S.
1970   *Cautantowwit's House: An Indian Burial Ground on the Island of Conanicut in Narragansett Bay*. Brown University Press, Providence, R.I.

Simon, Donald E.
1980   The Worldly Side of Paradise: Green-Wood Cemetery. In *A Time to Mourn: Expressions of Grief in Nineteenth Century America*, edited by Martha V. Pike and Janice Gray Armstrong, 51–66. Museums at Stony Brook, Stony Brook, N.Y.

Sloane, David Charles
1991   *The Last Great Necessity: Cemeteries in American History*. Johns Hopkins University Press, Baltimore, Md.

Smith, Bruce E., et al.
2010   Letter to the Honorable Ken Salazar, Secretary of the Interior, May 17, 2010, signed by 41 anthropologists. http://www.friendsofpast.org/nagpra/2010nagpra/nas-letter.html (accessed April 23, 2010).

Smith, Samuel D., and Stephen T. Rogers
1979   *A Survey of Historic Pottery Making in Tennessee*. Tennessee Department of Environment and Conservation, Nashville.

South, Stanley
1999   *Historical Archaeology in Wachovia: Excavating Eighteenth-Century Bethabara and Moravian Pottery*. Kluwer Academic Publishers, New York.

Spencer-Wood, Suzanne M. (editor)
1987   *Consumer Choice in Historical Archaeology*. Springer, New York.

Spencer-Wood, Suzanne M.
1996   Cultural Complexity, Non-linear Systems Theory, and Multi-scalar Analysis. In *Debating Complexity: Proceedings of the 26th Annual Chacmool Conference*. University of Calgary, Alberta.
2010   Gendered Power Dynamics among Religious Sects, Ethnic Groups, and Classes, in Jewish Communities on the Greater Boston Landscape at the Turn of the Century. In *Archaeology and Preservation of Gendered Landscapes*, edited by Sherene Baugher and Suzanne Spencer-Wood, 189–230. Springer, New York.

Sprague, Roderick
2005   *Burial Terminology: A Guide for Researchers.* AltaMira Press, Lanham, Md.
Stannard, David E.
1980   Where All Our Steps Were Tending: Death in the American Context. In *A Time to Mourn: Expressions of Grief in Nineteenth Century America*, edited by Martha V. Pike and Janice Gray Armstrong, 19–29. Museums at Stony Brook, Stony Brook, N.Y.
Statistical Research
2009   *The Skeletal Biology, Archaeology, and History of the New York African Burial Ground: A Synthesis of Volumes 1, 2, and 3.* Vol. 4 of *New York African Burial Ground.* Howard University Press, Washington, D.C.
St. George, Robert Blair
1988   Artifacts of Regional Consciousness in the Connecticut River Valley, 1700–1780. In *Material Life in America, 1600–1860*, edited by Robert Blair St. George, 335–57. Northeastern University Press, Boston.
Stilgoe, John R.
1982   *Common Landscape of America, 1580 to 1845.* Yale University Press, New Haven, Conn.
Stillwell, John E.
1903   *Historical and Genealogical Miscellany: Data Relating to the Settlement and Settlers of New York and New Jersey.* 4 vols. Reprint, 1970; Genealogical Publishing, Baltimore, Md.
Stone, Gaynell (also see Levine, Gaynell Stone)
1987   Spatial and Material Aspects of Culture: Ethnicity and Ideology in Long Island Gravestones, 1670–1820. Doctoral dissertation, Department of Anthropology, Stony Brook University, Stony Brook, N.Y.
2009   Sacred Landscapes: Material Evidence of Ideological and Ethnic Choice in Long Island, New York, Gravestones, 1680–1800. *Historical Archaeology* 43 (1): 142–59.
Strangstad, Lynette
1995   *A Graveyard Preservation Primer.* AltaMira Press, Lanham, Md.
Sutherland, Anne
1975   *Gypsies: The Hidden Americans.* Free Press, New York.
Sweeney, Kevin M.
1985   Where the Bay Meets the River: Gravestones and Stonecutters in the River Towns of Western Massachusetts, 1690–1810. *Markers* 3: 1–46.
Swidler, Nina, Kurt E. Dongoske, Roger Anyon, and Alan S. Downer (editors)
1997   *Native Americans and Archaeologists: Stepping Stones to Common Ground.* AltaMira Press, Walnut Creek, Calif.
Tainter, Joseph
1978   Mortuary Practices and the Study of Prehistoric Social Systems. In *Advances in Archaeological Method and Theory*, vol. 1, edited by Michael B. Schiffer, 105–41. Academic Press, New York.
Tarlow, Sarah
1999   Wormie Clay and Blessed Sleep: Death and Disgust in Later Historic Britain. In

The Familiar Past? Archaeologies of Britain, 1550–1950, edited by Sarah Tarlow and Susie West, 183–98. Routledge, London.

Tashjian, Ann, and Dickran Tashjian
1974   *Memorials for Children of Change: The Art of Early New England Stonecarving.* Wesleyan University Press, Middletown, Conn.

Taylor, Clarice
2001   *The African Burial Ground.* Pamphlet. U.S. General Services Administration, Washington, D.C.

Thomas, Brian W.
1994   Inclusion and Exclusion in the Moravian Settlement in North Carolina, 1770–1790. *Historical Archaeology* 28 (3): 15–29.

Thomas, David Hurst
1988   *St. Catherines: An Island in Time.* Georgia Endowment for the Humanities, Atlanta.
1990   The Spanish Mission in La Florida: An Overview. In *Columbian Consequences,* vol. 2, *Archaeological and Historical Perspectives on the Spanish Borderlands East,* edited by David Hurst Thomas, 327–97. Smithsonian Institution Press, Washington, D.C.
1993   The Archaeology of Mission Santa Catalina de Guale: Our First 15 Years. In *The Missions of La Florida,* edited by Bonnie G. McEwan, 1–34. University Press of Florida, Gainesville.
2000   *Skull Wars: Kennewick Man, Archaeology, and the Battle for Native American Identity.* Basic Books, New York.

Thompson, Robert Farris
1983   *Flash of the Spirit: African and Afro-American Art and Philosophy.* Random House, New York.

Tibensky, James
1983   The Evolution of Motifs on Colonial Gravestones in Central and Western Connecticut. In *Forgotten Places and Things: Archaeological Perspectives on American History,* edited by Albert E. Ward, 257–62. Contributions to Anthropological Studies no. 3. Center for Anthropological Studies, Albuquerque, N.Mex.

Trask, Deborah
1978   "J. W.": Folk Carver of Hants County, Nova Scotia. In *Puritan Gravestone Art II: The Dublin Seminar for New England Folklife; Annual Proceedings,* edited by Peter W. Benes, 58–65. Boston University, Boston.

Trinkley, Michael, and Debi Hackler
1999   *An Archaeological Excavation of Four Family Tombs at Colonial Park Cemetery, Savannah, Georgia.* Chicora Foundation Research Series 5. Chicora Foundation, Columbia, S.C.

Turnbaugh, William A.
1984   The Material Culture of RI-1000, A Mid-17th-Century Narragansett Indian Burial Site in North Kingstown, Rhode Island. Report on file with Department of Sociology and Anthropology, University of Rhode Island, Kingston.

Turner, C. G., II
1986   What Is Lost with Skeletal Reburial? *Quarterly Review of Archaeology* 7 (1): 1–3.
Turner, Jean Rae
1996   Evergreen Cemetery. In *Remove Not the Ancient Landmark*, edited by Donald Martin Reynolds, 191–98. Gordon and Breach Publishers, Amsterdam.
Ubelaker, D. H.
1989   *Human Skeletal Remains*. 2nd ed. Taraxacum, Washington, D.C.
Ucko, Peter
1969   Ethnography and Archaeological Interpretation of Funerary Remains. *World Archaeology* 1: 262–80.
Upton, Dell
1987   *Ethnic Groups That Built America*. Wiley, New York.
U.S. Department of the Interior
2010   43 CRF Part 10, Native American Graves Protection and Repatriation Act Regulations—Disposition of Culturally Unidentifiable Human Remains: Final Rule. *Federal Register* 75 (49): 12378–405, March 25, 2010.
U.S. Department of Veterans Affairs
2012   History of Government Furnished Headstones and Markers. http://www.cem.va.gov/hist/hmhist.asp (accessed June 11, 2012).
Van Gennep, A.
1960   *The Rites of Passage*. Translated by M. B. Vizedom and G. L. Caffee with an introduction by S. T. Kimball. University of Chicago Press, Chicago.
Veit, Richard F.
1991   Middlesex County, New Jersey, Gravestones, 1687–1799: Shadows of a Changing Culture. Master's thesis, Department of Anthropology, College of William and Mary, Williamsburg, Va.
1992   "Born a Slave, Died Free": The End of Slavery in New Jersey. *Bulletin of the Archaeological Society of New Jersey* 47: 23–28.
1993   Iron Gravemarkers in the Pine Barrens: Unusual Products of a Forgotten Industry. *Bulletin of the Archaeological Society of New Jersey* 48: 39–44.
1996   Grave Insights into Middlesex County's Colonial Culture. *New Jersey History* 114 (3–4): 75–94.
1997   Skyscrapers and Sepulchers: A Historic Ethnography of New Jersey's Terra Cotta Industry. Doctoral dissertation, Department of Anthropology, University of Pennsylvania, Philadelphia.
2000   John Solomon Teetzel and the Anglo-German Gravestone Carving Tradition of 18th Century Northwestern New Jersey. *Markers* 17: 124–62.
2007   Their Travels Have Ended: Gypsy Gravemarkers from New Jersey. Paper presented at the American Culture Association/Popular Culture Association Annual Meeting, Boston.
2009   "Resolved to Strike Out a New Path": Consumerism and Iconographic Change in New Jersey Gravestones, 1680–1820. *Historical Archaeology* 43 (1): 115–41.
Veit, Richard F., and Mark Nonestied
2003   Taken for Granite: Terracotta Gravemarkers from New Jersey and New York. In

Ceramics in America 2003, edited by Robert Hunter, 172–95. Chipstone Foundation and University Press of New England, Hanover, N.H.

2008 *New Jersey Cemeteries and Tombstones: History in the Landscape.* Rivergate Press, Rutgers University, New Brunswick, N.J.

2012 "Born a Slave, Died Free": Antebellum African-American Commemoration in a Northern State. Paper presented at the annual conference of the Society for Historical Archaeology, Baltimore, Md.

Venables, Robert W.

2004 *American Indian History: Five Centuries of Conflict* and *Coexistence,* vol. 1, *Conquest of a Continent, 1492–1783.* Clear Light Publishers, Santa Fe, N.Mex.

Vlach, John Michael

1978 *The Afro-American Tradition in the Decorative Arts.* Cleveland Museum of Art, Cleveland.

Walker, Sally

2009 *Written in Bone: Buried Lives of Jamestown and Colonial Maryland.* Carolrhoda Books, Minneapolis, Minn.

Warner, W. Lloyd

1959 *The Living and the Dead: A Study of the Symbolic Life in America.* Yale University Press, New Haven, Conn.

Warren, Nancy Hunter

1987 New Mexico Village Camposantos. *Markers* 4: 115–29.

Wasserman, Emily

1972 *Gravestone Designs: Rubbings and Photographs from Early New York and New Jersey.* Dover, New York.

Watkins, Joe E.

2000 *Indigenous Archaeology: American Indian Values and Scientific Practice.* AltaMira Press, Walnut Creek, Calif.

2003 Archaeological Ethics and American Indians. In *Ethical Issues in Archaeology,* edited by Larry J. Zimmerman, Karen D. Vitelli, and Julie Hollowell-Zimmer, 129–41. AltaMira Press, Walnut Creek, Calif.

Watkins, Joe

2004 Becoming American or Becoming Indian? NAGPRA, Kennewick and Cultural Affiliation. *Journal of Social Archaeology* 4 (1): 60–80.

2006 *Sacred Sites and Repatriation.* Chelsea House Publishers, New York.

2008 The Repatriation Arena: Control, Conflict, and Compromise. In *Opening Archaeology: Repatriation's Impact on Contemporary Research and Practice,* edited by Thomas W. Killian, 161–77. School for Advanced Research Press, Santa Fe, N.Mex.

Wegars, Priscilla (editor)

1993 *Hidden Heritage: Historical Archaeology of the Overseas Chinese.* Baywood, Amityville, N.Y.

Welch, Richard F.

1983 *Memento Mori: The Gravestones of Early Long Island, 1680–1810.* Friends for Long Island's Heritage, Syosset, N.Y.

1987   The New York and New Jersey Gravestone Carving Tradition. *Markers* 4: 1–54.

Welters, Linda, Margaret T. Ordoñez, Kathryn Tarleton, and Joyce Smith

1996   European Textiles from Seventeenth-Century New England Indian Cemeteries. In *Historical Archaeology and the Study of American Culture*, edited by Lu Ann De Cunzo and Bernard L. Herman, 193–232. Henry Francis du Pont Winterthur Museums, Winterthur, Del.

Werner, William, and Shannon A. Novak

2010   Archaeologists of Disease and Public Order in Nineteenth-Century New York: The View from Spring and Varick. *Northeast Historical Archaeology* 39: 97–120.

Weslager, C. A.

1945   The Indian Grave Robbers of Early Pennsylvania, Delaware, and Maryland. *Pennsylvania Archaeologist* 15 (4): 104–7.

West, Helen Ridgley

1908   *Historic Graves of Maryland and the District of Columbia.* Grafton Press, New York.

Wheeler, William Ogden, and Edmund D. Halsey

1892   *Inscriptions on Tombstones and Monuments in the Burying Grounds of the First Presbyterian Church and St. Johns Church at Elizabeth, New Jersey, 1664–1892.* Tuttle, Morehouse, and Taylor, New Haven, Conn.

White, Rebecca L., and Douglas B. Mooney

2010   Stories from the Rubble: Analysis of the Mortuary Artifacts from the Spring Street Presbyterian Church Vaults. *Northeast Historical Archaeology* 39: 40–65.

Wilczak, C., R. Watkins, C. C. Null, and M. L. Blakey

2009   Skeletal Indictors of Work: Musculoskeletal, Arthritic and Traumatic Effects. In *The New York African Burial Ground: Unearthing the African Presence in Colonial New York*, vol. 1, *The Skeletal Biology of the New York African Burial Ground*, edited by Michael L. Blakey and Lesley M. Rankin-Hill, 199–226. Howard University Press, Washington, D.C.

Willats, R. M.

1987   Iron Graveslabs: A Sideline of the Early Iron Industry. *Sussex Archaeological Collections* 125: 99–113.

Williams, Roger

1936 [1643]   *A Key into the Languages of America.* Reprint, Roger Williams Press, Providence, R.I.

Winters, Howard

1968   Value Systems and Trade Cycles of the Late Archaic in the Midwest. In *New Perspectives in Archaeology*, edited by Sally R. Binford and Lewis R. Binford, 175–222. Aldine, New York.

Wurst, LouAnn

1991   "Employees Must Be of Moral and Temperate Habits": Rural and Urban Elite Ideologies. In *The Archaeology of Inequality*, edited by Randall H. McGuire and Robert Paynter, 125–49. Blackwell, Cambridge, Mass.

Wurst, LouAnn, and Randall H. McGuire
1999   Immaculate Consumption: A Critique of the "Shop Till You Drop" School of Human Behavior. *International Journal of Historical Archaeology* 3 (3): 191–99.

Yalom, Marilyn
2008   *The American Resting Place: Four Hundred Years of History through Our Cemeteries and Burial Grounds.* Houghton Mifflin, Boston.

Yamin, Rebecca, Alexander A. Bartlett, and Nancy Donohue
2007   "Leaving No Stone Unturned": Archaeological Monitoring and the Transformation of Franklin Square. Prepared for Once Upon a Nation, by John Milner Associates, West Chester, Penn. http://www.phillyarchaeology.org/reports/pdf/Franklin-Square2.pdf (accessed August 11, 2011).

Yentsch, Anne Elizabeth
1963   Design Motifs on Scottish Gravestones. Paper prepared for Anthropology S-137, Harvard University. Manuscript on file at the Tozzer Library, Harvard University, Cambridge, Mass.
1978   To Remember Correctly: Epitaphs on Gravestones of New England Mariners. Paper presented at the 11th Annual Meeting of the Society for Historical Archaeology, San Antonio, Tex.
1992   Man and Vision in Historical Archaeology. In *The Art and Mystery of Historical Archaeology*, edited by Anne Elizabeth Yentsch and Mary C. Beaudry, 23–43. CRC Press, Boca Raton, Fla.

Young, Frank W.
1960   Graveyards and Social Structure. *Rural Sociology* 25 (4): 446–50.

Zelinsky, Wilbur
1973   *The Cultural Geography of the United States.* Prentice-Hall, Englewood, N.J.
1976   Unearthly Delights: Cemetery Names and the Map of the Changing American Afterworld. In *Geographies of the Mind: Essays in Historical Geography*, edited by David Lowenthal and Martyn J. Bowden, 171–95. Oxford University Press, New York.

Zielenski, John
2004   Shaping a Soul of Stone: The Soul Effigy Gravestones of Uzal Ward, William Grant, and the Anonymous Pear Head Carvers of Eighteenth-Century New Jersey: A Stylistic Study and Comprehensive Survey. Master's thesis, Department of Art History, Montclair State University, Montclair, N.J.

Zimmerman, Larry J.
1985   A Perspective on the Reburial Issue from South Dakota. In *Proceedings: Conference on Reburial Issue*, edited by Polly McW. Quick, 1–4. Society for American Archaeology and Society of Professional Archeologists, Newberry Library, Chicago, June 14–15, 1985.
1989   Made Radical by My Own: An Archaeologist Learns to Accept Reburial. In *Conflict in the Archaeology of Living Traditions*, edited by Robert Layton, 60–67. Unwin Hyman, London.
1996   Sharing Control of the Past. In *Archaeological Ethics*, edited by Karen D. Vitelli, 214–18. AltaMira Press, Walnut Creek, Calif.

1997   Anthropology and Responses to the Reburial Issue. In *Indians and Anthropologists: Vine Deloria, Jr., and the Critique of Anthropology*, edited by Thomas Biolsi and Larry J. Zimmerman, 92–112. University of Arizona Press, Tucson.

2000   A New and Different Archaeology? With a Postscript on the Impact of the Kennewick Dispute. In *Repatriation Reader: Who Owns American Indian Remains?* edited by Devon A. Mihesuah, 294–306. University of Nebraska Press, Lincoln.

Zucchi, Alberta

1997   Tombs and Testaments: Mortuary Practices during the Seventeenth to Nineteenth Centuries in the Spanish-Venezuelan Catholic Tradition. *Historical Archaeology* 31 (2): 31–41.

Zug, Charles C.

1986   *Turners and Burners: The Folk Potters of North Carolina*. University of North Carolina Press, Chapel Hill.

Index

Page numbers in *italics* refer to illustrations.

Abraham, Terry, 177
Act Prohibiting the Importation of Slaves, 116
African Americans: abandoned cemeteries of, 24, 169, 176–77; archaeology of cemeteries and, 52–58, 169; Baptist Church and, 54–55; beads and, 53–54; burial practices of, 54, 55–56, 57; burial sites of, 52–58, 77, 109–10, 162; burials of free people, 52, 55, 56–57, 174–75; clay smoking pipe and, 54; cultural retention by, 53; Dallas (Tex.) and, 57; dental analysis of, 52–53; descendant populations and, 55; enslavement in North of, 116; epitaphs of, 171, 173; grave goods of, 53–54, 57, 77, 169–70; gravemarkers for, 11, 115–17, 162, 169, 171–75; grave orientation of, 171, 175; human remains of, 52–53, 54, 55, 56, 169; infant mortality of, 55; modified teeth of, 53; Moravians and, 110; names of, 174; Philadelphia (Penn.) and, 54; portrait stones for, 117; scraped-earth burials of, 175; segregation of, 11; shell decorations of, 175; shells and, 169–70; slave burials of, 21–24, 25, 52–53, 64, 168–77; treatment of remains of, 52–53. *See also* African Burial Ground (NYC, N.Y.); African Union Church Cemetery (Polktown, Del.); Cedar Grove Baptist Cemetery (Ark.); Common Burying Ground (Newport, R.I.); Eighth Street Cemetery (Philadelphia, Penn.); First African Baptist Church Cemeteries (Philadelphia, Penn.); Freedman's Cemetery (Dallas, Tex.); Rahway Cemetery (Rahway, N.J.); Scotch Plains Baptist Church Cemetery (Scotch Plains, N.J.); Tenth Street Cemetery (Philadelphia, Penn.)
African Burial Ground (NYC, N.Y.): archaeological studies of, 14, 29–31, 36–37, 52–54, 162, 169; assimilation and, 14; dental analysis of, 52–53; descendant populations and, 31; grave goods of, 53–54; shells and, 54; study of human remains from, 52–53; treatment of remains of, 52–53
African Union Church Cemetery (Polktown, Del.), 176
Agua Mansa Cemetery (Colton, Calif.), 188–89
Albany Rural Cemetery (Albany, N.Y.), 134, *183*
Aleuts, 167–68
American Indians. *See* Aleuts; Brotherton (Brothertown); Guale Indians; Lenapes; Mohawks; Narragansetts; Navajos; Oneidas; Ottawas; Pequots; Tsimshians; Wampanoags; Zunis
Arminiansim, 40

Ashkenazim, 112, 182
Association for Gravestone Studies, 3, 93, 209

Barber, Russell, 188–89
Baugher, Sherene, 31, 96–98, 133, 184, 186
beads, 19, 45, 50, 53–54
Bello, Charles, 167–68
Benes, Peter, 88, 93–94
bone houses, 179
Brotherton (Brothertown), 163–65
Buddhism, 177
burial mounds, 11, 13, 19–20, 21, 164–65
"burner," 180–81, 202
buttons, 46, 55, 59, 68

Calvert, Anne Wolsey, 20–21, 42–43, 208
Calvert, Phillip, 20–21, 42–43, 208
Carlin Chinese Cemetery (Carlin, Nev.), 59–60
Cedar Grove Baptist Cemetery (Ark.), 56–57
cherub motif: in Bruton Parish Church-yard (Williamsburg, Va.), 111; in Colonial Park Cemetery (Savannah, Ga.), 83; Great Awakening and, 7–8, 86, 90; iconographic shift and, 81–82, 86–87, 93; as important artifact, 78; Jews and, 10, 91, 113, 114; in Massachusetts, 122; meaning of, 99, 200; in New Jersey, 104; in Pennsylvania, 121; Puritanism and, 85; religion and, 87–88, 98; seriation and, 97, 98; social status and, 86; stonecutters and, 84, 88, 89, 98, 103, 117; as typical colonial motif, 9
Chinese: assimilation of, 13, 14; burial practices of, 199, 202; cemeteries of, 58–60, 177–81; diversity of culture of, 162; DNA studies of, 77; exhumations of, 58–59, 60, 177, 178, 179, 206; gravemarkers of, 179–80; grave orientation of, 177–78, 206; in Hawaii, 180; relationship with the dead, 178–79;

segregation of, 11; temporary grave-markers of, 177; use of feng shui by, 178, 206; use of the "burner" by, 180–81, 202
Chinese New Year, 179
Chung, Sue Fawn, 177
Cipolla, Craig, 163–65
Civil War: changes in mourning customs after, 65–66, 126; gravemarker motifs and, 138; gravemarkers for soldiers of, 146, 147–49; impact on mortuary practices by, 16, 176
Clark, Lynn, 162–63, 190, 198
coffin hardware, 37, 38–39, 74, 168
coffin plates, 69, 71, 73, 74, 156
coffins: in African Burial Ground National Monument (NYC, N.Y.), 30–31, 52; attitudes toward death and, 14; in Carlin Chinese Cemetery (Carlin, Nev.), 59; cast iron, 65, 71, 176; for children, 36, 43; construction of, 37, 41; decoration of, 37, 38–39, 73, 74, 181; Ghanaian, 30–31, 204; growing use of, 41; identification of dead with, 42–44, 74; inner wooden, 44; lead, 42–43, 208; lead-lined, 73; lined with metal, 65, 69, 71, 73; made by cabinetmakers, 37; mass-produced, 37–38, 57, 65; metal-lined, 69, 71; mortuary studies and, 18, 33, 35, 36–37; mummiform, 1, 71, 72; religion and, 41; in Secaucus Potter's Field (Hudson County, N.J.), 68; shapes of, 41, 69, 76; social status and, 62, 64; St. Mary's City (Md.), 40, 41; vaults and, 135; viewing windows and, 74, 181; in Walton Family Cemetery (Griswold, Conn.), 66
Common Burying Ground (Newport, R.I.), 116–17
Confucianism, 177
consumer choice: advertising and, 151; attitudes toward death and, 57; cemeteries and, 12, 125, 133; ethnicity and, 123,

161, 198, 201, 202; gravemarkers and, 10–11, 78; gravestone motifs and, 89, 98, 117, 200; mass-production and, 127; social status and, 121, 162–63, 198–99, 201, 202; trade networks and, 206

cremation, 125, 126, 156–57, 158, 205

crematorium, 126, 156, 157

Crist, Thomas, 24, 54–55, 75

Crowell, Elizabeth, 105–7, 110–12

Cunningham, Keith, 165–67

Daoism, 177, 178, 206

day names, 174

death: changing American attitude toward, 2, 14, 16, 40, 176, 200; consumer choice and, 57; historic American attitude toward, 38; Jewish attitude toward, 186; modern American attitude toward, 149, 201; Narragansett attitude toward, 47

death's head motif: ethnicity and, 91; iconographic shift and, 7–8, 10, 81–82, 86–87, 93; Jews and, 90; in New Jersey, 104; Puritanism and, 8, 81–82; religion and, 87–88, 89–90, 91; stonecutters and, 84, 88–89

Deetz, James: Alan Ludwig and, 88–89; cemetery studies and, 11; challenges to, 10, 87–92; cherub motif and, 91–92; David Hall and, 88; death's head motif and, 89–90; demographic studies by, 86; gravemarker motifs and, 81–82, 84–85, 86–87; gravemarkers and, 80; gravemarker seriation by, 7–8, 80, 81–82; influence of, 8, 87; Kevin Sweeney and, 89; Peter Benes and, 88; seriation, 80–81; shortcomings of study of, 90; social status and, 86; stonecutters and, 84, 85, 86–87; structuralism, 8; urn and willow motif and, 92

descendant populations: of African Americans, 29–30, 55, 203; archaeologists and, 1, 18, 20, 31–34, 181–82; burial

removals and, 64–65, 66–67; Hudson County Burial Grounds (Hudson County, N.J.) and, 68–71; Native American Graves Protection and Repatriation Act and, 6, 24–29, 33–34, 50, 51, 209; power of, 15, 203–5; Spring Street Presbyterian Burial Ground (New York City, N.Y.) and, 71–72

Dethlefsen, Edwin: Alan Ludwig and, 88–89; cemetery studies and, 11; challenges to, 10, 87–92; cherub motif and, 91–92; David Hall and, 88; death's head motif and, 89–90; demographic studies by, 86; gravemarker motifs and, 81–82, 84–85, 86–87; gravemarkers and, 80; gravemarker seriation by, 7–8, 80, 81–82; influence of, 8, 87; Kevin Sweeney and, 89; Peter Benes and, 88; seriation, 80–81; shortcomings of study of, 90; social status and, 86; stonecutters and, 84, 85, 86–87; urn and willow motif and, 92

DiBlasi, Michael, 95–96

DNA studies, 28, 52, 77

Doppler Effect, 80–81

Dutch: diet of, 63; gravemarkers of, 102, 103, 201–2; in Gravesend Cemetery (Brooklyn, N.Y.), 98; immigration of, 101; influence of, 102–3; social status within, 117; in St. Andrew's Cemetery (Staten Island, N.Y.), 96; stonecutters and, 102, 104, 117

Eaton, Hubert, 149–50, 208

Edwards, Jonathan, 89, 90

Eighth Street Cemetery (Philadelphia, Penn.), 54–55

embalming: acceptance of, 206; green cemeteries and, 159, 204; at Hudson County Burial Grounds (Hudson County, N.J.), 68; as preservation method, 4; prevalence of, 36, 44, 125, 126, 176

Exclusion Act of 1882, 177
exhumations: of American Indians, 29; of
Chinese, 58–59, 60, 177, 178, 179, 206;
of Henry Opookiah, 181–82; at Hudson
County Burial Grounds (Hudson
County, N.J.), 68; of Opukaha'ia, 181–
82; in Spring Street Presbyterian Burial
Ground (New York City, N.Y.), 72

Fairmont Cemetery (Newark, N.J.), 71
feng shui, 178, 206
Ferguson, Leland, 109–10
fieldstones: decoration of, 103; as infor-
mal gravemarker, 99; Native Ameri-
cans and, 115, 164; Quakers and, 49; in
Uxbridge Almshouse burying ground
(Uxbridge, Mass.), 67
First African Baptist Church Cemeteries
(Philadelphia, Penn.), 54–55, 74
Fletcher Site (Mich.), 31–32
Forbes, Harriette Merrifield, 7, 79, 81
Freedman's Cemetery (Dallas, Tex.),
57–58, 208
functionalism, 7

Galt, Mary Jeffrey, 13, 14–15, 20
garden cemeteries, 125, 126, 130, 132. See
also rural cemeteries
Garman, James, 116–17
Giguere, Joy, 11, 114–15
Gilded Age, 116, 145, 202, 206
Gorman, Frederick, 95–96
Gosnell, Lynn, 189–90
Gott, Suzanne, 189–90
Gradwohl, David: cherub motif and, 10,
91–92; ethnicity and, 13; Jewish assimi-
lation and, 185; Jewish gravemarkers
and, 113–14, 182–83, 185–86, 198–99;
ledgers and, 185; Sephardic Jews and,
185
Gradwohl, Hanna Rosenberg, 113–14
Grafton Cemetery (Grafton, Ill.), 64, 144
gravemarkers: anthropomorphic, 175; of

cast concrete, 175; dating and, 81; ethnic diversity in, 202; idealized images
of slavery on, 170–71; "I.H.S." inscription on, 187; individuality in, 141–42;
Jewish motifs on, 140, 182, 185–86;
lamb motif on, 140; marital status
and, 102; materials for, 118–20, 150–56;
for military personnel, 147–49, 176;
monograms and, 173; pebbles and, 186;
photoengravings and, 186; purchasing
of, 162; in rural cemeteries, 133–34;
shape of, 105–6; social status and,
187–88; temporary, 177. See also cherub
motif; death's head motif; portrait
stones; urn and willow motif; wooden
gravemarkers
grave orientation: of African American
burials, 41; as dating method, 41; of
European Christians burials, 41, 164;
feng shui and, 178; of Narragansetts, 41;
remote sensing and, 34; at Waldo Farm
Site (Mass.), 49
graves, legal protections for, 29
Gravesend Cemetery (Brooklyn, N.Y.),
96, 98
Great Awakening: cherub motif and, 7–8,
86, 90; iconographic shift and, 82, 86,
88
green cemeteries, 204
Greenwood, Roberta, 179, 181
Green-Wood Cemetery (Brooklyn, N.Y.):
gravemarkers of, 138–39, 141; as rural
cemetery, 12, 133, 146, 184, 208; tourism
and, 144
Guale Indians, 50–51
Gypsy, 163, 190–93

Hall, David, 88, 92, 99
Hawaii: Chinese cemeteries in, 13, 179,
180; Chinese in, 180
Heinrich, Adam, 11, 98–99
Hispanics, 163
Hodge, Christina, 48–50, 52

Hrdlička, Aleš, 22, 51, 167
Hudson County Burial Grounds (Hudson County, N.J.), 24, 67–70

Industrial Revolution, 12, 201
Inguanti, Joseph, 193–94
Irish, 160, 161, 163, 195, 196–97, 199
Italians: in Catholic Calvary Cemetery (Queens, N.Y.), 194; cemeteries in Italy and, 194, 199; decorative plantings of, 194; gravemarkers of, 163, 186, 194; immigrant experience of, 13, 68; immigration of, 160, 194; portrait stones of, 193–94; relationship with the dead, 194; temporary burials of, 194; terra cotta gravemarkers of, 153

Jamestown (Va.): early excavations in, 13; ethics and, 14–15
Jefferson, Thomas, 20, 90
Jews: Ashkenazim, 112, 182; assimilation of, 13, 184, 185; attitudes toward death of, 186; burial practices of, 112; cemeteries of, 182–86; children, 140; Conservative, 185, 186; diversity of culture of, 161, 182, 186; emigration of, 112, 184; European Protestant perceptions of, 182; gravemarkers of, 113, 114, 182, 185–86; Ladino, 113, 182, 185; in multiethnic colonies, 101–2; in Newport (R.I.), 113–14; Orthodox, 185, 186; pebbles in cemeteries and, 186; Portuguese, 90; Reformed, 185; retention of burial practices by, 113, 182; Russian, 161, 186; Sephardic, 10, 91, 112, 113–14, 182, 185; stonecutters of, 113, 182; use of cherub motif by, 91, 92, 98, 113, 114; use of ledgers by, 120. See also Touro Synagogue (Newport, R.I.)
Jordan, Terry, 175

Kelso, William, 15, 62, 76

Ladino, 113, 182, 185
Laurel Hill Cemetery (Philadelphia, Penn.), 131, 133, 134, 142, 208
lawn-park cemeteries: Adolph Strauch and, 144; consumer choice and, 126; design of, 144, 145; as park, 145; popularity of, 145–46; rural cemeteries and, 12, 145–46; upkeep of, 144
ledgers: cost of, 124; prevalence of, 183; social status and, 110–11; in Tolomato Cemetery (St. Augustine, Fla.), 187; use of by Jews, 114, 120, 182, 185
Lenapes, 22
Levine, Gaynell. See Stone, Gaynell (Levine)
Little, Ruth, 175
looting, 19–20
Ludwig, Alan, 85, 89–90, 92–93, 99

Mackie, Norman, 110
Marxism, 10, 195, 196
Masonic emblems, 138, 200
McGuire, Randall, 10, 133, 190, 195–98
memorial parks, 126, 149, 150, 158–59, 201, 208
Methodists, 31, 92
Mexican, 165, 188–90
military cemeteries: African Americans in, 147; the Civil War and, 146–47; Confederate soldiers in, 147–49; consumer choice and, 126; gravemarkers in, 147–49
Minisink Burial Ground (Minisink, N.J.), 21–23, 49
Mohawks, 161
Moravians, 108–10
Mormons, 165–66, 206
Mount Auburn Cemetery (Cambridge, Mass.), 12, 129–31, 133, 134, 146, 208
Mytum, Harold, 3, 90

Narragansetts, 33, 45–47
Nassaney, Michael, 47–48

Native American Graves Protection and
  Repatriation Act, 6–7, 22–23, 24–29,
  50, 51, 209
Navajos, 26, 161, 165–66
neutron activation, 44
New Archaeology, 5, 6, 7, 87
New Haven Burying Ground (New Haven, Conn.), 129
Newport (R.I.): African American
  gravemarkers in, 116–17; gravemarkers
  in, 91–92, 99; Jewish colonists to, 10,
  90, 112; Jewish gravemarkers in, 113–14,
  182, 183
New York City Marble, 129
New York Marble Cemetery, 129
nitrogen isotope analysis, 63, 64

obelisks: prevalence of, 137, 138, 141, 183;
  social status and, 188; in Tolomato
  Cemetery (St. Augustine, Fla.), 187;
  type of, 153; in Virginia, 110
Old First Presbyterian Burial Ground
  (Newark, N.J.), 24, 70–71
Old Settlers' Vault (Newark, N.J.), 71
Oneidas, 164
Opookiah, Henry (Opukaha'ia), 181–82
Opukaha'ia (Henry Opookiah), 181–82
Orr, David, 176–77
Orser, Charles, 160–61, 162
Osborn, Jonathan Hand, 172–73
Ottawas, 47–48

Page Law of 1875, 177
Pequots, 163–65
photoengravings, 186
Polktown (Del.), 176–78
pollen analysis, 42, 44
portrait stones: of African Americans,
  117; in Green-Wood Cemetery (Brooklyn, N.Y.), 139; iconographic shift and,
  88; of Italians, 194; of Romany, 191;
  stonecutters and, 121–22
postprocessualism, 5, 8

Price, Ebenezer, 83
processualism, 7
Puritanism, 8
putti, 99, 100, 111

Qingming, 179
Quakers: in Cape May (N.J.), 105; gravemarker motifs and, 98; as gravemarker
  suppliers, 106; influence of, 107; Native
  Americans and, 49–50, 115; in Philadelphia (Penn.), 106; plain gravemarkers
  of, 8, 107–8; in Plymouth Colony, 88;
  shroud burials of, 49

Rahway Cemetery (Rahway, N.J.), 173–74
Rainville, Lynn, 95, 168–69, 170
Romani, 163, 190–93
Rubertone, Patricia, 31, 33, 45–47
rural cemeteries: clutter of, 145–46;
  consumer choice in, 133–34; design of,
  128, 134–35; fencing in, 130, 134, 146;
  gravemarkers, 130–31; gravemarkers in,
  133–34, 140–42, 145; individuality in,
  141–42; as park, 125, 144–45; permanent plots in, 132–33; preservation of,
  146; Second Great Awakening and,
  140; social status in, 125, 130, 133–34,
  140–41; symbolism in, 140–41; tourism and, 144; upkeep of, 144. See also
  Green-Wood Cemetery (Brooklyn,
  N.Y.); Laurel Hill Cemetery (Philadelphia, Penn.); Mount Auburn Cemetery
  (Cambridge, Mass.)
rural cemetery movement, 12, 65, 126,
  129–32, 146

sandblasting, 147
San Fernando Cemetery (San Antonio,
  Tex.), 189–90
Sankofa symbol, 37
Scotch Plains Baptist Church Cemetery
  (Scotch Plains, N.J.), 172–73
Scott Act of 1888, 177

scraped-earth burials, 175
Secaucus Potter's Field (Hudson
   County, N.J.), 24, 67–70
Second Great Awakening, 10, 140–41
secularism, 8
Sephardic Jews, 10, 91, 112, 113–14, 182,
   185
shell: as African American grave goods,
   54, 169, 175; American Indian beads
   of, 45; American Indian gorget of, 50;
   as American Indian grave goods, 112;
   as inset of gravemarker, 156; meaning
   of, 169–70
shroud pins, 18, 36, 49, 55, 66
shrouds, 14, 36, 40, 47, 49, 62
Smith, John Jay, 12
social status: archaeological studies
   of, 47–48; coffins and, 62, 64; coffin
   shape and, 76; consumer choice
   and, 121, 162–63, 198–99, 201, 202;
   diet and, 63; grave goods and, 5, 20,
   46, 49; gravemarkers and, 187–88;
   gravemarker selection and, 86, 96,
   101, 114, 122, 190, 195–96; lead in
   isotope analysis and, 63–64; in rural
   cemeteries, 125, 130, 133–34, 140–41;
   vaults and, 73, 129, 187–88
Soule, Ebenezer, 85
Spanish: box tombs of, 112; Catholics,
   9–10, 187–88; gravemarkers of, 9–10;
   graves of, 50–51; Jews, 9–10, 101,
   113, 114, 184; missions to America
   by, 13–14, 20, 50, 112, 166. See also
   Ladino; Tolomato Cemetery (St.
   Augustine, Fla.)
Spencer-Wood, Suzanne, 10, 121–22
Spring Street Presbyterian Burial
   Ground (NYC, N.Y.), 71–76, 209
St. Andrew's Cemetery (Staten Island,
   N.Y.), 96, 97–98, 105
St. Catherines Island (Ga.), 50–52
St. Mary's City (Md.), 14, 40–44, 45,
   62, 77

Stone, Gaynell (Levine), 99–102, 106–7
stonecutters: advertisements for, 89, 117;
   of African American gravemarkers,
   116; changing styles of, 85, 86–87, 94;
   cherub motif and, 98; differing styles
   of, 84, 86, 88, 89, 103, 117; Dutch and,
   102; Ebenezer Price and, 83; Edwin
   Dethlefsen and, 84, 85; enslaved
   Africans, 175; ethnicity and, 104; of folk
   gravemarkers, 103; identification of,
   79; influence of, 7, 10, 103; James Deetz
   and, 84, 85; of Jewish gravemarkers,
   113, 182; John Solomon Teetzel and,
   103; John Zuricher and, 102, 104; Long
   Island and, 101; modernization of,
   151; Old Mortality and, 142; patronage
   networks of, 89, 117; of Philadelphia,
   106; signing work by, 117; stones for
   enslaved Africans by, 172–73; studies
   of, 94–95; written records of, 123
Strauch, Adolph, 144, 145, 208
structuralism, 8, 93
Sweeney, Kevin, 89

Tenth Street Cemetery (Philadelphia,
   Penn.), 55
Titus, Thomas, 174–75
tobacco pipes: in African Burial Ground
   National Monument, 54; American
   Indian burial practices and, 46–47; as
   Chinese American grave goods, 59, 60;
   consumer choice and, 161; at Hudson
   County Burial Grounds (Hudson
   County, N.J.), 68; in Long Island (N.Y.)
   burials, 45
Tolomato Cemetery (St. Augustine, Fla.),
   112, 187–88
Touro Synagogue (Newport, R.I.), 90,
   91–92, 91, 113–14, 116, 182–84, 183
Trinity Cemetery (NYC, N.Y.), 52–54,
   96–97, 98, 102, 117, 118, 127
Tsimshians, 165
tympana, 103, 106, 120

Unitarians, 82, 92
urn and willow motif: in Colonial Park
    Cemetery (Savannah, Ga.), *83*; icono-
    graphic shift and, 81–82, 93; influence
    of, 87; meaning of, 200; neoclassical
    fashion and, 99; prevalence of, 104;
    secularism and, 8, 92; seriation and, 97

vaults: design of, 134–35; in Fairmount
    Cemetery (Newark, N.J.), 71; in Maple
    Grove Cemetery (Hackensack, N.J.),
    70; mausoleums and, 136; in New York
    Marble Cemetery (NYC, N.Y.), 129;
    rural cemeteries and, 134; social status
    and, 73, 129, 187–88; in Spring Street
    Presbyterian Burial Ground (NYC,
    N.Y.), 72, 73–75, 208–9; in Tolomato
    Cemetery (St. Augustine, Fla.), 187–88
Veit, Richard, 11–12, 96–98, 103–4, 117,
    171, 190

Waldo Farm Site (Mass.), 48–49
Wampanoags, 47, 49–50
Wegars, Priscilla, 177–79, 180, 181

Welch, Richard, 118
Wier Family Cemetery (Manassas, Va.),
    65–66
Winter, Frederick A., 96–98
wooden gravemarkers: of African Ameri-
    cans in, 175; in Agua Mansa Cemetery
    (Colton, Calif.), 188; on Aleutian
    Islands, 168; of Chinese women, 179;
    Civil War and, 176; cost of, 124, 162; in
    Gettysburg National Cemetery (Get-
    tysburg, Penn.), *148*; loss of, 124, 162,
    188, 200; prevalence of, 118, 123–24,
    146–47, 187, 200, 206; social status and,
    123–24, 162; in Tolomato Cemetery (St.
    Augustine, Fla.), 187; in Vander Wagen
    Cemetery (N.Mex.), 166
Worcester, Jonathon, 81
Wurst, LouAnn, 10, 140–41

Yulanpen, 179

Ziegler boxes, 69
Zunis, 165, 166–67
Zuricher, John, 102, 104, 117

Sherene Baugher is professor of archaeology and landscape architecture at Cornell University. She is a coeditor of *Archaeology and Preservation of Gendered Landscapes* and *Past Meets Present: Archaeologists Partnering with Museum Curators, Teachers, and Community Groups.*

Richard F. Veit is professor of anthropology at Monmouth University. He is the author of *Digging New Jersey's Past: Historical Archaeology in the Garden State* and coauthor of *Stranger Stop and Cast an Eye: New Jersey's Historic Cemeteries and Burial Grounds through Four Centuries.*

THE AMERICAN EXPERIENCE IN ARCHAEOLOGICAL PERSPECTIVE

Edited by Michael S. Nassaney

The books in this series explore an event, process, setting, or institution that was significant in the formative experience of contemporary America. Each volume will frame the topic beyond an individual site and attempt to give the reader a flavor of the theoretical, methodological, and substantive issues that researchers face in their examination of that topic or theme. These books will be comprehensive overviews that will allow serious students and scholars to get a good sense of contemporary and past inquiries on a broad theme in American history and culture.

The Archaeology of Collective Action, by Dean J. Saitta (2007)

The Archaeology of Institutional Confinement, by Eleanor Conlin Casella (2007)

The Archaeology of Race and Racialization in Historic America, by Charles E. Orser Jr. (2007)

The Archaeology of North American Farmsteads, by Mark D. Groover (2008)

The Archaeology of Alcohol and Drinking, by Frederick H. Smith (2008)

The Archaeology of American Labor and Working-Class Life, by Paul A. Shackel (2009; first paperback edition, 2011)

The Archaeology of Clothing and Bodily Adornment in Colonial America, by Diana DiPaolo Loren (2010; first paperback edition, 2011)

The Archaeology of American Capitalism, by Christopher N. Matthews (2010; first paperback edition, 2012)

The Archaeology of Forts and Battlefields, by David R. Starbuck (2011; first paperback edition, 2012)

The Archaeology of Consumer Culture, by Paul R. Mullins (2011; first paperback edition, 2012)

The Archaeology of Antislavery Resistance, by Terrance M. Weik (2012; first paperback edition, 2013)

The Archaeology of Citizenship, by Stacey Lynn Camp (2013)

The Archaeology of American Cities, by Nan A. Rothschild and Diana diZerega Wall (2014)

The Archaeology of American Cemeteries and Gravemarkers, by Sherene Baugher and Richard F. Veit (2014)

CPSIA information can be obtained
at www.ICGtesting.com
Printed in the USA
BVHW071234280620
582062BV00007B/102